ZANE GREY:

OUTDOORSMAN

ZANE GREY'S
BEST HUNTING
AND FISHING TALES
PUBLISHED
IN COMMEMORATION
OF HIS
CENTENNIAL YEAR

SELECTED AND EDITED BY GEORGE REIGER

PRENTICE-HALL, INC., Englewood Cliffs, N.J.

(endpapers) *Zane Grey called these "wild white horses of the sea."*

Zane Grey: Outdoorsman Zane Grey's best hunting and fishing tales published in commemoration of his centennial year
Selected and Edited by George Reiger

Library of Congress Cataloging in Publication Data
Grey, Zane, 1872–1939.
Zane Grey: outdoorsman.
CONTENTS: The lord of Lackawaxen Creek.—Fighting
qualities of black bass–1907.—Roping lions in the
Grand Canyon.—Byme-by-tarpon. [etc.]
1. Fishing. 2. Hunting. I. Title.
SH441.G615 1972   799.1'2   75–178136
ISBN 0–13–983841–4

For Admiral Ben
who set so many wheels in motion

ABOUT GEORGE REIGER

George Reiger has fished and hunted throughout North and Central Americas. He caught his first sailfish when he was eight and has angled in many of Zane Grey's favorite haunts including the Florida Keys, Catalina Island, Baja California, and Tahiti.

Free-lance writing for more than a decade, Mr. Reiger's by-line has appeared in most of America's outdoor magazines. Educated at Princeton (A.B.) and Columbia (M.A.) Universities, he served two tours in Vietnam as a Naval Lieutenant and was awarded the U.S. Navy Commendation Medal, Purple Heart, and the Vietnamese Armed Forces Medal of Honor, among other decorations. After two years as Boating and Outdoors Editor for *Popular Mechanics*, he is currently Washington (D.C.) Editor for *National* and *International Wildlife* magazines.

INTRODUCTION

Not one in a hundred who've ever heard of Zane Grey—not even a majority of those who read his Western novels—know of him as an outdoorsman and conservationist. Yet his personal life was far more romantic, more rambunctious, than anything found in his novels.

For starters, few writers in history have known greater wealth. For years the total sales of Zane Grey's books were surpassed only by the Holy Bible and McGuffey's Readers. Even today his novels, in various editions, sell better than a million copies a year in the United States alone. And when he was alive, Zane Grey invested the major share of his fabulous income in doing the kinds of things most men only dream of doing.

He roped lions in the Grand Canyon, hiked through Death Valley ("to see what it must have been like for those who hadn't made it"), mapped wild rivers in Mexico, and fished seas never before explored by a sportsman. He held a number of world records attesting to his determination as an angler and was the first man ever to catch a fish over a thousand pounds on rod and reel.

The best of Zane Grey's fiction is nothing less than a dramatization of his outdoor experiences. His largest characters are patterned after men with whom he hunted bear beneath the Tonto Rim in Arizona or trolled for marlin off New Zealand. His heroes' virtues—strength, loyalty, courage—are qualities he felt inherent in men of the outdoors. And this is why the best of ZG's writings are in effect diaries immortalizing a rugged outdoor landscape that, even as he wrote, was changing, fading. Working against time like a painter hoping to fix an impression of a particular sunset, Zane Grey wrote for all of us who will never see an undammed Rogue River or an undeveloped Florida Keys.

The finest of Zane Grey's nonfiction is a blend of adventure, humor, and how-to information which is as relevant today as it was half a century ago. Whether ZG is advocating the use of particular tackle or instructing his reader in what makes the best wood for camp fires, he does so in terms of anecdote and you usually don't realize you've been "learned" until you're actually out camping or fishing.

But learning woodlore or recovering a sense of the past are not the only reasons to read his tales of hunting and fishing. In his concern for environment, Zane Grey is our contemporary. In his campaigns against the overgrazing of rangeland and the reckless cutting of timber, in his condemnation of the noise and exhaust of automobiles, and in his prediction that indiscriminate netting would dangerously deplete certain fishes even in the so-called limitless seas, Zane Grey was ahead of his time. More than half a century ago Zane Grey wrote:

> *Thousands and millions of men exploit what is not really theirs for their own selfish ends. Coal, oil, timber, minerals, the great schools of food fishes are all natural products of our great outdoors. I do not advocate that they should belong to the government, but the government should see to it that the men dealing with those resources should not gut them and not spoil the beauty and health-giving properties of the forests and rivers.*

He publicized the release of any fish he or his companions could not use in a time when most anglers measured their success by the number of fish creeled. Partly as a result of ZG's efforts, no outdoors magazine today will print a picture of a man posing proudly with a pile of dead fish or game without running the risk of losing its readership.

And in the light of nineteenth-century disregard for the welfare of the outdoors, it is marvelous to consider that as early as 1909 Zane Grey wrote a novel whose background is the feud between timber barons and the federal government for control of vast forest reserves of the West (a struggle, incidentally, that continues to this day in more subtle form). In *The Young Forester*, Grey leaves little doubt that the "men in black hats" are those whose sole interest in woodlands is profit. The author's appeal is for the national government to guide industry in considering the people's needs for recreation to be on a par with their requirements for lumber.

Zane Grey is part of a tradition that grew from a handful of men confronting an inert majority to thousands of conservationists today seeking remedies on behalf of millions more at last aware of the devastation of decades.

But if Zane Grey was ahead of his time, he was also after it. His spirit was attuned to the great age of exploration. He was fascinated by the achievements of early Spanish adventurers and, temperamentally, he was akin to them.[1] Hugely romantic, Zane Grey trusted best those men who agreed with him or who supplemented his own imagination. Single-minded, he organized complex expeditions and carried them through with people whose loyalty he required—and occasionally tested. Like the *conquistadores*, Zane Grey was obsessed by El Dorado. Yet his dream was not of gold but of pristine lands where game abounded and of purple seas where giant marlin fed on shoals of breaking tuna. When he first visited New Zealand, he called it El Dorado. Later, Tahiti also qualified as an El Dorado. Zane Grey relentlessly tracked down each legend of enormity or mystery in nature the way Cortez and Pizarro pursued their visions through the conquest of nations. And finally, like the *conquistadores*, he brought back fragments of reality nearly as large as the legends themselves.

*

Had Zane Grey lived in the eighteenth century, he would have been a pioneer like his great-grandfather, Colonel Ebenezer Zane, who led settlers west and founded Zanesville, Ohio, where Grey was born on January 31, 1872. During the Revolutionary War the Colonel's sister carried powder through a storm of British and Indian fire at the siege of Fort Henry[2] on the Ohio River. Her act saved the American defenders and inspired Zane Grey's first book, *Betty Zane*.

But Zane Grey was born more than 100 years after his great-grandfather set out from Hardy County, Virginia, and the boy was only five when George Armstrong Custer and his men died at Little Big Horn. By the time Zane Grey was a home-run-hitting left fielder for an undefeated University of Pennsylvania baseball team, the Indian Wars in the West had been settled and only a few Arizona

---

[1] In *The Young Lion Hunter*, ZG devotes a chapter to the tales of Lopez de Cardeñas, who discovered the Grand Canyon sixty-seven years before the colony at Jamestown was established, and of Alvar Nuñez Cabeza de Vaca, who crossed the North American continent more than eighty years before the *Mayflower* anchored off Plymouth.

[2] Named for Patrick Henry by Colonel Zane and his men, this island fort was later expanded to become the hub of Wheeling, West Virginia.

[ix]

towns retained an active memory of the good and bad men who were to supply the characters for Grey's novels.

In 1896 Grey completed his studies in dentistry and opened an office at 100 West 74th Street in Manhattan (now the Graystone Apartments). Very quickly he realized that neither dentistry nor city life suited him. But, knowing no other way to earn a living, Grey stayed with his practice and sought recreation in regular visits to East Orange, New Jersey, where he was a member of the Orange Athletic Club; to Westchester County for monthly meetings of the Camp Fire Club[3]; and on weekend trips to Pennsylvania, where he fished the Delaware with his brothers, Ellsworth (also called Cedar) and Romer Carl (known more familiarly as "Reddy" or "R. C."), and where in August, 1900, he met his future bride, Lina Elise ("Dolly") Roth.

*

These Delaware River trips meant much to Grey. His first published story was an angling yarn in May, 1902, called "A Day on the Delaware" for *Recreation Magazine*, and retrospective reference to these bachelor days with his brothers, particularly R. C., are found throughout his later outdoor writings.

Grey started to contribute to several outdoor magazines and suddenly found that writing was as important, if not as satisfying, a form of escape from the city as actually getting away to the woods and water. All one Manhattan winter he labored over *Betty Zane*, and when spring came and he couldn't find a publisher, he borrowed money from Dolly Roth to publish the novel himself.

Despite indifferent sales, Grey now felt he was destined to be a writer. At least he saw this profession as his only hope for independence. So marrying the girl he met on the Delaware five years before, he gave up dentistry and moved to a cottage in Lackawaxen, Pennsylvania.

Grey was literate—and determined—but the story of his early years of independence are bleak. He read the masters. He studied grammar and rhetoric to make up for his indifferent academic years

---

[3] This distinguished organization, founded by naturalist William T. Hornaday in 1897, soon included such important members as Theodore Roosevelt, Gifford Pinchot, Ernest Thompson Seton—and Zane Grey.

when his strongest subjects had been daydreaming and fighting—often a result of boys teasing him about his Christian name, Pearl.[4] He wrote books and stories, and when they were rejected, he rewrote them to the editors' specifications—only to have them rejected again. But one day while visiting New York to see still another publisher, he was taken by a friend, Alvah James,[5] to see some wildlife films presented by Charles Jesse "Buffalo" Jones.

Legend has it that only Zane Grey was enthralled by Jones' tales of the Far West—the rest of Jones' audience sat politely, but unbelievingly, through the old man's ramblings; then, not until Grey followed Jones back to his hotel room and persuaded him that he would be valuable to Jones as a companion on future adventures in the Arizona territories, did the old plainsman feel the trip east had been worthwhile.

Actually, "Buffalo" Jones was a successful and respected farmer/rancher, and Zane Grey may have met him at a Camp Fire Club dinner given in Jones' honor, or been recommended to him by George O. Shields, publisher of *Recreation* and a member of the exclusive club's executive committee. The outdoor world in those days was a tight little island of pedigreed talents. It stands to reason that Zane Grey met his opportunity to travel west through a formal introduction rather than through nursing a disillusioned oldster in a back room

---

[4] ZG's family name was spelled *Gray*. Shortly before he was born, Queen Victoria had gone into semi-mourning to mark the tenth anniversary of the Prince Consort's death. Her favorite mourning color was a shade known as *pearl gray*. Since the Queen was the taste-maker of her time, pearl gray soon became the most fashionable color in the English-speaking world, and Zane Grey's mother thought it would be clever to name her newborn son *à la mode*.

[5] Though Alvah D. James was seven years younger than Zane Grey, he had already achieved success as a writer in the outdoor and adventure field. Zane Grey admired him for several exotic expeditions he'd been on, including one up the Amazon and across the Andes. *Field and Stream*, September, 1906, includes a story by Zane Grey entitled "James' Waterloo," in which "Doctor [Grey] arranges a canoe trip on a flooded creek and persuades Alvah he cannot safely poke fun at Pike County." In the story, Grey nearly kills James and himself by impetuously tackling an unknown stretch of the Lackawaxen. But all ends well when James crawls ashore and "with a quiet smile" calls Zane Grey a "chump." That James could forgive ZG for his folly forever made Grey loyal to him. When James' fortune was lost in the Great Depression, ZG turned over his home in Lackawaxen to him. Today the house, now the Zane Grey Inn, is owned and managed by James' daughter Helen, and the two friends, Zane Grey and Alvah James, are buried not far from each other in the Lackawaxen Cemetery.

of the Grand Hotel, even though the latter tale undeniably has more appeal.

However initiated, Zane Grey's first trip was a tremendous success. It resulted in memorable descriptions of Arizona hunting and provided the background for books like *The Last of the Plainsmen*, *Heritage of the Desert*, and *Riders of the Purple Sage*. Zane Grey's career as the world's foremost Western writer was launched, and his adventures as America's premier outdoorsman had begun.

*

Most of the material for this anthology has been drawn from Zane Grey's many books on hunting and fishing. Their contents were often first published, or later serialized, in magazines like *American*, *Everybody's*, *Popular* and *Recreation*, which are no longer with us, and in many such as *Field and Stream*, *Outdoor Life*, *Sports Afield*, and *Motor Boating*, which are. Zane Grey's family maintains the rights to all his writings and I'm grateful for the guidance of his two sons, Romer and Loren, for suggesting material and offering five stories that have never before appeared in book form, plus an introduction to "The North Umpqua, Oregon," that has never before appeared in print.

My selections represent less than 100,000 words of the millions Zane Grey wrote on the outdoors. Many stories have been extensively cut, and I've altered some words and expressions for the sake of clarity. In addition, in an attempt to maintain continuity, I have suspended the ordinary use of ellipses and brackets and recommend that a "purist" Zane Grey reader turn to his local library or bookstore for the entire text.

This anthology is roughly in chronological order. Though total wordage is divided about evenly between hunting and fishing selections, there is actually more variety in the fishing material—simply because in life Zane Grey was more of a fisherman than a hunter. The chapters are so arranged that each hunting tale is bracketed by a pair of fishing adventures.

In addition to the Grey family, I would like to thank Mr. Norris F. Schneider of Zanesville, Ohio; the Reverend G. M. Farley of Williamsport, Maryland; and Mrs. Helen Laudenslager of Lackawaxen, Pennsylvania, for their kind assistance. Also, I want to thank artist Roy Grinnell for sharing my enthusiasm for the project; Prentice-

Hall editor Dennis Fawcett for his everlasting patience; and my wife, Barbara, who typed and retyped Zane Grey so many times she can quote entire paragraphs of his tales from memory. Finally, my appreciation to Clare Conley of *Field and Stream*, William Rae of *Outdoor Life*, and Lamar Underwood of *Sports Afield* for giving me permission to spend hours in their office libraries, reading through ancient issues of their magazines.

One of the most interesting aspects of my homework was to see how much outdoor and recreation magazines have changed since the turn of the century. They once provided their readers with poetry, short stories, travel sketches, and science articles by the leading naturalists of the day. Today specialty publications cover each one of these categories, and contemporary outdoor magazines are devoted to a how-to, where-to, how-much, and new-product perspective of hunting and fishing.

The editors of *Field and Stream*, *Outdoor Life*, and *Sports Afield* all assure me this is a successful approach to the outdoors, and my experience as Boating and Outdoors Editor at *Popular Mechanics* corroborates their opinion. Today's readers *are* more impatient about getting to the outback themselves than were their grandparents seventy years ago. But it would be pleasant to see more pieces concerned with the total experience of outdoor living in order to balance those devoted only to the cost of getting there.

Zane Grey was a fine photographer and a competent how-to writer (for example, he did a safety feature for the June, 1910, *Field and Stream* entitled "Accidents in Camp"), but he felt his first duty as an outdoors reporter was to cultivate a feeling for the majesty and meaning of nature. When a critic once accused Zane Grey of writing "mere romances," ZG retorted that since *romance* is simply another word for *idealism*, he was proud to create "romances." Hunting and fishing tales reflecting the idealism of those you will find in this anthology are all too uncommon in today's outdoor literature.

George Reiger
Locustville, Virginia

[xiii]

CONTENTS

A Zane Grey Album
follows page 292

1

THE LORD OF LACKAWAXEN CREEK

Look at any map of Pennsylvania and you'll find in its upper right-hand corner—not far upstream from where New Jersey and New York State meet at the Delaware River—the little town of Lackawaxen. It lies some 30 miles east of Scranton, less than 15 miles north of Interstate Highway 84. Still relatively unsettled, the area is nevertheless popular with canoeists and float fishermen in the spring and summer, the majority of whom drift past what is today the Zane Grey Inn without any knowledge of its history or any interest in the Lackawaxen River that joins the Delaware there.

It's appropriate that we start with a Zane Grey tale of fresh-water fishing, for fresh-water angling is how ZG began his outdoor career. And when the last bear had been shot and the final swordfish fought, it was to fresh water he returned for sport in his elder years. The first stroke of the heart condition that eventually took his life occurred on a steelhead fishing trip to the Umpqua River, Oregon, in 1937. But the following story, written for the May, 1909, issue of *Outing* magazine, harks back to an early time in this century when Zane Grey—and our country—were both a good deal younger.

GWR

THE LORD OF LACKAWAXEN CREEK[1]

Winding among the Blue Hills of Pennsylvania there is a swift amber stream that the Indians named Lack-a-wax-en. The literal translation no one seems to know, but it must mean, in mystical and imaginative Delaware, "the brown water that turns and whispers and tumbles."[2] It is a little river hidden away under gray cliffs and hills black with ragged pines. It is full of mossy stones and rapid ripples.

All its tributaries, dashing white-sheeted over ferny cliffs, wine-brown where the whirling pools suck the stain from the hemlock root, harbor the speckled trout. Wise in their generation, the black and red-spotted little beauties keep to their brooks; for, farther down, below the rush and fall, a newcomer is lord of the stream. He

---

[1] Reprinted with the permission of A. S. Barnes & Company, Cranbury, New Jersey, from *Tales of Fresh-Water Fishing*, first published by Harper & Brothers in 1928.

[2] ZG's interpretation is close; *Lackawaxen* actually means "swift waters."

[2]

is an archenemy, a scorner of beauty and blood, the wolf-jawed, red-eyed, bronze-backed black bass.[3]

A mile or more from its mouth the Lackawaxen leaves the shelter of the hills and seeks the open sunlight and slows down to widen into long lanes that glide reluctantly over the few last restraining barriers to the Delaware. In a curve between two of these level lanes, there is a place where barefoot boys wade and fish for chubs and bask on the big boulders like turtles. It is a famous hole of chubs and bright-sided shiners and sunfish. And, perhaps because it is so known, and so shallow, so open to the sky, few fishermen ever learned that in its secret stony caverns hid a great golden-bronze treasure of a bass.

In vain had many a flimsy feathered hook been flung over his lair by fly casters and whisked gracefully across the gliding surface of his pool. In vain had many a shiny spoon and pearly minnow reflected sun glints through the watery windows of his home. In vain had many a hellgrammite and frog and grasshopper been dropped in front of his broad nose.

Chance plays the star part on a fisherman's luck. One still, cloudy day, when the pool glanced dark under a leaden sky, I saw a wave that reminded me of the wake of a rolling tarpon; then followed an angry swirl, the skitter of a frantically leaping chub, and a splash that ended with a sound like the deep chung of water sharply turned by an oar.

Big bass choose strange hiding places. They should be looked for in just such holes and rifts and shallows as will cover their backs. But to corral a six-pounder in the boys' swimming hole was a circumstance to temper a fisherman's vanity with experience.

Thrillingly conscious of the possibilities of this pool, I studied it thoughtfully. It was a wide, shallow bend in the stream, with dark channels between submerged rocks, suggestive of underlying shelves. It had a current, too, not noticeable at first glance. And this pool looked at long and carefully, colored by the certainty of its guardian, took on an aspect most alluring to an angler's spirit. It

---

[3] ZG calls the smallmouth bass a "newcomer" because, up to 1869, this fish was largely confined to the Lake Ontario and Ohio River drainage systems. After that date, compliments of the Baltimore & Ohio Railroad, the smallmouth was introduced to many waters east, south, and west of its original range.

[3]

had changed from a pond girt by stony banks, to a foam-flecked running stream, clear, yet hiding its secrets, shallow, yet full of labyrinthine watercourses. It presented problems which, difficult as they were, faded in a breath before a fisherman's optimism.

I tested my leader, changed the small hook for a large one, and selecting a white shiner fully six inches long, I lightly hooked it through the side of the upper lip. A sensation never outgrown since boyhood, a familiar mingling of strange fear and joyous anticipation, made me stoop low and tread the slippery stones as if I were a stalking Indian. I knew that a glimpse of me or a faint jar vibrating under the water, or an unnatural ripple on its surface, would be fatal to my enterprise.

I swung the lively minnow and instinctively dropped it with a splash over a dark space between two yellow sunken stones. Out of the amber depths started a broad bar of bronze, rose and flashed into gold. A little dimpling eddying circle, most fascinating of all watery forms, appeared round where the minnow had sunk. The golden moving flash went down and vanished in the greenish gloom like a tiger stealing into a jungle. The line trembled, slowly swept out and straightened. How fraught that instant with a wild yet waiting suspense, with a thrill potent and blissful!

Did the fisherman ever live who could wait in such a moment? My arms twitched involuntarily. Then I struck hard, but not half hard enough. The bass leaped out of a flying splash, shook himself in a tussle plainly audible, and slung the hook back at me like a bullet.

In such moments one never sees the fish distinctly; excitement deranges the vision, and the picture, though impressive, is dim and dreamlike. But a blind man would have known this bass to be enormous, for when he fell he cut the water as a heavy stone.

The best of fishing is that a mild philosophy attends even the greatest misfortunes. It is a delusion peculiar to fishermen, and I went on my way upstream, cheerfully, as one who minded not at all an incident of angling practice; spiritedly, as one who had seen many a big bass go by the board. I found myself thinking about my two brothers, Cedar and Reddy for short, both anglers of long standing and some reputation. It was a sore point with me and a stock subject for endless disputes that they could never appreciate

[4]

my superiority as a fisherman. Brothers are singularly prone to such points of view. So when I thought of them I felt the incipient stirring of a mighty plot. It occurred to me that the iron-mouthed old bass, impregnable of jaw as well as of stronghold, might be made to serve a turn. And all the afternoon the thing grew and grew in my mind.

Luck otherwise favored me, and I took home a fair string of fish. I remarked to my brothers that the conditions for fishing the stream were favorable. Thereafter morning on morning my eyes sought the heavens, appealing for a cloudy day. At last one came, and I invited Reddy to go with me. With childish pleasure that would have caused weakness in any but an unscrupulous villain, he eagerly accepted. He looked over a great assortment of tackle, and finally selected a five-ounce Leonard bait rod carrying a light reel and fine line. When I thought of what would happen if Reddy hooked that powerful bass, an unholy glee fastened upon my soul.

We never started out that way together, swinging rods and pails, but old associations were awakened. We called up the time when we had left the imprints of bare feet on the country roads; we lived over many a boyhood adventure by a running stream. And at last we wound up on the never threadbare question as to the merit and use of tackle.

"I always claimed," said Reddy, "that a fisherman should choose tackle for a day's work after the fashion of a hunter in choosing his gun. A hunter knows what kind of game he's after, and takes a small or large caliber accordingly. Of course a fisherman has more rods than there are calibers of guns, but the rule holds. Now today I have brought this light rod and thin line because I don't need weight. I don't see why you've brought that heavy rod. Even a two-pound bass would be a great surprise up this stream."

"You're right," I replied, "but I sort of lean to possibilities. Besides I'm fond of this rod. You know I've caught a half dozen bass of from five to six pounds with it. I wonder what you would do if you hooked a big one on your delicate rod."

"Do?" exclaimed my brother. "I'd have a fit! I might handle a big bass in deep water with this outfit, but here in this shallow stream with its rocks and holes I couldn't. And that is the reason so few big bass are taken from the Delaware. We know they are there, great

[5]

lusty fellows! Every day in season we hear some tale of woe from some fisherman. 'Hooked a big one—broke this—broke that—got under a stone.' That's why no five- or six-pound bass are taken from shallow, swift, rock-bedded streams on light tackle."

When we reached the pool I sat down and began to fumble with my leader. How generously I let Reddy have the first cast! My iniquity carried me to the extreme of bidding him steal softly and stoop low. I saw a fat chub swinging in the air; I saw it alight to disappear in a churning commotion of the water, and I heard Reddy's startled, "Gee!"

Hard upon his exclamation followed action of striking swiftness. A shrieking reel, willow wand of a rod wavering like a buggy whip in the wind, curving splashes round a foam-lashed swell, a crack of dry wood, a sound as of a banjo string snapping, a sharp splash, then a heavy sullen souse; these, with Reddy standing voiceless, eyes glaring on the broken rod and limp trailing line, were the essentials of the tragedy.

Somehow the joke did not ring true when Reddy waded ashore calm and self-contained, with only his burning eyes to show how deeply he felt. What he said to me in a quiet voice must not, owing to family pride, go on record. It most assuredly would not be an addition to the fish literature of the day.

But he never mentioned the incident to Cedar, which omission laid the way open for my further machinations. I realized that I should have tried Cedar first. He was one of those white-duck-pants-on-a-dry-rock sort of a fisherman, anyway. And in due time I had him wading out toward the center of that pool.

I always experienced a painful sensation while watching Cedar cast. One moment he resembled Ajax defying the lightning and the next he looked like the fellow who stood on a monument, smiling at grief. Cedar's execution was wonderful. I have seen him cast a frog a mile—but the frog had left the hook. It was remarkable to see him catch his hat, and terrifying to hear the language he used at such an ordinary angling event. It was not safe to be in his vicinity, but if this was unavoidable, the better course was to face him; because if you turned your back an instant, his flying hook would have a fiendish affinity for your trousers, and it was not beyond his powers to swing you kicking out over the stream. All of which, considering the frailties of human nature and of fishermen, could be forgiven; he had, however, one great fault impossible to overlook, and it was that he made more noise than a playful hippopotamus.

I hoped, despite all these things, that the big bass would rise to the occasion. He did rise. He must have recognized the situation of his life. He spread the waters of his shallow pool and accommodatingly hooked himself.

Cedar's next graceful move was to fall off the slippery stone on which he had been standing and to go out of sight. His hat floated downstream; the arched tip of his rod came up, then his arm, and his dripping shoulders and body. He yelled like a savage and pulled on the fish hard enough to turn a tuna in the air. The big bass leaped three times, made a long shoot with his black dorsal fin showing, and then, with a lunge, headed for some place remote from there. Cedar plowed after him, sending the water in sheets, and then he slipped, wildly swung his arms, and fell again.

I was sinking to the ground, owing to unutterable and overpowering sensations of joy, when a yell and a commotion in the bushes heralded the appearance of Reddy.

"Hang on, Cedar! Hang on!" he cried, and began an Indian war dance.

The few succeeding moments were somewhat blurred because of my excess of motion. When I returned to consciousness, Cedar was wading out with a hookless leader, a bloody shin, and a disposition utterly and irretrievably ruined.

"Put a job on me!" he roared.

Thereafter during the summer each of us made solitary and sneaking expeditions, bent on the capture of the lord of the Lackawaxen. And somehow each would return to find the other two derisively speculative as to what caused his clouded brow. Leader on leader went to grace the rocks of the old bronze warrior's home. At length Cedar and Reddy gave up, leaving the pool to me. I fed more than one choice shiner to the bass and more than once he sprang into the air to return my hook.

Summer and autumn passed; winter came to lock the Lackawaxen in icy fetters; I fished under Southern skies where lagoons and moss-shaded waters teemed with great and gamy fish, but I

[7]

never forgot him. I knew that when the season rolled around, when a June sun warmed the cold spring-fed Lackawaxen, he would be waiting for me.

Who was it spoke of the fleeting of time? Obviously he had never waited for the opening of the fishing season. At last the tedious time, like the water, flowed by. But then I found I had another long wait. Brilliant June days without a cloud were a joy to live, but worthless for fishing. Through all that beautiful month I plodded up to the pool, only to be unrewarded. Doubt began to assail me. Might not the ice, during the spring break-up, have scared him from the shallow hole? No. I felt that not even a rolling glacier could have moved him from his subterranean home.

Often as I reached the pool I saw fishermen wading down the stream, and on these occasions I sat on the bank and lazily waited for the intruders to pass on. Once, the first time I saw them, I had an agonizing fear that one of the yellow-helmeted, khaki-coated anglers would hook my bass. The fear, of course, was groundless. The idea of that grand fish rising to a feathery imitation of a bug or a lank dead bait had nothing in my experience to warrant its consideration. Small, lively bass, full of play, fond of chasing their golden shadows, and belligerent and hungry, were ready to fight and eat whatever swam into their ken. But a six-pound bass, slow to reach such weight in swift-running water, was old and wise and full of years. He did not feed often, and when he did he wanted a live fish big enough for a good mouthful. So, with these facts to soothe me I rested my fears, and got to look humorously at the invasions of the summer-hotel fishers.

They came wading, slipping, splashing downstream, blowing like porpoises, slapping at the water with all kinds of artificial and dead bait. And they called to me in a humor inspired by my fishing garb and the rustic environment:

"Hey, Rube! Ketchin' any?"

I said the suckers were bitin' right pert.

"What d'you call this stream?"

I replied, giving the Indian name.

"Lack-a-what? Can't you whistle it? Lack-awhacken? You mean Lack-afishin'."

"Lack-arotten," joined in another.

[8]

"Do you live here?" questioned a third.

I said yes.

"Why don't you move?" Whereupon they all laughed and pursued the noisy tenor of their way downstream, pitching their baits around.

"Say, fellows," I shouted after them, "are you training for the casting tournament in Madison Square Garden or do you think you're playing lacrosse?"

The laugh that came back proved the joke on them, and that it would be remembered as part of the glorious time they were having.

July brought the misty, dark, lowering days. Not only did I find the old king at home on these days, but just as contemptuous of hooks and leaders as he had been the summer before. About the middle of the month he stopped giving me paralysis of the heart; that is to say, he quit rising to my tempting chums and shiners. So I left him alone to rest, to rust out hooks and grow less suspicious.

By the time August came, the desire to call on him again was well-nigh irresistible. But I waited, and fished the Delaware, and still waited. I would get him when the harvest moon was full. Like all the old mossbacked denizens of the shady holes, he would come out then for a last range over the feeding shoals. At length a morning broke humid and warm, almost dark as twilight, with little gusts of fine rain. Of all days this was the day! I chose a stiff rod, a heavy silk line, a stout brown leader, and a large hook. From my bait box I took two five-inch red catfish, the little "stone-rollers" of the Delaware, and several long shiners. Thus equipped, I sallied forth.

The walk up the towpath, along the canal with its rushes and sedges, across the meadows white with late-blooming daisies, lost nothing because of its familiarity. When I reached the pool I saw in the low water near shore several small bass scouting among the schools of minnows. I did not want these pugnacious fellows to kill my bait, so, procuring a hellgrammite from under a stone, I put it on my hook and promptly caught two of them, and gave the other a scare he would not soon forget.

I decided to try the bass with one of his favorite shiners. With this trailing in the water I silently waded out, making not so much as a ripple. The old familiar oppression weighed on my breast; the old

[9]

throbbing boyish excitement tingled through my blood. I made a long cast and dropped the shiner lightly. He went under and then came up to swim about on the surface. This was a sign that made my heart leap. Then the water bulged, and a black bar shot across the middle of the long shiner. He went down out of sight, the last gleams of his divided brightness fading slowly. I did not need to see the little shower of silver scales floating up to know that the black bar had been the rounded nose of the old bass and that he had taken the shiner across the middle. I struck hard, and my hook came whistling at me. I had scored a clean miss.

I waded ashore very carefully, sat down on a stone by my bait pail, and meditated. Would he rise again? I had never known him to do so twice in one day. But then there had never been occasion. I thought of the "stone-rollers" and thrilled with certainty. Whatever he might resist, he could not resist one of those little red catfish. Long ago, when he was only a three- or four-pounder, roaming the deep eddies and swift rapids of the Delaware, before he had isolated himself to a peaceful old age in this quiet pool, he must have poked his nose under many a stone, with red eyes keen for one of those dainty morsels.

My excitation thrilled itself out to the calm assurance of the experienced fisherman. I firmly fastened on one of the catfish and stole out into the pool. I waded farther than ever before; I was careful but confident. Then I saw the two flat rocks dimly shining. The water was dark as it rippled by, gurgling softly; it gleamed with lengthening shadows and glints of amber.

I swung the catfish. A dull flash of sunshine seemed to come up to meet him. The water swirled and broke with a splash. The broad black head of the bass just skimmed the surface; his jaws opened wide to take in the bait; he turned and flapped a huge spread tail on the water.

Then I struck with all the power the tackle would stand. I felt the hook catch solidly as if in a sunken log. Swift as flashing light the bass leaped. The drops of water hissed and the leader whizzed. But the hook held. I let out one exultant yell. He did not leap again. He dashed to the right, then the left, in bursts of surprising speed. I had hardly warmed to the work when he settled down and made for the dark channel between the yellow rocks. My triumph

[10]

was to be short-lived. Where was the beautiful spectacular surface fight I expected of him? Cunning old monarch! He laid his great weight dead on the line and lunged for his sunken throne. I held him with a grim surety of the impossibility of stopping him. How I longed for deep, open water! The rod bent, the line strained and stretched. I removed my thumb and the reel sang one short shrill song. Then the bass was as still as the rock under which he had gone.

I had never dislodged a big bass from under a stone, and I saw herein further defeat; but I persevered, wading to different angles, and working all the tricks of the trade. I could not drag the fish out, nor pull the hook loose. I sat down on a stone and patiently waited for a long time, hoping he would come out on his own accord.

As a final resort I waded out. The water rose to my waist, then to my shoulders, my chin, and all but covered my raised face. When I reached the stone under which he had planted himself, I stood in water about four feet deep. I saw my leader, and tugged upon it, and kicked under the stone, all to no good.

Then I calculated I had a chance to dislodge him if I could get my arm under the shelf. So I went, hat, rod, and all. The current was just swift enough to lift my feet, making my task most difficult. At the third trial I got my hand on a sharp corner of stone and held fast. I ran my right hand along the leader, under the projecting slab of rock, till I touched the bass. I tried to get hold of him, but had to rise for air.

I dove again. The space was narrow, so narrow that I wondered how so large a fish could have gotten there. He had gone under sidewise, turned, and wedged his dorsal fin, fixing himself as solidly as the rock itself. I pulled frantically till I feared I would break the leader.

When I floundered up to breathe again, the thought occurred to me that I could rip him with my knife and, by taking the life out of him, loosen the powerful fin so he could be dragged out. Still, much as I wanted him, I could not do that. I resolved to make one more fair attempt. In a quick determined plunge I secured a more favorable hold for my left hand and reached under with my right. I felt his whole long length and I could not force a finger behind him anywhere. The gill toward me was shut tight like a trap door. But I

[11]

got a thumb and forefinger fastened to his lip. I tugged till a severe cramp numbed my hand; I saw red and my head whirled; a noise roared in my ears. I stayed until one more second would have made me a drowning man, then rose gasping and choking.

I broke off the leader close to the stone and waded ashore. I looked back at the pool, faintly circled by widening ripples. What a great hole and what a grand fish! I was glad I did not get him and knew I would never again disturb his peace.

So I took my rod and pail and the two little bass, and brushed the meadow daisies, and threaded the familiar green-lined towpath toward home.

2

FIGHTING QUALITIES OF BLACK BASS—1907

Though Dr. James A. Henshall published his definitive *Book of the Black Bass* in 1881, controversy concerning the game qualities of these species, both largemouth and smallmouth, extended well into this century. One pleasant result was that such controversy made for exciting magazine copy. Entire articles were devoted to whether treble-hooked plugs—practically invented for bass fishing—were sporting lures, and whether a trout fisherman would demean himself and his fly tackle by trying to take such unruly game.

By 1912 the black bass was happily accepted everywhere, including transplants to Europe. But a new controversy had flickered up: which of the two species was the better game fish. W. P. Corbett suggested in the pages of *Field and Stream* that the smallmouth, pound for pound, was superior to the largemouth as a game fish. Will H. Dilg, a popular angling writer of the time and future founder with Zane Grey of the Izaak Walton League, replied that such testimony was nonsense, and that the fighting qualities of any bass depended entirely on the conditions and temperature of the water he came from and what the fish had been eating. Largemouth and smallmouth bass taken from the same lake, he argued, were identical in taste and in behavior at the end of a line. Mr. C. replied that he had indeed taken largemouth and smallmouth bass from the same waters, and the smallmouth was still unquestionably superior. But Mr. Corbett's reply was a mite more sarcastic than his opening article, and at one point he called the big pot-bellied Florida bass "flabby monsters" and compared them to carp, and, in another context, he casually mentioned taking many smallmouths with fly tackle from the Delaware.

Suddenly, like a champion of insulted virtue, Zane Grey appeared on the stage. He was there to support Dilg's thesis and friendship; he was also aggravated by any comparison between bass and carp—not because he considered the bass lordly and the carp base, but because he knew that Mr. Corbett thought so. (Actually, ZG considered the carp as worthy an opponent as the bass but in a different class.) Mostly, however, Zane Grey was annoyed to find someone who pretended to know more about the Delaware than did ZG himself. Here is the last half of his reply.

GWR

FIGHTING QUALITIES OF BLACK BASS—1907[1]

If I know any fishing water at all it is the Delaware River. I live on it. I own nearly a thousand acres of land along it. I have fished it for ten years. I know every rapid, every eddy, almost, I might say, every stone from Callicoon to Port Jervis. This fifty-mile stretch of fast water I consider the very finest bass ground that I have fished. The mountains are heavily wooded and bold and rugged; the river is winding and picturesque and a succession of white rapids and foam-flecked eddies. The bass that grow from four to six and one-half pounds in this swift water are magnificent game fish. And that is why I am always at home in late summer when these big fish bite.

Mr. C. remarked that "thousands of bass are taken every summer with the fly on the Delaware." If it was meant seriously, I think it should have been made clear. I fancy that in his enthusiasm Mr. C. just "talked." He was not clear, deliberate, and absolutely sure of his facts.

There are black bass in the Delaware from its source down to Trenton. And at certain times during the season a few fish might rise to a fly somewhere above Milford, and very probably below in the quieter waters. The West Branch and the East Branch, joining at Hancock, are both shallow streams. Both branches furnish good fly-fishing for those who are content to catch little bass. Neither stream can be compared to the Lackawaxen River, which empties into the Delaware in front of my cottage. But I have never had a rise from a big bass in the Lackawaxen or the Delaware.

The Delaware proper only comes into existence at Hancock, and really is not a river until about Long Eddy. Cochecton Falls, five miles below Callicoon, marks the development of the best water. In ten years, during hundreds of trips between Cochecton Falls and

---

[1] Reprinted with the permission of A. S. Barnes & Company, Cranbury, New Jersey, from *Tales of Fresh-Water Fishing*, first published by Harper & Brothers in 1928. The date 1907 is the one given in *Tales of Fresh-Water Fishing*. Actually, this "Historic Controversy" (as *Field and Stream* called it) raged over many months five years later. "Fighting Qualities of Black Bass" first appeared in the May, 1912, issue of *Field and Stream*, and the debate was concluded with a last-licks reply on behalf of the largemouth by Will H. Dilg in the September, 1912, issue.

Cedar Rapids, perhaps thirty miles of swift water and positively the best of the river, I have never encountered a fly fisherman. At the boarding houses and camps, I have met, in that time, perhaps half a dozen men who had fly rods in their outfits.

The best of these fishermen, Mr. Patterson, a man of wide experience and much skill, told me he caught a good many bass. But he admitted the fish ran small, a two-pounder being the largest. The bass I have caught on a fly with few exceptions ran less than half a pound in weight. A small gold spoon with a fly attached appeared to be more attractive, and bass up to three pounds would take it. But for me, the real bass, the big fellows, never batted an eye or twitched a fin at these artificial lures. Possibly they may have done so for some better fisherman than I am. However, I find it hard to believe. If I saw it I would put it down as the exception that proved the rule.

I see hundreds of canoeists and fishermen come down the Delaware every summer. If they were fly fishermen I would know it. They all stop at the hotel opposite my place.[2] Many of them are kind enough to pay me a little visit. Whatever style of fishermen they were, if they caught a big bass or even made a good catch I would be likely to find it out. Most of them, amateurs or otherwise, had good fishing. Some were inclined to ridicule sport on the Delaware. To these I usually told a few bass stories and always had the pleasure of seeing them try politely to hide their convictions of what an awful liar I was. Then I paralyzed them by showing a 26-inch mounted bass, and upon occasions a few live bass of six pounds and more; and upon one remarkable occasion I made several well-meaning but doubtful fishermen speechless and sick. These men had fished around the hotel for days. They were disgusted. They could not catch any bass. Somebody sent them to me. I am sorry to state that they hurt my feelings by asking me if I had bait to sell. That little interview ended in my advising them to learn the rudiments of the sport—to make their own flies and catch their own bait. And they delicately implied that they did not believe there were any

---

[2] The Delaware House, where ZG often stayed himself before moving to Lackawaxen, and in front of which he first met his wife. The hotel is gone, and today New York State Highway 97 runs opposite ZG's old home, now the Zane Grey Inn.

[16]

more bass in the Delaware than there were brains in my head. So I sarcastically told them to come down to the hotel float on the following evening at sunset. Next morning at daylight my brother and I started up the river. We had *rather* a good day. At sunset we were on time with the boat at the float. The disgruntled anglers were on hand. In fact, so many people crowded down on the float that it sank an inch or so under water. I wish all my readers could have heard the plunging of the big bass in my fish box as I lifted the lid. When I bent over to take out a bass I was deluged with water. But this was great! I captured a fine black fellow—about four and a half pounds—and he gaped and spread his great dorsal fin and curved his broad tail, and then savagely shook himself. I pitched him out. Souse! Then, deliberately, one after another, I lifted big bass out of the fish box under the seat of my boat and threw them into the water. Forty bass, not one under three pounds and some over four!

This is history now up along that section of the Delaware, and I am not considered so much of a liar as I used to be.

I have caught a good many Delaware bass running over six pounds, and I want to say that these long, black and bronze fellows, peculiar to the swift water of this river, are the most beautiful and gamy fish that swim. I never get tired of studying them and catching them. It took me years to learn how to catch them. Perhaps some day I shall tell how to do it. But not until I have had the pleasure of seeing Dilg and Davis, and other celebrated fishermen who have not yet honored me with a visit, breaking their arms and hearts trying to induce one of these grand fish to rise to an artificial lure. Because, gentlemen, they will not do it.

Every fishing water has its secrets. A river or a lake is not a dead thing. It has beauty and wisdom and content. And to yield up these mysteries it must be fished with more than hooks and for more than fish. Strange things happen to the inquiring fisherman. Nature meets him halfway on his adventure. He must have eyes that see. One fisherman may have keener eyes than another, but no one fisherman's observation is enough.

I can learn from anyone, yet I do not stop at that, and go on trying to learn for myself. And so amazing experience and singular knowledge have become my possession. Let me close with one more word about the Delaware. In July, when the water gets low and clear, I go up the river. I build a raft and lie flat upon it and drift down. I see the bottom everywhere, except in rough water. I see the rocks, the shelves, the caverns. I see where the big bass live. And I remember. When the time comes for me to fish I know where the big bass are. Nevertheless, it is far from easy to catch them. They are old and wary. I never caught one in deep water. I never had one take hold nearer than 100 feet from the boat. I never use a casting rod or fish with a short line. I never caught one on the day I first saw him. I never caught one on any day he saw me or the boat. I never caught a very large bass, say over five pounds, until after the beginning of the harvest moon. Furthermore, I know that these big bass do not feed often.

One day at a certain place I caught a smallmouth bass, next day a largemouth, then a *salt-water striped bass*, all out of the same hole. They were about the same size, upward of two pounds; none of the fish jumped and they all fought well and equally. I could not have told the difference. This was in the Delaware, not a mile from my home. I have seen striped bass with the shad, and once I think I saw a sturgeon. While fishing for bass I have caught big trout. I have had small bass bite my bare toes in the water. I have seen bass engaged in a pitched battle with what appeared to be some kind of order. I have seen a bass tear a water snake to pieces. These last two instances I heard of from other fishermen before I saw them myself.

I repeat, no one fisherman's observation or experience is enough. We must get together or forever be at dagger's point.

3

ROPING LIONS IN THE GRAND CANYON

Colonel C. J. "Buffalo" Jones. The name sounds corny, and Americans already have one Buffalo Somebody to accept as a Western hero. Yet it's our loss that Jones is so little known, for he earned his Buffalo sobriquet for saving the bison from extinction, not for having contributed to its destruction.

Born in Tazewell County, Illinois, in 1844, Charles Jesse Jones was the second son in a family of twelve. His father owned 160 acres of land bought from the government, and when once asked for childhood memories, Charles Jesse replied, "Work, work, work."

One afternoon in his youth Jones caught an immature fox squirrel instead of working and got a beating for his indulgence. However, the "pet" squirrel was later converted to two dollars in an exchange that shaped Jones' life:

> *The buyer's offer almost took my breath. . . . It was that transaction which fixed upon me the ruling passion that has adhered so closely through life. From that time until this, I have never lost an opportunity in my power to capture every wild animal that runs on legs, as well as some that creep upon their bellies.*[1]

It was doubtless this same "ruling passion" that years later led to his desire to capture mountain lions alive, for the market value of a live cougar at the turn of the century was better than one hundred dollars; for a lion skin, less than ten.

But Jones' work wasn't entirely mercenary. He shared with the leading conservationists of his day the naive faith that eliminating predators would bring about another Garden of Eden inhabited only by "beneficial" (i.e., non-competitive and edible) birds and animals. And for a man who had never seen disease and starvation in entire herds of deer and elk due to overpopulation and overgrazed rangelands, these early conservation notions seemed logical.

Jones also helped popularize natural history studies. He supplied the newly created zoos in St. Louis, Philadelphia, and New York with live specimens, and he even managed to get some bison packed off to Britain as a gift to the Prince of Wales. In 1910 he capped his career with a safari to Africa, where he thoroughly one-upped Teddy Roosevelt by roping and *capturing alive* many of the same species the former President had *shot* during his safari the previous year. (TR showed excellent grace on Jones' return by sending him a letter of praise.)

Jones' life was not merely a carnival of fabulous exploits. He knew that his trips and the films he made and the lectures he gave were an excellent means to publicize the cause of wildlife. President Roosevelt made Jones an honorary game warden and appointed him a "field commander" in the nation's conservation campaign. When the Yellowstone herd of bison all but vanished, Jones packed 26 of his own animals north to refurbish the

---

[1] *Buffalo Jones' Forty Years of Adventure*—A Volume of Facts Gathered from Experience, by Hon. C. J. Jones, whose Eventful Life has been Devoted to the Preservation of the American Bison and Other Wild Animals, etc., compiled by Henry Inman, London: S. Low, Marston & Company, Ltd., 1899, p. 22.

herd. He also sent bison to the Wainwright ranch in Canada for breeding and distribution, and wherever he went, Jones tried to interest ranchers in domesticating bison for food stock rather than introducing foreign cattles. In an experiment, he crossbred black Galloway cattle with bison to produce an animal he called "catalo," which he claimed had a finer flavored meat than longhorn and was better able to withstand the rigors of a plains' winter than ordinary cattle. Jones even visited the Arctic and tried to bring back musk ox (after roping them, of course!) to see whether they, too, might be domesticated. Just two years before his death, the federal government issued a new five-cent coin showing a bison on its reverse side, and Jones must have felt pride in the role he'd played in saving these animals from extinction.

*

The year the Buffalo nickel appeared—1913—Zane Grey was about to leave on another Arizona trip, but with a new guide, Al Doyle of Flagstaff. It's doubtful whether ZG ever saw Jones after their second trip together to rope mountain lions, in what is today the Kaibab National Forest. But their association was mutually beneficial while it lasted: Jones and his activities were given excellent publicity, and Grey was introduced to people and a way of life that forever affected his own lifestyle and writing. *The Last of the Plainsmen* is a profile of Jones, and after he died in 1915, Zane Grey summed up his larger debt to this pioneer:

> *Buffalo Jones was great in all those remarkable qualities common to the men who opened up the West. Courage, endurance, determination, and hardihood were developed in him to the supermost degree. No doubt something of Buffalo Jones crept unconsciously into all the great fiction characters I have created.*

When "Roping Lions in the Grand Canyon" was serialized in *Field and Stream* beginning January, 1909, a picture of the author was run on a separate page with the following caption:

> *It is one thing to bag mountain lions at safe distances with a modern rifle, and quite another to toss a rope around their necks, drag them fighting and snarling from a tree, and bind them securely with loops and knots. This is the newest of sports, strenuous and replete with peril, but alive with the thrills which sportsmen accept as full payment for their toils and risks. But few men have as yet shared in its delights, and one of these few is Zane Grey, the novelist, who, by a strange chance, after chronicling the wildest adventures of Kentucky's daring pioneers, has voluntarily taken part in adventures from which even Boone or Kenton would have withheld their hands.*

Today the mountain lion has been tremendously reduced from its former range which once extended throughout North America. According to J. Lloyd Cahill of the University of California's Department of Zoology at Berkeley, the total number of wild pumas probably does not exceed 17,500 with better than half that figure residing in western Canada. Many states still maintain bounties on the big cats, and Zane Grey's favorite hunting state, Arizona,

[21]

alone paid over $350,000 in public funds for the slaughter of 4,954 mountain lions beween 1947 and 1969. In 1970, Arizona eliminated the bounty, but most experts find the mountain lion's future dim there. Nonbounty hunting continues, and the human population of the state is increasing, squeezing out the last wild areas.

Some outfitters nowadays "guarantee" mountain lions to hunters and make good their promise by releasing a caged animal for their clients to pursue in a jeep. When the lion is treed (often after just a short run), the "hunters" shoot the immobile target and return directly to camp for the next plane home.

Zane Grey and Buffalo Jones would have been outraged by such behavior. For them, one of the supreme values of hunting lay in matching exertion to the prize. A bear or mountain lion was not fair game until the rituals of camping, tracking, and the chase had entitled the hunter to the animal's life. And wrestling lions from a tree and capturing them alive were what both men relished in the way of high adventure. Certainly the anguish they felt at the death of even one of these fine animals is well documented in the following excerpts from "Roping Lions in the Grand Canyon."

GWR

ROPING LIONS IN THE GRAND CANYON

The Grand Canyon of Arizona is over two hundred miles long, thirteen wide, and a mile and a half deep; a titanic gorge in which mountains, tablelands, chasms and cliffs lie half veiled in purple haze. It is wild and sublime, a thing of wonder, of mystery— beyond all else a place to grip the heart of a man, to unleash his daring spirit.

On April 20th, 1908, after days on the hot desert, my weary party and pack train reached the summit of Powell's Plateau, the most isolated, inaccessible and remarkable mesa of any size in all the canyon country. Cut off from the mainland it appeared insurmountable; standing aloof from the towers and escarpments, rugged and bold in outline, its forest covering like a strip of black velvet, its giant granite walls gold in the sun, it seemed apart from the world, haunting with its beauty, isolation and wild promise.

The members of my party harmoniously fitted the scene. Buffalo Jones, burly-shouldered, bronze-faced, and grim, proved in his appearance what a lifetime on the plains could make of a man. Emett[1] was a Mormon, a massively built gray-bearded son of the desert; he had lived his life on it; he had conquered it and in his falcon eyes shone all its fire and freedom. Ranger Jim Owens had the wiry, supple body and careless, tidy garb of the cowboy, and the watchful gaze, quiet face and locked lips of the frontiersman.

While we were pitching camp among magnificent pine trees, and above a hollow where a heavy bank of snow still lay, a sodden pounding in the turf attracted our attention.

"Hold the horses!" yelled Emett.

As we all made a dive among our snorting and plunging horses the sound seemed to be coming right into camp. In a moment I saw a string of wild horses thundering by. A noble black stallion led them, and as he ran with beautiful stride he curved his fine head backward to look at us, and whistled his wild challenge.

Later a herd of large white-tailed deer trooped up the hollow. Nothing could have pleased me better, incident to the settling into permanent camp. The wild horses and tame deer added the all-satisfying touch to the background of forest, flowers and mighty pines and sunlit patches of grass, the white tents and red blankets, the sleeping hounds and blazing fire-logs all making a picture like that of a hunter's dream.

"Come, saddle up," called the never restful Jones, "and we'll get the lay of the land." All afternoon we spent riding the plateau. What a wonderful place! We were completely bewildered with its physical properties, and surprised at the abundance of wild horses and mustangs, deer, coyotes, foxes, grouse and other birds, and over-joyed to find innumerable lion trails. When we returned to camp I drew a rough map, which Jones laid flat on the ground as he called us around him.

"Now, boys, let's get our heads together."

In shape the plateau resembled the ace of clubs. The center and side wings were high and well wooded with heavy pines; the middle

---

[1] ZG uses two spellings for this man's name: Emett and Emmet. For consistency's sake, we chose the former. Emett impressed Zane Grey nearly as much as did Buffalo Jones. Years later, in the August, 1926, issue of *American Magazine*, ZG published a story about this "mighty Mormon" entitled "The Man Who Influenced Me Most."

[23]

wing was longest, sloped west, had no pine, but a dense growth of cedar. Numerous ridges and canyons cut up this middle wing. Middle Canyon, the longest and deepest, bisected the plateau, headed near camp, and ran parallel with two smaller ones, which we named Right and Left Canyons. These three were lion runways, and deer carcasses lined the thickets. North Hollow was the only depression, as well as runway, on the northwest rim. West Point formed the extreme western cape of the plateau. To the left of West Point was a deep cut-in of the rim wall, called the Bay. The three important canyons opened into it. From the Bay, the south rim was regular and impassable all the way round to the narrow Saddle, which connected it to the mainland.

"Now then," said Jones, when we assured him that we were pretty well informed as to the important features, "you can readily see our advantage. The plateau is about nine or ten miles long, and six wide at its widest. We can't get lost, at least for long. We know where lions can go over the rim and we'll head them off, make shortcut chases, something new in lion hunting. We are positive the lions cannot get over the second wall, except where we came up, at the Saddle. In regard to lion signs, I'm doubtful of the evidence of my own eyes. This is virgin ground. No white man or Indian has ever hunted lions here. We have stumbled on a lion home, the breeding place of hundreds of lions that infest the north rim of the canyon."

The old plainsman struck a big fist into the palm of his hand, a rare action with him. Jim lifted his broad hat and ran his fingers through his white hair. In Emett's clear desert-eagle eyes shown a furtive, anxious look, which yet could not overshadow the smouldering fire.

"If only we don't kill the horses!" he said.

More than anything else that remark from such a man thrilled me with its subtle suggestion. He loved those beautiful horses. What wild rides he saw in his mind's eye! In cold calculation we perceived the wonderful possibilities never before experienced by hunters.

During supper we talked incessantly, and afterward around the camp fire. Twilight fell with the dark shadows sweeping under the silent pines; the night wind rose and began its moan.

[24]

"Shore there's some scent on the wind," said Jim, lighting his pipe with a red ember. "See how uneasy Don is."

The hound raised his fine, dark head and repeatedly sniffed the air, then walked to and fro as if on guard for his pack. Moze ground his teeth on a bone and growled at one of the pups. Sounder was sleepy, but he watched Don with suspicious eyes. The other hounds, mature and somber, lay stretched before the fire.

"Tie them up, Jim," said Jones, "and let's turn in."

*

When I awakened next morning the sound of Emett's axe rang out sharply. Little streaks of light from the camp fire played between the flaps of the tent. I saw old Moze get up and stretch himself.

"All rustle for breakfast," called Jim.

We ate in the semi-darkness with the gray shadow ever brightening. Dawn broke as we saddled our horses. The pups were limber, and ran to and fro on their chains, scenting the air; the older hounds stood quietly waiting.

"Climb up, you fellows," said Jones, impatiently. "Have I got everything—rope, chains, collars, wire, nippers? Yes, all right. Hyar, you lazy dogs—out of this!"

We struck out of the pines at half past five. Floating mist hid the lower end of the plateau. The morning had a cool touch but there was no frost. Crossing Middle Canyon about halfway down we jogged on. Cedar trees began to show bright green against the soft gray sage. We were nearing the dark line of the cedar forest when Jim, who led, held up his hand in a warning check. We closed in around him.

"Watch Don," he said.

The hound stood stiff, head well up, nose working, and the hair on his back bristling. All the other hounds whined and kept close to him.

"Don scents a lion," whispered Jim.

"Hunt 'em up Don, old boy," called Jones.

The pack commenced to work back and forth along the ridge. We neared a hollow when Don barked eagerly. Sounder answered and likewise Jude. Moze's short angry "bow-wow" showed the old gladiator to be in line.

[25]

"Ranger's gone," cried Jim. "He was farthest ahead. I'll bet he's struck it. We'll know in a minute, for we're close."

The hounds were tearing through the sage, working harder and harder, calling and answering one another, all the time getting down into the hollow.

Don suddenly let out a string of yelps. I saw him, running head up, pass into the cedars like a yellow dart. Sounder howled his deep, full bay, and led the rest of the pack up the slope in angry clamor.

"They're off!" yelled Jim, and so were we.

In less than a minute we had lost one another. Crashings among the dry cedars, thud of hoofs and yells kept me going in one direction. The fiery burst of the hounds had surprised me. I remembered that Jim had said Emett and his charger might keep the pack in sight, but that none of the rest of us could.

We climbed a ridge, and found the cedars thinning out into open patches. Then we faced a bare slope of sage and I saw Emett below on his big horse. For what seemed a long time, I threaded the maze of cedar, galloped the open sage flats, always on Emett's track.

A signal cry, sharp to the right, turned me. I answered, and with the exchange of signal cries found my way into an open glade where Jones and Jim awaited me.

"Here's one," said Jim. "Emett must be with the hounds. Listen."

The baying came closer and closer. Our horses threw up long ears. It was hard to sit still and wait. At a quick cry from Jim we saw Don cross the lower end of the flat.

No need to spur our mounts! The lifting of bridles served, and away we raced. My mustang passed the others in short order. Don had long disappeared, but with blended bays, Jude, Moze, and Sounder broke out of the cedars hot on the trail. They, too, were out of sight in a moment.

We crossed a canyon, and presently reached another which, from its depth, must have been Middle Canyon. From a bare ridge we distinguished the line of pines above us, and decided that our location was in about the center of the plateau. We came to a halt where the canyon widened and was not so deep, with cliffs and cedars opposite us, and an easy slope leading down. Sounder bayed incessantly; Moze emitted harsh, eager howls, and both hounds, in plain sight, began working in circles.

[26]

"The lion has gone up somewhere," cried Jim. "Look sharp!"

Repeatedly Moze worked to the edge of a low wall of stone and looked over; then he barked and ran back to the slope, only to return. When I saw him slide down a steep place, make for the bottom of the stone wall, and jump into the low branches of a cedar I knew where to look. Then I descried the lion, a round yellow ball, cunningly curled up in a mass of dark branches. He had leaped into the tree from the wall.

"There he is! Treed! Treed!" I yelled. "Moze has found him."

"Down boys, down into the canyon," shouted Jones, in sharp voice. "Make a racket, we don't want him to jump."

How he and Jim and Emett rolled and cracked the stone! For a moment I could not get off my horse; I was chained to my saddle by a strange vacillation that could have been no other thing than fear.

"Are you afraid?" called Jones from below.

"Yes, but I am coming," I replied, and dismounted to plunge down the hill. It may have been shame or anger that dominated me then; whatever it was, I made directly for the cedar, and did not halt until I was under the snarling lion.

"Not too close!" warned Jones. "He might jump. It's a tom, a two-year-old, and full of fight."

It did not matter to me then whether he jumped or not. I knew I had to be cured of my dread, and the sooner it was done the better.

Old Moze had already climbed a third of the distance up to the lion.

"Hyar Moze! Out of there, you rascal coon chaser!" Jones yelled as he threw stones and sticks at the hound. Moze, however, replied with his snarly bark and climbed on steadily.

"I've got to pull him out. Watch close, boys, and tell me if the lion starts down."

When Jones climbed the first few branches of the tree, Tom let out an ominous growl.

"Make ready to jump. Shore he's comin'," called Jim.

The lion, snarling viciously, started to descend. It was a ticklish moment for all of us, particularly Jones. Warily he backed down.

"Boys, maybe he's bluffing," said Jones. "Try him out. Grab sticks and run at the tree and yell, as if you were going to kill him."

Not improbably the demonstration we executed under the tree

[27]

would have frightened even an African lion. Tom hesitated, showed his white fangs, returned to his first perch, and from there climbed as far as he could. The forked branch on which he stood swayed alarmingly.

"Here, punch Moze out," said Jim handing up a long pole.

The old hound hung like a leech to the tree, making it difficult to dislodge him. At length he fell heavily, and venting his thick battle cry, attempted to climb again.

Jim seized him, made him fast to the rope with which Sounder had already been tied.

"Say, Emett, I've no chance here," called Jones. "You try to throw at him from the rock."

Emett ran up the rock, coiled his lasso and cast the noose. It sailed perfectly in between the branches and circled Tom's head. Before it could be slipped tight the lion threw it off. Then he hid behind the branches.

"I'm going farther up," said Jones.

"Be quick," yelled Jim.

Jones evidently had that in mind. When he reached the middle fork of the cedar, he stood erect and extended the noose of his lasso on the point of his pole. Tom, with a hiss and snap, struck at it savagely. The second trial tempted the lion to saw the rope with his teeth. In a flash Jones withdrew the pole, and lifted a loop of the slack rope over the lion's ears.

"Pull!" he yelled.

Emett, at the other end of the lasso, threw his great strength into action, pulling the lion out with a crash, and giving the cedar such a tremendous shaking that Jones lost his footing and fell heavily.

Thrilling as the moment was, I had to laugh, for Jones came up out of a cloud of dust, as angry as a wet hornet, and made prodigious leaps to get out of the reach of the whirling lion.

"Look out!—" he bawled.

Tom, certainly none the worse for his tumble, made three leaps, two at Jones, one at Jim, which was checked by the short length of the rope in Emett's hands. Then for a moment, a thick cloud of dust enveloped the wrestling lion, during which the quick-witted Jones tied the free end of the lasso to a sapling.

"Dod gast the luck!" yelled Jones, reaching for another lasso. "I

[28]

didn't mean for you to pull him out of the tree. Now he'll get loose or kill himself."

When the dust cleared away, we discovered our prize stretched out at full length and frothing at the mouth. As Jones approached, the lion began a series of evolutions so rapid as to be almost indiscernible to the eye. I saw a wheel of dust and yellow fur. Then came a thud and the lion lay inert.

Jones pounced upon him and loosed the lasso around his neck.

"I think he's done for, but maybe not. He's breathing yet. Here, help me tie his paws together. Look out! He's coming to!"

The lion stirred and raised his head. Jones ran the loop of the second lasso around the two hind paws and stretched the lion out. While in this helpless position and with no strength and hardly any breath left in him the lion was easy to handle. With Emett's help Jones quickly clipped the sharp claws, tied the four paws together, took off the neck lasso and substituted a collar and chain.

"There, that's one. He'll come to all right," said Jones. "But we are lucky. Emett, never pull another lion clear out of a tree. Pull him over a limb and hang him there while someone below ropes his hind paws. That's the only way, and if we don't stick to it, somebody is going to get done for. Come, now, we'll leave this fellow here and hunt up Don and Jude. They've treed another lion by this time."

Remarkable to me was to see how, as soon as the lion lay helpless, Sounder lost his interest. Moze growled, yet readily left the spot. Before we reached the level, both hounds had disappeared.

"Hear that?" yelled Jones, digging spurs into his horse. "Hi! Hi! Hi!"

From the cedars rang the thrilling, blending chorus of bays that told of a treed lion. The forest was almost impenetrable. We had to pick our way. Emett forged ahead; we heard him smashing the deadwood; and soon a yell proclaimed the truth of Jones' assertion.

First I saw the men looking upward; then Moze climbed the cedar, and the other hounds with noses skyward; and last, in the dead top of the tree, a dark blot against the blue, a big tawny lion.

"Whoop!" The yell leaped past my lips. Quiet Jim was yelling;

[29]

and Emett, silent man of the desert, let from his wide cavernous chest a booming roar that drowned ours.

Jones' next decisive action turned us from exultation to the grim business of the thing. He pulled Moze out of the cedar, and while he climbed up, Emett ran his rope under the collars of all of the hounds. Quick as the idea flashed over me I leaped into the cedar adjoining the one Jones was in, and went up hand over hand. A few pulls brought me to the top, and then my blood ran hot and quick, for I was level with the lion, too close for comfort, but in excellent position for taking pictures.

The lion, not heeding me, peered down at Jones, between wide-spread paws. I could hear nothing except the hounds. Jones' gray hat came pushing up between the dead snags; then his burly shoulders. The quivering muscles of the lion gathered tense, and his lithe body crouched low on the branches. He was about to jump. His open dripping jaws, his wild eyes, roving in terror for some means of escape, his tufted tail, swinging against the twigs and breaking them, manifested his extremity. The eager hounds waited below, howling, leaping.

It bothered me considerably to keep my balance, regulate my camera, and watch the proceedings. Jones climbed on with his rope between his teeth, and a long stick. The very next instant it seemed to me, I heard the cracking of branches and saw the lion biting hard at the noose which circled his neck.

Here I swung down, branch to branch, and dropped to the ground, for I wanted to see what went on below. Above the howls and yelps, I distinguished Jones' yell. Emett ran directly under the lion with a spread noose in his hands. Jones pulled and pulled, but the lion held on firmly. Throwing the end of the lasso down to Jim, Jones yelled again, and then they both pulled. The lion was too strong. Suddenly, however, the branch broke, letting the lion fall, kicking frantically with all four paws. Emett grasped one of the four whipping paws, and even as the powerful animal sent him staggering, he dexterously left the noose fast on the paw. Jim and Jones in unison let go of their lasso, which streaked up through the branches as the lion fell, and then it dropped to the ground, where Jim made a flying grab for it. Jones, plunging out of the tree, fell upon the rope at the same instant.

[30]

If the action up to then had been fast, it was slow to what followed. It seemed impossible for two strong men with one lasso, and a giant with another, to straighten out that lion. He was all over the little space under the trees at once. The dust flew, the sticks snapped, the gravel pattered like shot against the cedars. Jones plowed the ground flat on his stomach, holding on with one hand, with the other trying to fasten the rope to something; Jim went to his knees; and on the other side of the lion, Emett's huge bulk tipped a sharp angle, and then fell.

I shouted and ran forward, having no idea what to do, but Emett rolled backward, at the same instant the other men got a strong haul on the lion. Short as that moment was in which the lasso slackened, it sufficed for Jones to make the rope fast to a tree. Whereupon with the three men pulling on the other side of the leaping lion, somehow I had flashed into my mind the game that children play, called skipping the rope, for the lion and lasso shot up and down.

This lasted for only a few seconds. They stretched the beast from tree to tree, and Jones running with the third lasso, made fast the front paws.

"It's a female," said Jones, as the lion lay helpless, her sides swelling; "a good-sized female. She's nearly eight feet from tip to tip, but not very heavy. Hand me another rope."

When all four lassos had been stretched, the lioness could not move. Jones strapped a collar around her neck and clipped the sharp yellow claws.

"Now to muzzle her," he continued.

Jones' method of performing this most hazardous part of the work was characteristic of him. He thrust a stick between her open jaws, and when she crushed it to splinters he tried another, and yet another, until he found one that she could not break. Then while she bit on it, he placed a wire loop over her nose, slowly tightening it, leaving the stick back of her big canines.

The hounds ceased their yelping and when untied, Sounder wagged his tail as if to say, "Well done," and then lay down; Don walked within three feet of the lion, as if she were now beneath his dignity; Jude began to nurse and lick her sore paw; only Moze, the incorrigible, retained antipathy for the captive, and he growled, as

[31]

always, low and deep. And on the moment, Ranger, dusty and lame from travel, trotted wearily into the glade and, looking at the lioness, gave one disgusted bark and flopped down.

Transporting our captives to camp bade fair to make us work. Jones had brought a packsaddle and two panniers. When Emett essayed to lead the horse which carried these, the animal stood straight up and began to show some of his primal desert instincts. It certainly was good luck that we unbuckled the packsaddle straps before he left the vicinity. In about three jumps he had separated himself from the panniers, which were then placed upon the back of another horse. This one, a fine-looking beast, and amiable under surroundings where his life and health were considered even a little, immediately disclaimed any intention of entering the forest.

"They scent the lions," said Jones. "I was afraid of it; never had but one nag that would pack lions."

"Maybe we can't pack them at all," replied Emett dubiously. "It's certainly new to me."

"We've got to," Jones asserted; "try the sorrel."

For the first time in a serviceable and honorable life, according to Emett, the sorrel broke his halter and kicked like a plantation mule.

"It's a matter of fright. Try the stallion. He doesn't look afraid," said Jones, who never knew when he was beaten.

Emett gazed at Jones as if he had not heard right.

"Go ahead, try the stallion. I like the way he looks."

No wonder! The big stallion looked a king of horses—just what he would have been if Emett had not taken him, when a colt, from his wild desert brothers. He scented the lions, and he held his proud head up, his ears erect, and his large, dark eyes shone fiery and expressive.

"I'll try to lead him in and let him see the lions. We can't fool him," said Emett.

Marc showed no hesitation, nor anything we expected. He stood stiff-legged, and looked as if he wanted to fight.

"He's all right; he'll pack them," declared Jones.

The packsaddle being strapped on and the panniers hooked to the horns, Jones and Jim lifted Tom and shoved him down into the left pannier while Emett held the horse. A madder lion than Tom

[32]

never lived. It was cruel enough to be lassoed and disgrace enough to be "hog-tied," as Jim called it, but to be thrust down into a bag and packed on a horse was adding insult to injury. Tom frothed at the mouth and seemed like a fizzing torpedo about to explode. The lioness being considerably longer and larger, was with difficulty gotten into the other pannier, and her head and paws hung out. Both lions kept growling and snarling.

Marc packed the lions to camp in short order, and, quoting Jones, "without turning a hair." Jim and Emett unhooked one of the panniers and dumped out the lioness. Jones fastened her chain to a small pine tree, and as she lay powerless he pulled out the stick back of her canines. This allowed the wire muzzle to fall off. She signalled this freedom with a roar that showed her health to be still unimpaired. The last action in releasing her from her painful bonds Jones performed with sleight-of-hand dexterity. He slipped the loop fastening one paw, which loosened the rope, and in a twinkling let her work all of her other paws free. Up she sprang, ears flat, eyes ablaze, mouth wide, once more capable of defense, true to her instinct and her name.

Before the men lowered Tom from Marc's back I stepped closer and put my face within six inches of the lion's. He promptly spat on me. I had to steel my nerve to keep so close. But I wanted to see a wild lion's eyes at close range. They were exquisitely beautiful, their physical properties as wonderful as their expression. Great half globes of tawny amber, streaked with delicate wavy lines of black, surrounding pupils of intense purple fire. Pictures shone and faded in the amber light—the shaggy-tipped plateau, the dark pines and smoky canyons, the great dotted downward slopes, the yellow cliffs and crags. Deep in those live pupils, changing, quickening with a thousand vibrations, quivered the soul of this savage beast, the wildest of all wild Nature, unquenchable love of life and freedom, flame of defiance and hate.

Jones disposed of Tom in the same manner as he had the lioness, chaining him to an adjoining small pine, where he leaped and wrestled.

*

That night the wind switched and blew cold from the north, and so strong that the camp fire roared like a furnace. Next morning, we

[33]

had breakfast and got into our saddles by the time the sun, a red ball low down among the pines, began to brighten and turn to gold. No snow had fallen but a thick frost encrusted the ground. The hounds, wearing cloth moccasins, which plainly they detested, trotted in front.

Jones led down the big hollow to which he kept after we had passed the edge of the pines; then marking a herd of deer ahead, he turned his horse up the bank.

We breasted the ridge and jogged toward the cedar forest, which we entered without having seen the hounds show interest in anything. Under the cedars in the soft yellow dust we crossed lion tracks, many of them, but too old to carry a scent. Even North Hollow with its regular beaten runway failed to win a murmur from the pack.

"Spread out," said Jones, "and look for tracks. I'll keep the center and hold in the hounds."

Signalling occasionally to one another we crossed almost the breadth of the cedar forest to its western end, where the open sage flats inclined to the rim. In one of those flats I came upon a broken sage bush, the grass being thick thereabout. I discovered no track but dismounted and scrutinized the surroundings carefully. A heavy body had been dragged across the sage, crushing it. The ends of broken bushes were green, the leaves showed bruises.

I began to feel like Don when he scented game. Leading my mustang I slowly proceeded across the open, guided by an occasional downtrodden bush or tuft of grass. As I neared the cedars again, my horse snorted. Under the first three I found a ghastly bunch of red bones, a spread of grayish hairs, and a split skull. The bones were yet wet; two long doe ears were still warm. Then I saw big lion tracks in the dust and even a well-pressed imprint of a lion's body where he had rolled or lain.

The two yells I sent ringing into the forest were productive of interesting results. Answers came from near and far. Then, what with my calling and the replies, the forest rang so steadily with shrill cries that the echoes had no chance to follow.

An elephant in the jungle could not have caused more crashing and breaking of brush than did Emett as he made his way to me. He arrived from the forest just as Jim galloped across the flat. Mutely I held up the two long ears.

"Get on your horse!" cried Jim after one quick glance at the spread of bones and hair.

It was well he said that, for I might have been left behind. I ran to Foxie and vaulted upon him. A flash of yellow appeared among the sage and a string of yelps split the air.

"It's Don!" yelled Jim.

Well we knew that. What a sight to see him running straight for us! He passed, a savage yellow wolf in his ferocity, and disappeared like a gleam under the gloomy cedars.

We spurred after him. The other hounds sped by. Jones closed in on us from the left, and in a few minutes we were strung out behind Emett, fighting the branches, dodging and swerving, hugging the saddle, and always sending out our sharp yells.

The race was furious but short. The three of us coming up together found Emett dismounted on the extreme end of West Point.

"The hounds have gone down," he said, pointing to the runway.

We all listened to the bays.

"Shore they've got him up!" asserted Jim. "Like as not they found him under the rim here, sleeping off his gorge. Now fellows, I'll go down. It might be a good idea for you to spread along the rim."

With that we turned our horses eastward and rode as close to the rim as possible. Clumps of cedars and deep fissures often forced us to circle them. The hounds, traveling under the walls below, kept pace with us and then forged ahead, which fact caused Jones to dispatch Emett on the gallop for the next runway at North Hollow.

Soon Jones bade me dismount and make my way out upon one of the promontories, while he rode a little farther on. As I tied my mustang I heard the hounds, faint and far beneath. I waded through the sage and cedar to the rim.

Cape after cape jutted out over the abyss. Some were very sharp and bare, others covered with cedar; some tottering crags with a crumbling bridge leading to their rims; and some ran down like giant steps. From one of these I watched below. The slope here

[35]

under the wall was like the side of a rugged mountain. Somewhere down among the dark patches of cedar and the great blocks of stone the hounds were hunting the lion, but I could not see one of them.

The promontory I had chosen had a split, and choked as this was with brush, rock, and shale, it seemed a place where I might climb down. Once started, I could not turn back, and sliding, clinging to what afforded, I worked down the crack. A wall of stone hid the sky from me part of the way. I came out a hundred feet below upon a second promontory of huge slabs of yellow stone. Over these I clambered, to sit with my feet swinging over the last one.

Straight before my gaze yawned the awful expanse of the canyon. In the soft morning light the red mesas, the yellow walls, the black domes were less harsh than in the full noonday sun, purer than in the tender shadow of twilight. Below me were slopes and slides divided by ravines full of stones as large as houses, with here and there a lonesome leaning crag, giving irresistible proof of the downward trend, of the rolling, weathering ruins of the rim. Above, the wall bulged out full of fissures, ragged and rotten shelves, toppling columns of yellow limestone, beaded with quartz and colored by wild flowers wonderfully growing in crannies.

Wild and rare as was this environment, I gave it but a glance and a thought. The bay of the hounds caused me to bend sharp and eager eyes to the open spaces of stone and slide below. Luck was mine as usual; the hounds were working up toward me. How I strained my sight! Hearing a single cry I looked eastward to see Jones silhouetted against the blue on a black promontory. He seemed a giant primeval man overlooking the ruin of a former world. I signalled him to make for my point.

Black Ranger hove in sight at the top of a yellow slide. He was at fault but hunting hard. Jude and Sounder bayed off to his left. I heard Don's clear voice permeating the thin, cool air, seemingly to leave a quality of wildness upon it; yet I could not locate him. Ranger disappeared. Then for a time I only heard Jim. Moze was next to appear and he, too, was upward bound. A jumble of stone hid him, and then Ranger again showed. Evidently he wanted to get around the bottom of a low crag, for he jumped only to fall back.

[36]

Quite naturally my eyes searched that crag. Stretched out upon the top of it was the long, slender body of a lion.

"Hi! Hi! Hi! Hi! Hi!" I yelled till my lungs failed me.

"Where are you?" came from above.

"Here! Here!" I cried, seeing Jones on the rim. "Come down. Climb down the crack. The lion is here; on top of that round crag. He's fooled the hounds and they can't find him."

"I see him! I see him!" yelled Jones. Then he roared out a single call for Emett that pealed like a clear clarion along the curved broken rim wall, opening up echoes which clapped like thunder.

While Jones clattered down I turned again to the lion. He lay with head hidden under a little shelf and he moved not a muscle. What a place for him to choose! But for my accidental venturing down the broken fragments and steps of the rim he could have remained safe from pursuit.

On the moment from my right somewhere Don pealed out, and immediately after, Sounder and Jude joining him, sent up the thrice welcome news of a treed lion.

"There're two! There're two!" I yelled to Jones, now working down to my right.

"He's treed down here. I've got him spotted!" replied Jones. "You stay there and watch your lion. Yell for Emett."

Signal after signal for Emett earned no response, though Jim far below to the left sent me an answer.

The next few minutes, or more likely half an hour, passed with Jones and me separated from each other by a wall of broken stone, waiting impatiently for Jim and Emett, while the hounds bayed one lion and I watched the other.

Calmness was impossible under such circumstances. No man could have gazed into that marvel of color and distance, with wild life about him, with wild sounds ringing in his ears, without yielding to the throb and race of his wild blood.

Emett did not come. Jim had not answered a yell for minutes. No doubt he needed his breath. He came into sight just to the left of our position, and he ran down one side of the ravine to toil up the other. I hailed him, Jones hailed him, and the hounds hailed him.

"Steer to your left Jim!" I called. "There's a lion on that crag

[37]

above you. He might jump. Round the cliff to the left—Jones is there!"

The most painful task it was for me to sit there and listen to the sound rising from below without being able to see what happened. My lion had peeped up once, and, seeing me, had crouched closer to his crag, evidently believing he was unseen, which obviously made it imperative for me to keep my seat and hold him there as long as possible.

But to hear the various exclamations thrilled me enough.

"Hyar Moze—get out of that. Catch him—hold him! Damn these rotten limbs. Hand me a pole—Jones, back down—back down! He's comin'—Hi! Hi! Whoop! There—now you've got him! No, no; it slipped! Now! Look out, Jim, from under—he's going to jump!"

A smashing and rattling of loose stones and a fiery burst of yelps with trumpet-like yells followed close upon Jones' last words. Then two yellow streaks leaped down the ravine. The first was the lion, the second was Don. The rest of the pack came tumbling helter-skelter in their wake. Following them raced Jim in long kangaroo leaps, with Jones in the rear, running for all he was worth. The animated and musical procession passed up out of the ravine and gradually lengthened as the lion gained and Jones lost, till it passed altogether from my jealous sight.

On the other side of the ridge of cedars the hounds treed their quarry again, as was easy to tell by their change from sharp inter-mittent yelping to an unbroken, full, deep chorus. Then presently all quieted down, and for long moments at a time the still silence enfolded the slope. Shouts now and then floated up on the wind and an occasional bark.

I sat there for an hour by my watch, though it seemed only a few minutes, and all that time my lion lay crouched on his crag and never moved.

I looked across the curve of the canyon to the purple breaks of the Siwash and the shaggy side of Buckskin Mountain and far be-yond to where Kanab Canyon opened its dark mouth, and farther still to the Pink Cliffs of Utah, weird and dim in the distance.

Something swelled within my breast at the thought that for the time I was part of that wild scene. The eye of an eagle soaring above would have placed me as well as my lion among the few living

[38]

things in the range of his all-compassing vision. Therefore, all was mine, not merely the lion—for he was only the means to an end— but the stupendous, unnamable thing beneath me, this chasm that hid mountains in the shades of its cliffs, and the granite tombs, some gleaming pale, passionless, others red and warm, painted by a master hand; and the wind-caves, dark-portaled under their mist curtains, and all that was deep and far off, unapproachable, unattainable, of beauty exceeding, dressed in ever-changing hues, was mine by right of presence, by right of the eye to see and the mind to keep.

"Waa-hoo!"

The cry lifted itself out of the depths. I saw Jones on the ridge of cedars.

"All right here—have you kept your lion there?" he yelled.

"All's well—come along, come along," I replied.

I watched them coming, and all the while my lion never moved. The hounds reached the cliff under me, but they could not find the lion, though they scented him, for they kept up a continual baying. Jim got up to the shelf under me and said they had tied up the lion and left him below. Jones toiled slowly up the slope.

"Someone ought to stay down there; he might jump," I called in warning.

"That crag is forty feet high on this side," he replied.

I clambered back over the uneven mass, let myself down between the boulders, and crawled under a dark ridge, and finally with Jim catching my rifle and camera and then lending his shoulders, I reached the bench below. Jones came puffing around a corner of the cliff, and soon all three of us with the hounds stood out on the rocky shelf with only a narrow space between us and the crouching lion.

Before we had a moment to speak, much less form a plan of attack, the lion rose, spat at us defiantly, and deliberately jumped off the crag. We heard him strike with a frightful thud.

Surprise held us dumb. To take the leap to the slope below seemed beyond any beast not endowed with wings. We saw the lion bounding down the identical trail which the other lion had taken. Jones came out of his momentary indecision.

"Hold the dogs! Call them back!" he yelled hoarsely. "They'll kill the lion we tied! They'll kill him!"

[39]

The hounds had scattered off the bench here and there, everywhere, to come together on the trail below. Already they were in full cry with the matchless Don at the fore. Manifestly to call them back was an injustice, as well as impossible. In ten seconds they were out of sight.

In silence we waited, each listening, each feeling the tragedy of the situation, each praying that they would pass by the poor, helpless, bound lion. Suddenly the regular baying swelled to a burst of savage, snarling fury, such as the pack made in a vicious fight. This ceased—short silence ensued; Don's sharp voice woke the echoes, then the regular baying continued.

As with one thought, we all sat down. Painful as the certainty was, it was not so painful as that listening, hoping suspense.

"Shore they can't be blamed," said Jim finally. "Bumping their nose into a tied lion that way—how'd they know?"

"Who could guess the second lion would jump off that quick and run back to our captive?" burst out Jones.

"Shore we might have knowed it," replied Jim. "Well, I'm goin' after the pack."

He gathered up his lasso and strode off the bench. Jones said he would climb back to the rim, and I followed Jim.

Why the lions ran in that particular direction was clear to me when I saw the trail. It was a runway, smooth and hard packed. I trudged along it with rather less enjoyment than on any trail I had ever followed to the canyon. Jim waited for me over the cedar ridge and showed me where the captive lion lay dead. The hounds had not torn him. They had killed him and passed on after the other.

"He was a fine fellow, all of seven feet. We'll skin him on our way back."

Only dogged determination coupled with a sense of duty to the hounds kept us on that trail. For the time being, enthusiasm had been submerged. But we had to follow the pack.

Jim, less weighted down and perhaps less discouraged, forged ahead. The sun had burned all the morning coolness out of the air. I perspired and panted and began to grow weary. Jim's signal called me to hurry. I took to a trot and came upon him and the hounds under a small cedar. The lion stood among the dead branches. His sides were shaking convulsively and his short breaths could be

[40]

plainly heard. He had the most blazing eyes and most untamed expression of any wild creature I have ever seen; and this amazed me, considering I had kept him on a crag for over an hour and had come to look upon him as my own.

"What'll we do, Jim, now that we have him treed?"

"Shore, we'll tie him up," declared Jim.

The lion stayed in the cedar long enough for me to photograph him twice, then he leaped down again and took to his back trail. We followed as fast as we could, soon to find that the hounds had put him up another cedar. From this he jumped down among the dogs, scattered them as if they had been so many leaves, and bounded up the slope out of sight.

I laid aside my rifle and camera and tried to keep up with Jim. The lion ran straight up the slope and treed again under the wall. Before we covered half the distance he was on the go once more, flying down in clouds of dust.

"Don is makin' him hump," said Jim.

And that alone was enough to spur us on. We would reward the noble hound if we had the staying power. Don and his pack ran westward this time, and along a mile of the beaten trail put him up two more trees. But these we could not see and judged only by the sound.

"Look there!" cried Jim. "Darn me if he ain't comin' right at us."

It was true. Ahead of us the lion appeared, loping wearily. We stopped in our tracks undecided. Jim drew his revolver. Once or twice the lion disappeared behind stones and cedars. When he sighted us he stopped, looked back, then again turning toward us, he left the trail to plunge down. He had barely got out of sight when old Don came pattering along the trail; then Ranger leading the others. Don did not even put his nose to the ground where the lion had switched, but leaped aside and went down. Here the long section of slope between the lion's runway and the second wall had been weathered and worn, racked and convulsed into deep ravines, with ridges between. We climbed and fell and toiled on, always with the bay of the hounds in our ears. We leaped fissures, we loosened avalanches, rolling them to crash and roar below, and send long, rumbling echoes out into the canyon.

[41]

A gorge in the yellow rock opened suddenly before us. We stood at the constricted neck of one of the great splits in the second wall. The side opposite was almost perpendicular, and formed a mass on mass of broken stones. This was a weathered slope on a gigantic scale. Points of cliffs jutted out; caves and cracks lined the wall.

"This is a rough place," said Jim, "but a lion could get over the second wall here, an' I believe a man could, too. The hounds seemed to be back further toward where the split narrows."

Through densely massed cedars and thickets of prickly thorns we wormed our way to come out at the neck of the gorge.

"There ye are!" sang out Jim. The hounds were all on a flat shelf some few feet below us, and on a sharp point of rock close by, but too far for the dogs to reach, crouched the lion. He was gasping and frothing at the mouth.

"Shore if he'd only stay there—" said Jim.

He loosened his lasso, and stationing himself just above the tired beast, he prepared to cast down the loop. The first throw failed of its purpose, but the rope hit the lion. He got up painfully it seemed, and faced the dogs. That way barred he turned to the cliff. Almost opposite him a shelf leaned out. He looked at it, then paced to and fro like a beast in a cage.

He looked again at the hounds, then up at us, all around, and finally concentrated his attention on the shelf; his long length sagged in the middle, he stretched low, his muscles gathered and strung, and he sprang like a tawny streak.

His aim was true, the whole forepart of his body landed on the shelf and he hung there. Then he slipped. We distinctly heard his claws scrape the hard, smooth rock. He fell, turning a somersault, struck twenty feet below on the rough slant, bounded from that to fall down, striking suddenly and then to roll, a yellow wheel that lodged behind a rock and stretched out to move no more.

The hounds were silent; Jim and I were silent; a few little stones rattled, then were still. The dead silence of the canyon seemed to pay tribute to the lion's unquenchable spirit and to the freedom he had earned to the last.

*

Morning found us all rather subdued, yet more inclined to a philosophical resignation as regarded the difficulties of our special kind of hunting. Capturing the lions on the level of the plateau was easy compared to following them down into canyons and bringing them up alone. We all agreed that that was next to impossible. Another feature, which before we had not considered, added to our perplexity, and it was a dawning consciousness that we would be perhaps less cruel if we killed the lions outright. Jones and Emett arrayed themselves on the side that life even in captivity was preferable; while Jim and I, no doubt still under the poignant influence of the last lion's heroic race and end, inclined to freedom or death. We compromised on the reasonable fact that as yet we had shown only a jackass kind of intelligence.

*

"Shore, they'll be somethin' doin' today," said Jim, fatalistically.

"We haven't crippled a horse yet," put in Emett hopefully. Don led the pack and us down the ridge, out of the pines into the sage. The sun, a red ball, glared out of the eastern mist, shedding a dull glow on the ramparts of the far canyon walls. A herd of white-tailed deer scattered before the hounds. Blue grouse whirred from under our horses' feet.

"Spread out," ordered Jones, and though he meant the hounds, we all followed his suggestion, as the wisest course.

Ranger began to work up the sage ridge to the right. Jones, Emett and I followed, while Jim rode away to the left. Gradually the space widened, and as we neared the cedars, a sharply defined, deep canyon separated us.

We heard Don open up, then Sounder. Ranger left the trail he was trying to work out in the thick sage, and bounded in the direction of the rest of the pack. We reined in to listen.

First Don, then Sounder, then Jude, then one of the pups bayed eagerly, telling us they were hunting hard. Suddenly the bays blended in one savage sound.

"Hi! Hi! Hi!" cracked the cool, thin air. We saw Jim wave his hand from the far side of the canyon, spur his horse into action, and disappear into the cedars.

"Stick close together," yelled Jones, as we launched forward. We made the mistake of not going back to cross the canyon, for the hounds soon went up the opposite side. As we rode on and on, the sounds of the chase lessened, and finally ceased. To our great

[43]

chagrin we found it necessary to retrace our steps, and when we did get over the deep gully, so much time had elapsed that we despaired of coming up with Jim. Emett led, keeping close on Jim's trail, which showed plain in the dust, and we followed.

We found him in the small glade engaged in binding up the leg of his horse. The baying of the hounds floated up over the rim.

"What's up?" queried Jones.

"It's that big one we call old Sultan," replied Jim. "We run plumb into him. We've had him in five trees. It ain't been long since he was in that cedar there. When he jumped the yellow pup was in the way an' got killed. My horse just managed to jump clear of the lion, an' as it was, nearly broke his leg."

Emett examined the leg and pronounced it badly strained, and advised him to lead the horse back to camp. Jones and I stood a moment over the remains of the yellow pup, and presently Emett joined us.

"He was the most playful one of the pack," said Emett, and then he placed the limp, bloody body in a crack, and laid several slabs of stone over it.

"Hurry after the other hounds," said Jim. "That lion will kill them one by one. An' look out for him!"

If we needed an incentive, the danger threatening the hounds furnished one; but I calculated the death of the pup was enough. Emett had a flare in his eye, Jones looked darker and more grim than ever, and I had sensations that boded ill to old Sultan.

"Fellows," I said, "I've been down this place, and I know where the old brute has gone; so come on."

I laid aside my coat, chaps and rifle, feeling that the business ahead was stern and difficult. Then I faced the canyon. Down slopes, among rocks, under piñons, around yellow walls, along slides, the two big men followed with heavy steps. We reached the white stream-bed, and sliding, slipping, jumping, always down and down, we came at last within sound of the hounds. We found them baying wildly under a piñon on the brink of the deep cove.

Then, at once, we all saw old Sultan close at hand. He was of immense size; his color was almost gray, his head huge, his paws heavy and round. He did not spit, nor snarl, nor growl; he did not look at the hounds, but kept his half-shut eyes upon us.

[44]

We had no time to make a move before he left his perch and hit the ground with a thud. He walked by the baying hounds, looked over the brink of the cove, and without an instant of hesitation, leaped down. The rattling crash of sliding stones came up with a cloud of dust. Then we saw him leisurely picking his way among the rough stones.

Exclamations from the three of us attested to what we thought of that leap.

"Look the place over," called Jones. "I think we've got him."

The cove was a hold hollowed out by running water. At its head, where the perpendicular wall curved, the height was not less than forty feet. The walls became higher as the cove deepened toward the canyon. It had a length of perhaps a hundred yards, and a width of perhaps half as many. The floor was mass on mass of splintered rock.

"Let the hounds down on a lasso," said Jones.

Easier said than done! Sounder, Ranger, Jude refused. Old Moze grumbled and broke away. But Don, stern and savage, allowed Jones to tie him in a slip noose.

"It's a shame to send that grand hound to his death," protested Emett.

"We'll all go down," declared Jones.

"We can't. One will have to stay up here to help the other two out," replied Emett.

"You're the strongest; you stay up," said Jones. "Better work along the wall and see if you can locate the lion."

We let Don down into the hole. He kicked himself loose before reaching the bottom and then, yelping, he went out of sight among the boulders. Moze, as if ashamed, came whining to us. We slipped a noose around him and lowered him, kicking and barking, to the rocky floor. Jones made the lasso fast to a cedar root, and I slid down, like a flash, burning my hands. Jones swung himself over, wrapped his leg around the rope, and came down, to hit the ground with a thump. Then, lassos in hands, we began clambering over the broken fragments.

For a few moments we were lost to sights and sounds away from our immediate vicinity. The bottom of the cove afforded hard going. Dead piñons and cedars blocked our way; the great, jagged

[45]

stones offered no passage. We crawled, climbed, and jumped from piece to piece.

A yell from Emett halted us. We saw him above waving his arms. He yelled unintelligible commands to us. The fierce baying of Don and Moze added to our desperate energy.

The last jumble of splintered rock cleared, we faced a terrible and wonderful scene.

"Look! Look!" I gasped to Jones.

A wide, bare strip of stone lay a few yards beneath us; and in the center of this last step sat the great lion on his haunches with his long tail lashing out over the precipice. Back to the canyon, he confronted the furious hounds; his demeanor had changed to one of savage apprehension.

When Jones and I appeared, old Sultan abruptly turned his back to the hounds and looked down into the canyon. He walked the whole length of the bare rock with his head stretched over. He was looking for a niche or a step whereby he might again elude his foes.

Faster lashed his tail; farther and farther stretched his neck. He stopped, and with head bent so far over the abyss that it seemed he must fall, he looked and looked.

How grandly he fitted the savage sublimity of that place! The tremendous purple canyon depths lay beneath him. He stood on the last step of his mighty throne. The great downward slopes had failed him. Majestically and slowly he turned from the deep that offered no hope.

As he turned, Jones cast the noose of his lasso perfectly round the burly neck. Sultan roared and worked his jaws, but he did not leap. Jones must have expected such a move, for he fastened his rope to a spur of rock. Standing there, revolver gripped, hearing the baying hounds, the roaring lion, and Jones' yells mingled with Emett's, I had no idea what to do. I was in a trance of sensations.

Old Sultan ran rather than leaped at us. Jones evaded the rush by falling behind a stone, but still did not get out of danger. Don flew at the lion's neck and Moze buried his teeth in a flank. Then the three rolled on the rock dangerously near the verge.

Bellowing, Jones grasped the lasso and pulled. Still holding my revolver, I leaped to his assistance, and together we pulled and jerked. Don got away from the lion with remarkable quickness. But Moze, slow and dogged, could not elude the outstretched paws, which fastened in his side and leg. We pulled so hard we slowly raised the lion. Moze, never simpering, clawed and scratched at the rock in his efforts to escape. The lion's red tongue protruded from his dripping jaws. We heard the rend of hide as our efforts, combined with those of Moze, loosed him from the great yellow claws.

The lion, whirling and wrestling, rolled over the precipice. When the rope straightened with a twang, had it not been fastened to the rock Jones and I would have been jerked over the wall. The shock threw us to our knees.

For a moment we did not realize the situation. Emett's yells awakened us.

"Pull! Pull! Pull!" he roared.

Then, knowing that old Sultan would hang himself in a few moments, we attempted to lift him. Jones pulled till his back cracked; I pulled till I saw red before my eyes. Again and again we tried. We could lift him only a few feet. Soon exhausted, we had to desist altogether. How Emett roared and raged from his vantage point above! He could see the lion in death throes.

Suddenly he quieted down with the words: "All over; all over!" Then he sat still, looking into space. Jones sat mopping his brow. And I, all my hot resentment vanished, lay on the rock, with eyes on the distant mesas.

Presently Jones leaned over the verge with my lasso. "There," he said, "I've roped one of his hind legs. Now we'll pull him up a little, then we'll fasten this rope, and pull on the other."

So, foot by foot, we worked the heavy lion up over the wall. He must have been dead, though his sides heaved. Don sniffed at him in disdain. Moze, dusty and bloody, with a large strip of hide hanging from his flank, came up growling low and deep, and gave the lion a last vengeful bite.

"We've been fools," observed Jones, meditatively. "The excitement of the game made us lose our wits. I'll never rope another lion."

I said nothing. While Moze licked his bloody leg and Don lay with his fine head on my knees, Jones began to skin old Sultan. Once more the strange, infinite silence enfolded the canyon. The far-off golden walls glistened in the sun; farther down, the purple clefts smoked. The many-hued peaks and mesas, aloof from each other, rose out of the depths. It was a grand and gloomy scene of ruin where every glistening descent of rock was but a page of earth's history.

It brought to my mind a faint appreciation of what time really meant; it spoke of an age of former men; it showed me the lonesome crags of eagles, and the cliff lairs of lions; and it taught mutely, eloquently, a lesson of life—that men are still savage, still driven by a spirit to roam, to hunt, and to slay.

4

BYME-BY-TARPON

From 1885 until well into this century the tarpon reigned as the supreme game fish of salt water. Before then, tarpon were usually caught on hand-lines or speared. Dr. James A. Henshall, the black bass authority who thirty years later claimed to have caught small tarpon on fly tackle as early as 1878, described in Louis L. Babcock's *The Tarpon* the hunting of six-foot Silver Kings with a harpoon as the only reasonable way to deal with these over-grown herring!

Yet on March 25, 1885, Mr. W. H. Wood of New York City caught a 93-pounder on regulation tackle in Tarpon Bay, Florida. After the deed was reported in *Forest and Stream*,[1] it set off a mad rush south by competitive anglers seeking to better, or at least duplicate, Wood's success. The news crossed the Atlantic, and the *London Observer* on August 26, 1886, had this to say:

> *Here, at last, there is a rival to the black bass of North America, to the Siluria glanis [a giant catfish] of the Danube, to our own European salmon, and possibly even to the sturgeon. . . . Sportsmen may go to Florida for the tarpon, as they now go to the Arctic Zone for the reindeer, walrus and musk-ox!*

As soon as Zane Grey acquired enough money and leisure through his writings, he too wanted to test his angling mettle on the Silver King. By 1900 the focus of fishing activity had shifted from Florida to Aransas Pass, Texas, and Tampico, Mexico. Characteristically Zane Grey chose the more distant port for his initiation into tarpon fishing. The following story first appeared in the December 1907 issue of *Field and Stream*, but it purports to describe an outing made some years before.

GWR

BYME-BY-TARPON

To capture the fish is not all of the fishing. Yet there are circumstances which make this philosophy hard to accept. I have in mind an incident of angling tribulation which rivals the most poignant instant of my boyhood, when a great trout flopped for one sharp moment on a mossy stone and then was gone like a golden flash into the depths of the pool.

---

[1] *Forest and Stream*, founded in 1873, was long America's leading outdoor journal. It was absorbed by *Field and Stream* in 1930.

Some years ago I followed Attalano, my guide, down the narrow Mexican street of Tampico to the bank of the broad Panuco. Under the rosy dawn the river quivered like a restless opal. The air, sweet with the song of blackbird and meadowlark, was full of cheer; the rising sun shone in splendor on the water and the long line of graceful palms lining the opposite bank, and on the tropical forest beyond, with its luxuriant foliage festooned by gray moss. Here was a day to warm the heart of any fisherman; here was the beautiful river, celebrated in many a story; here was the famous guide, skilled with oar and gaff, rich in experience. What sport I would have; what treasure of keen sensation would I store; what flavor of life would I taste this day! Hope burns always in the heart of a fisherman.

Attalano was in harmony with the day and the scene. He had a cheering figure, lithe and erect, with a springy stride, bespeaking the Montezuma blood said to flow in his Indian veins. Clad in a colored cotton shirt, blue jeans, and Spanish girdle, and treading the path with brown feet never deformed by shoes, he would have stopped an artist. Soon he bent his muscular shoulders to the oars, and the ripples circling from each stroke hardly disturbed the calm Panuco. Down the stream glided long Indian canoes, hewn from trees and laden with oranges and bananas. In each stern stood a dark native wielding an enormous paddle with ease. Wild fowl dotted the glassy expanse; white cranes and pink flamingoes graced the reedy bars; red-breasted kingfishers flew over with friendly screech. The salt breeze kissed my cheek; the sun shone with the comfortable warmth Northerners welcome in spring; from over the white sand dunes far below came the faint boom of the ever-restless Gulf.

We trolled up the river and down, across from one rush-lined shore to the other, for miles and miles with never a strike. But I was content, for over me had been cast the dreamy, care-dispelling languor of the South.

When the first long, low swell of the changing tide rolled in, a stronger breeze raised little dimpling waves and chased along the water in dark, quick-moving frowns. All at once the tarpon began to show, to splash, to play, to roll. It was as though they had been awakened by the stir and murmur of the miniature breakers. Broad

[51]

bars of silver flashed in the sunlight, green backs cleft the little billows, wide tails slapped lazily on the water. Every yard of river seemed to hold a rolling fish. This sport increased until the long stretch of water, which had been as calm as a lake at twilight, resembled the quick current of a Canadian stream. It was a fascinating, wonderful sight. But it was also peculiarly exasperating, because when the fish roll in this sportive, lazy way, they will not bite. For an hour I trolled through this whirlpool of flying spray and twisting tarpon, with many a salty drop on my face, hearing all around me the whipping crash of breaking water.

"Byme-by-tarpon," presently remarked Attalano, favoring me with the first specimen of his English.

The rolling of the tarpon diminished, and finally ceased as noon advanced.

No more did I cast longing eyes upon those huge bars of silver. They were buried treasure. The breeze quickened as the flowing tide gathered strength, and together they drove the waves higher. Attalano rowed across the river into the outlet of one of the lagoons. This narrow stream was unruffled by wind; its current was sluggish and its muddy waters were clarifying under the influence of the now fast-rising tide.

By a sunken log near shore we rested for lunch. I found the shade of the trees on the bank rather pleasant, and became interested in a blue heron, a russet-colored duck, and a brown and black snipe, all sitting on the sunken log. Nearby stood a tall crane watching us solemnly, and above in the treetop a parrot vociferously proclaimed his knowledge of our presence. I was wondering if he objected to our invasion, at the same time taking a most welcome bite for lunch, when directly in front of me the water flew up as if propelled by some submarine power. Framed in a shower of spray I saw an immense tarpon, with mouth agape and fins stiff, close in pursuit of frantically leaping little fish.

The fact that Attalano dropped his sandwich attested to the large size and close proximity of the tarpon. He uttered a grunt of satisfaction and pushed the boat. A school of feeding tarpon closed the mouth of the lagoon. Thousands of mullet had been cut off from their river haunts and were now leaping, flying, darting in wild haste to elude the great white monsters.

[52]

"Byme-by-tarpon!" called Attalano, warningly.

Shrewd guide! I had forgotten that I held a rod. When the realization dawned on me that sooner or later I would feel the strike of one of those silver tigers, a keen, tingling thrill of excitement quivered over me. The primitive man asserted himself and I leaned forward, tense and strained with suspended breath and swelling throat.

Suddenly the strike came, so tremendous in its energy that it almost pulled me from my seat; so quick, fierce, bewildering that I could think of nothing but to hold on. Then the water split with a hissing sound to let out a great tarpon, long as a door, seemingly as wide, who shot up and up into the air. He wagged his head and shook it like a struggling wolf. When he fell back with a heavy splash, a rainbow, exquisitely beautiful and delicate, stood out of the spray, glowed, paled, and faded.

Five times he sprang toward the blue sky, and as many he plunged down with a thunderous crash. The reel screamed. The line sang. The rod, which I had thought stiff as a tree, bent like a willow wand. The silver king came up far astern and sheered to the right in a long, wide curve, leaving behind a white wake. Then he sounded, while I watched the line with troubled eyes. But not long did he sulk. He began a series of magnificent tactics new in my experience. He stood on his tail, then on his head; he sailed like a bird; he shook himself so violently as to make a convulsive, shuffling sound; he dove, to come up covered with mud, marring his bright sides; he closed his huge gills with a slap and, most remarkable of all, he rose in the shape of a crescent, to straighten out with such marvelous power that he seemed to actually crack like a whip.

After this performance, which left me in a condition of mental aberration, he sounded again, to begin a persistent, dragging pull which was the most disheartening of all his maneuvers; for he took yard after yard of line until he was far away from me, out in the Panuco. We followed him, and for an hour crossed to and fro, up and down, humoring him, responding to his every caprice, as if he verily were a king. At last, with a strange inconsistency more human than fishlike, he returned to the scene of his fatal error, and here in the mouth of the smaller stream he leaped once more. But it was only a ghost of his former efforts—a slow, weary rise, showing he

[53]

was tired. I could see it in the weakening wag of his head. He no longer made the line whistle.

I began to recover the long line. I pumped and reeled him closer. Reluctantly he came, not yet broken in spirit, though his strength had sped. He rolled at times with a shade of the old vigor, with a pathetic manifestation of the temper that became a hero. I could see the long, slender tip of his dorsal fin, then his broad tail, and finally the gleam of his silver side. Closer he came and slowly circled around the boat, eying me with great, accusing eyes. I measured him with a fisherman's glance. What a great fish! Seven feet, I calculated, at the very least.

At this triumphant moment I made a horrible discovery. About six feet from the leader the strands of the line had frayed, leaving only one thread intact. My blood ran cold and the clammy sweat broke out on my brow. My empire was not won; my first tarpon was as if he had never been. But true to my fishing instincts, I held on morosely; my eye on the frail place in my line, and gently, ever so gently, I began to lead the silver king shoreward. Every smallest move of his tail meant disaster to me, so when he moved it I let go of the reel. Then I would have to coax him to swim back again.

The boat touched the bank. I stood up and carefully headed my fish toward the shore, and slid his head and shoulders out on the mud. One moment he lay there, glowing like mother-of-pearl, a rare fish, fresh from the sea. Then, as Attalano warily reached for the leader, he gave a gasp, a flop that deluged us with water, and a lunge that spelled freedom.

I watched him swim slowly away with my bright leader dragging beside him. Is it not the loss of things which makes life bitter? What we have gained is ours; what is lost is gone, whether fish, or love, or fame.

I tried to put on a cheerful aspect for my guide. But it was too soon. Attalano, wise fellow, understood my case. A smile, warm and living, flashed across his dark face as he spoke:

"Byme-by-tarpon."

Which defined his optimism and revived the failing spark within my breast. It was, too, in the nature of a prophecy.

[54]

5

MAST HOPE BROOK IN JUNE

By 1910 Zane Grey was an established novelist and free-lance contributor to various recreational magazines. He had already made several hunting and fishing trips to remote places, and had he been a poseur or fake, it would have been a natural time for him to begin exaggerating his own worth as an outdoorsman. But all his life ZG avoided a professional outdoorman's standing, knowing that his readers preferred seeing his world through an amateur's eyes. Read Zane Grey carefully, and you'll generally find him fishing or hunting with men who are superior anglers or better shots. He jokes continually about his awkwardness and miserable luck. Only later in his career, when other writers who had never been to Tahiti or the Galapagos began to tell their readers that Zane Grey could not possibly have seen or done this-and-such in Tahiti or the Galapagos, did ZG sacrifice his amateur standing in defense of his own experience and tend toward that syndrome of old age: being an authority.

But let's return to a humbler time when Zane Grey and his brothers used the Lackawaxen house (which ZG actively maintained from 1905 to 1918 and still visited as late as 1929) as their regular meeting ground and celebrated their reunions by fishing the Delaware and its local tributaries. Had ZG been a poseur, it's doubtful that the following story, written in 1910, would have quite the candor it has. After all, respectable fly fishermen aren't supposed to use the tactics he describes to get trout from Mast Hope Brook.

GWR

MAST HOPE BROOK IN JUNE[1]

Of the myriad of streams that Cedar, Reddy, and I have fished in, Mast Hope Brook is the one beyond compare. It is a joy, the substance of which are low tinkle and gurgle of unseen current beneath green banks; glancing sheets of hemlock-brown water shining in the sun, rushing soft and swift around the stones; and in the distance, dreamy hum of waterfall, now lulling, now deepening to mellow boom.

We left the road at the little village and took to the brook trail

[1] Reprinted with the permission of A. S. Barnes & Company, Cranbury, New Jersey, from *Tales of Fresh-Water Fishing*, first published by Harper & Brothers in 1928.

winding through mass thickets of rhododendron. The buds showed ambitious glints of pink. There were swampy, grassy places, blue with violets, and cool, fragrant, dewy dells to cross before we came out into an open valley. On the hill some men were cutting timber and burning brush. Long after we had entered the forest above, the smell of wood smoke lingered with us, seeming to have penetrated our very clothes. The trees were full-foliaged, the maples blowing like billows of green ocean. The sun was dazzlingly bright. From time to time we caught alluring glimpses of the dancing brook. Everything was bathed in the rich thick amber light of June.

We were wearing khaki suits and wading boots; we carried the lightest of rods, the finest of lines, the thinnest leaders, the flimsiest flies; we were equipped with all the modern paraphernalia of up-to-date anglers; but for all that we had reverted to the barefoot days, the memorable days of cut rods and twisted threads and stubby hooks and angleworms. Moreover, our conversation could not have been considered that of expert scientific fishermen; the wildest stretch of imagination would still have left it boys' talk.

"The crick's in bully shape," said Reddy, for the tenth time. We had been there often that spring; we had always found some unfavorable condition; we had watched the lowering of the brook, the weather, the many things involved. But this was the day!

"I know where my big fellow I lost last year is," added Cedar. "Mind you, steer clear of me when we get to that hole."

"Wonder how many we'll ketch," I put in, all aglow with hope.

At last we reached the head of the valley and turned off the trail into the forest. It was as if we had suddenly stepped among pink and white patches of snow. Mountain laurel bloomed everywhere. How fresh, exquisite were these blossoms! It was an open hardwood forest, from which the large timber had been cut, and except for a few thickets of hemlock all the underbrush was laurel. We swept aside the low bushes with our knees and buried ourselves in the tall ones, to be showered with rosy snowy petals. We were confronted by beautiful walls of green and white through which only ruthless fishermen could have crushed their way.

Strange to say, once we stood upon the bank of the brawling brook, the boyish eagerness resurging with memories of long-past pleasures gave place somewhat to the selfish zest of the battle of

[57]

men. Yet, after all, it was the old, youthful, playful rivalry augmented to matured pride in achievement.

"You fellows may as well consider yourselves out of my class from the start," suggested Cedar, loftily, as he jointed his rod. "Then you won't be disappointed at the finish."

Reddy regarded his elder brother with pity and me with thoughtful scorn. "Have either of you guys any money you can afford to lose?"

If there were trout in Mast Hope Brook that could jump at a bait as quickly as we snapped at Reddy's offer, they certainly were hungry fish.

"Boys, I'll be sorry to take this money," I said. "It'll be as easy as picking blossoms from these laurels. Now, as we're ready, how shall we divide up the stream? We can't fish together."

"As usual, you'd like to go ahead and get first whack at all the pools, eh?" queried Reddy. "I've fished down a stream behind you. Not again! Here's an idea. I'll fish the branch. Cedar will start in here, and you go down to the little island and fish from there. We'll meet at the log bridge for lunch."

His suggestion was accepted as a capital one, and he and I were making ready to start for our respective points when Cedar whipped his rod. Naturally we waited to see the first cast. I was not very charitable in my opinion of his casting, but I had to admit that he made a wonderful picture. He jerked his line back over his head, tore off about a basketful of laurel blossoms, and completed his cast. I saw the brown hackle alight and float down and sink; then came a swirl of the water and a surge of the line. On his very first try Cedar raised and hooked a trout. The fish executed a few interesting maneuvers and then playfully leaped over a snag and fouled the leader. Cedar pulled on the line and lifted the trout clear of the water, but could not get him any further. To our surprise, the frantically wriggling silver-sided trout proved to be a lusty broad fellow nearly twelve inches long.

"Climb down, get him, one of you!" yelled Cedar, excitedly.

"Go yourself. I'll hold your rod," replied Reddy, running back.

"Too late! All over!" I warned. "That's a bad place, Cedar. Look out!"

Of course the trout wriggled off; of course Cedar slipped in, the

[58]

top of one boot under water; of course he floundered out, red in the face, and inclined to a remarkable flow of unprintable language. We gathered presently that for some occult reason we were to blame for the disaster.

"I'm afraid it's a bad start," remarked Reddy, soberly. Fishermen know that when a day begins badly very seldom does it end favorably. But there is never any telling and certainty about luck.

Reddy separated from me below where the branch tumbled off the mountain into the main brook, and with a last cheery call for me to bear in mind the issue of the day he disappeared under the trees. I cut across a corner of the wooded valley, through which the stream described wide curves. My stretch of water from the island to the bridge was a long one, open to the sun, free of brush, and presented no obstacles to easy wading. The brook babbled merrily onward, yet it was in no great hurry. I flipped out my fly across a brown dimpled shallow and let it float downward. From then, time was annihilated, or it stood still, I did not know which. I stepped along from wet stones to dry ones, wading little coves, casting my fly into the likely places. I covered much ground and cast many times before I had a rise, and then I missed. I caught a flash of the trout as he darted away into the shady depths. The brook widened, lingering in flat reaches, and softened its rippling song. The yellow and green of willows curled over the bank; from the wet grass growing out of the trickling springs peeped long-stemmed purple violets. In places a deep gush of blue invited rest of the eye. The caw of a crow from a hillside died gradually away in the distance, and the screech of a kingfisher followed me downstream. In a long sunny channel I caught a small trout. He was by far too small to keep, so I unhooked him gently, and taking one glance at the beauty of glistening dots and black-tipped fins and wondrous blend of silver and gold, I let him go. Strikes came few and far between, but that seemed of small matter. The whole day with its possibilities, its certainties, its fulfillments, lay long ahead. Then I saw a bridge. Surely it could not be the one where I was to wait for my brothers! In bewilderment I looked up for the sun. It shone hot and white directly over my head. A vague and pleasant sense of movement, song of brook and bird and stir of breeze, one little trout, a few rises, and the hours had flown!

[59]

I climbed up the bank and lay down upon a brown needle-mat under a pine tree. The wind blew over me with fervent breath, sweet and warm and laden with the smell of pine. I was far away from the world, held drowsily still by the spell of a summer day, by the thrall of the wilderness.

Cedar and Reddy burst noisily into my solitude, and enchantment filtered out to the mountings of mingled emotions—fear that my brothers had more to tell and show than I, hope that they had each caught big ones, surprise at Reddy's clouded brow, and mirth at Cedar's wrecked rod and bedraggled clothes and flashing eyes. We were all rather uncommunicative while we ate lunch, whether from ravenous appetites or disheartening experiences and prospects, I did not know; but the pleasure of eating when hungry, the genial sunshine, and roar of the rapids in the glen below roused anew the hopes of fishermen.

"They're not rising to flies," said Reddy. "Maybe they will this afternoon."

Cedar lit his pipe and puffed clouds of smoke. His eyes lost their flame and the lines of his face softened. "I got only two strikes this morning, and that's a blamed hard stretch to fish. The second trout! Oh! Say! but he was a whale! It was this way——"

Then followed the gripping story, familiar, yet ever new; the shaded pool with its circle of foam, a brown hackle slowly floating down—a gleam of gold. Splash! Swish! Tug! Powerful fish in head-long irresistible fight—whizzing reel—slippery rocks and slippery boots. Crash!—crippled knee and broken rod—wild rush—flying water—pull, hard over hand, pull—stretching, tangled line—agonized hope ending in despair. Snap! a trailing, limp, sagging, weightless leader!

Wisely, Reddy and I let silence speak fittingly of our deep understanding of this tragedy. How many times it had been our fortune! We rested a while and then portioned off the remaining two miles of the brook. The glen just below fell to my lot and I had difficulty in repressing my gratification. My brothers strode off into the forest with the parting shot that I might just as well find a sunny spot and go to sleep.

When I was well into the glen I took off my brown hackle and substituted a short, stubby, black, common fishhook. Then stealthily looking above and below to see if by chance my brothers might be in sight, I slipped my hand into my pocket to bring forth a flat tin box. It contained a few choice common angleworms. These were the backbone of my campaign; these were the strength of my boast to my brothers; these were the secret source of my assurance. I stifled a feeling of guilt. All was fair in love, in war—why not in fishing? I acquitted Cedar and Reddy of such an underhand game, but I could not elevate myself to the heights upon which I raised them.

I passed by many good places in my hurry, and climbing over a jumble of stones in a narrow construction of the ravine I reached my pool. How my pulse danced! The brook swept down a six-foot chute between broken fragments of cliff. There was a great round pool with a lashing current on my side close to the rocky shore, a swirling, foamy back-eddy on the other. Here the sun was excluded. The shore was cool, the stones were wet with spray, the roar of the fall was deafening and filled the gorge with reverberating sound.

A perturbing thrilling portent of something about to be, rushed stirringly over me as I crouched low and crawled behind a big boulder. I had been there before. Before I had had the same presaging breathlessness that now tightened my chest. Ample reason there was for my quiver of expectation.

I cast my bait over the rushing channel into the slow-circling pool. A vicious, active, black-nosed trout broke water and spilled sparkling drops over the foam. My line swept away, then sagged. I jerked—too late! My bait was gone. I put on another, suddenly awfully aware that there were only four angleworms left. This time I cast short of the pool; my leader raced with the yellow-eyed bubbles. I was about to reel in when I got a tug. I hooked the trout and led him, fighting hard, out of the back-eddy. Once in the current he bent my rod double. I played him and reeled him out of the swift water and unskillfully lifted him to the bank. He was a fine ten-inch trout, dark blue, a silver-sided, black-spotted beauty. Crawling back behind the boulder I cast again and raised another fish and landed him. Then I caught two more in rapid succession, making four in less than as many minutes. Each time I had failed to reach the back-eddy, as I had done on the first cast.

The big hungry trout was still there and I had but one bait left.

[61]

Circumstances like these make the great crises in a fisherman's experience. In that tense moment, what could have gotten from me my last angleworm? Putting him on my hook, I raised a taut arm and made a long cast.

The bait alighted perfectly in the center of the pool and slowly drifted upstream, sinking the while . . . No rise! I felt the cold quaking sensation known only to anglers. Down, down sank my bait. How deep the pool! Suddenly there came a fierce onslaught upon my line; it nearly jerked the rod out of my hands. Loosing my thumb from the reel, I let the line play out steadily. The big trout was going deep into the depths, far under the dark shelving stone. Then the line ceased running out but did not slacken. There were little vibrations and sudden strains; I knew he had not let go; I was absolutely certain that the bait had been in his mouth long enough, too long, but I could not strike. For an instant of eternity I was bound between hope and dread.

I got up cautiously and yanked with a regular old-time boyish yank on the rod. The heavy weight of the trout, his lightning-swift movement, brought a yell to my lips. He fought deep, making me shudder as I felt the line twang from contact with stones. After that one wild outward rush he turned for his subterranean home and tugged and plugged. It was land him quickly or not at all, that I knew; and I pulled him in a way to delight my more expert brothers, could they have been there to see. A broad bar, dull glow, shone in the pool; then a black streak flashed into the seething white air-filled current of the chute. But he failed to make the leap over the narrow ledge, and plunged back to be swept down with the rapid, a dead weight on my line. I ran with him as far as I could go, forty, fifty feet down, and saw him swing in close to the shore, where, out of the drowning current, he began to fight again. I reeled in with all the speed at my command, and knowing it would be fatal if he once got out of that comparatively smooth little cove, I yielded to a wild impulse and began to lift. I lifted with all my strength, and I saw the dangerously full bend of the rod. Out of the water I lifted him, up, up, and swung him in upon the bank.

The leader snapped. He dropped to the moss and began a series of incredibly rapid flops. I bounded for him; I fell to gather him in my arms, grabbed with fingers seemingly incapable of holding anything.

How infernally slippery he was! A million times I had him; a million times he slipped out of my hands. He splashed in the shallow water just as a lucky random clutch ran my thumb in his mouth. His teeth were sharp, but if he had been a sawfish I would have held on. With grim foreboding of possibilities I killed him. Then, washing off the dirt and slime, I laid him upon the moss and gloated over him. Fifteen inches—no—fourteen he was—a broad heavy-shouldered trout, brilliant as a rainbow, with the most delicate and rare coloring of anything in nature.

The afternoon had waned when I strode out of the forest into the open valley below. The sun rimmed fleecy clouds with rose tints and the sky was as blue as the violets underfoot. The roar of the brook receded and died away, yet lingered in my mind. In fact, my mind was full, full of the thronging sensations of this day that had passed as a dream.

Cedar and Reddy were waiting for me under a chestnut tree on the outskirts of the village. Even in the joyous certainty of victory, when my eyes were dazzled by anticipation, I seemed to see them as strangely calm and self-contained.

"Any luck?" queried Reddy.

"Great! . . . Look!" I burst out, producing my trout and laying them side by side on the grass. I waited eagerly for the acclaim due me, but it was not forthcoming.

"Pretty fair," said Cedar.

"Not so bad," said Reddy. "Did you catch those on a fly?"

"Wasn't I using a fly when we separated?" I demanded.

"My boy, you're not one-two-six." Reddy deliberately opened his basket—I hate those baskets, for you can never tell what they will hold—and laid out upon the ground, one by one, ten beautiful trout, not one under ten inches.

I gasped weakly. "What—did you get them—on?"

"Worms," replied Reddy, smilingly.

Cedar manifested the facial agitation habitual with him when he has a fellow in a corner and can kill him at will. He began to pull something wrapped in a napkin out of his pocket, and he seemed to have difficulty. But he got it out finally. That bundle could not be a fish! I was in danger of collapse. Deliberately he laid the long white thing on the grass, slowly he put back the first fold of napkin,

[63]

leisurely he turned back the second, and with many a pause, and glance at me, and calm cool smile, he unwrapped a great trout and stretched him overlappingly beside the others.

Professional pride went into eclipse; I gazed in admiration at an eighteen-inch trout, the massive many-hued monarch of Mast Hope Brook.

"Lord! You got him!" I exclaimed. "After all your bad luck—losing the other. Say! What did you catch him on?"

"My boy, he broke his back reaching for a big fat worm."

NONNEZOSHE

When you share the great outdoors with Zane Grey, you sometimes discover an American wilderness that is no more. Today, the dammed and rising waters of the Colorado River are creeping up Forbidding Canyon that shelters Utah's Rainbow Bridge. Water skiers sweep up the canyon, and not many years hence, picnickers will beach their boats and lunch in the high-noon shadow of the arch and, perhaps, carve their names there—not far from Zane Grey's own. For in the illusion that Nonnezoshe (Navajo for "a rainbow turned to stone") would maintain its isolation and that he'd be one of the few to see its perfect shape and to hear its cathedral silence, Zane Grey succumbed to a temptation older than Kilroy, and left "Zane Grey" in a recess at the base of the great arch just above his guide's own "J. Wetherill."

"Nonnezoshe" was originally published in *Recreation Magazine* in February, 1915, and later combined with "Colorado Trails," "Roping Lions in the Grand Canyon," "Tonto Basin," and a story about a trip to Death Valley to make up *Tales of Lonely Trails*, published in 1922 by Hodder and Stoughton, Limited, in London.

The story provides some hint as to Zane Grey's feelings for Indians. First of all, he believed himself 1/32 Indian, supposedly inherited from his mother's side of the family. But there was a more profound reason for his tolerance and interest in Indians in a day when some Westerners still sniped at them as casually as they would at coyotes or crows. Zane Grey believed the white men of Arizona and Utah represented the highest evolutionary form of humanity—a development as much due to their environment as to inheritance. Since the Indians shared this Western experience, they, too, were superior to most mortals. But because they had lost their struggle for the West, they were necessarily inferior to the Western whites who had defeated them. This may be simplistic reasoning—couched in superficial Darwinism—but it describes how ZG felt. And it is this faith that lends his novel an epic tone and illuminates such nonfiction as "Nonnezoshe" with awe.

GWR

NONNEZOSHE

John Wetherill, one of the famous Wetherill brothers[1] and trader at Kayenta, Arizona, is the man who discovered Nonnezoshe, which is probably the most beautiful and wonderful natural phenomenon in the world. Wetherill owes the credit to his wife, who, through her influence with the Indians, finally after years succeeded in getting the secret of the great bridge.

After three trips to Marsh Pass and Kayenta with my old guide, Al Doyle of Flagstaff, I finally succeeded in getting Wetherill to take me in to Nonnezoshe. This was in the spring of 1913 and my party was the second one, not scientific, to make the trip. Later this same year Wetherill took in the Roosevelt party and after that the Kolb[2] brothers. It is a safe thing to say that this trip is one of the most beautiful in the West. It is a hard one and not for everybody. There is no guide except Wetherill, who knows how to get there. And after Doyle and I came out we admitted that we would not care to try to return over our back trail. We doubted if we could find the way. This is the only place I have ever visited which I am not sure I could find again alone.

My trip to Nonnezoshe gave me the opportunity to see also Monument Valley, and the mysterious and labyrinthine Canyon Segi with its great prehistoric cliff dwellings.

The desert beyond Kayenta spread out impressively, bare red flats and plains of sage leading to the rugged, vividly colored and wind-sculpted sandstone heights typical of the Painted Desert of Arizona. Laguna Creek, at that season, became flooded after every thunderstorm; and it was a treacherous red-mired quicksand where I convinced myself we would have stuck forever had it not been for Wetherill's Navajos.

We rode all day, for the most part closed in by ridges and bluffs, so that no extended view was possible. It was hot, too, and the sand blew and the dust rose. Travel in northern Arizona is never easy,

---

[1] Richard Wetherill was a contributor to *Sports Afield* and *Outdoor Life* magazines in the late 1800's. His writings on natural history and travel also served to publicize the guide services offered by his brother John.

[2] Explorers Emery and Ellsworth Kolb.

and this grew harder and steeper. There was one long slope of heavy sand that I was sure would prove too much for Wetherill's pack mules. But they surmounted it apparently less breathless than I was. Toward sunset a storm gathered ahead of us to the north with a promise of cooling and sultry air.

At length we turned into a long canyon with straight rugged red walls, and a sandy floor with quite a perceptible ascent. It appeared endless. Far ahead I could see the black storm-clouds, and by and by began to hear the rumble of thunder. Darkness had overtaken us by the time we had reached the head of this canyon; and my first sight of Monument Valley came with a dazzling flash of lightning. It revealed a vast valley, a strange world of colossal shafts and buttes of rock, magnificently sculpted, standing isolated and aloof, dark, weird, lonely. When the sheet lightning flared across the sky, showing the monuments silhouetted black against that strange horizon, the effect was marvelously beautiful. I watched until the storm died away.

Dawn, with the desert sunrise, changed Monument Valley, bereft it of its night gloom and weird shadow, and showed it in another aspect of beauty. It was hard for me to realize that those monuments were not the works of man. The great valley must once have been a plateau of red rock from which the softer strata had eroded, leaving the gentle league-long slopes marked here and there by upstanding pillars and columns of singular shape and beauty. I rode down the sweet-scented sage slopes under the shadow of the lofty Mittens, and around and across the valley, and back again to the height of land. And when I had completed the ride a story had woven itself into my mind; and the spot where I stood was to be the place where Lin Slone taught Lucy Bostil to ride the great stallion Wildfire.[3]

---

[3] Lin Slone and Lucy Bostil are characters from *Wildfire*, published three years after ZG's visit to Nonnezoshe. Some readers have criticized ZG for plugging his Westerns in his nonfiction books. But these occasional references to his novels may have been a means of justifying his extensive outdoor trips and expenses to the Internal Revenue Service. Despite the many books and articles stemming from his trips, the tax men were reluctant to view ZG's guns and tackle, his horses and guide fees, as deductible expenses. As a result, Zane Grey was paying as much as $54,000 in federal income taxes by 1924. The situation became so oppressive that ZG and his wife went to Washington, D.C. in 1931 to plead their case—unsuccessfully. And the only pleasant result of this Washington trip was an invitation to lunch at the White House with fellow angling writer, President Herbert Hoover.

Two days' ride took us across country to the Segi. With this wonderful canyon I was familiar, that is, as familiar as several visits could make a man with such a bewildering place. In fact I had named it Deception Pass. The Segi had innumerable branches, all more or less the same size, and sometimes it was difficult to tell the main canyon from one of its tributaries. The walls were rugged and crumbling, of a red or yellow hue, upward of a thousand feet in height, and indented by spruce-sided notches.

There were a number of ruined cliff dwellings, the most accessible of which was Keet Seel. I could imagine no more picturesque spot. A huge wind-worn cavern with a vast slanted stained wall held upon a projecting ledge or shelf the long line of cliff dwellings. These silent little stone houses with their vacant black eye-like windows had strange power to make me ponder, and then dream. In many places there was no trail at all, and I encountered difficulties, but in the end without much loss of time I entered the narrow rugged entrance of the canyon I had named Surprise Valley. The sight of the great dark cave thrilled me as I thought it might have thrilled Bess and Venters, who had lived for me their imagined lives of loneliness here in this wild spot. With the sight of those lofty walls and the scent of the dry sweet sage, there rushed over me a strange feeling that *Riders of the Purple Sage* was true. My dream people of romance had really lived there once upon a time. I climbed high upon the huge stones, and along the smooth red walls where Fay Larkin once had glided with swift sure steps, and I entered the musty cliff dwellings, and called out to hear the weird and sonorous echoes, and I wandered through the thickets and upon the grassy spruce-shaded benches, never for a moment free of the story I had conceived there. Something of awe and sadness abided with me. I could not enter into the merry pranks and investigations of my party. Surprise Valley seemed a part of my past, my dreams, my very self. I left it, haunted by its loneliness and silence and beauty, by the story it had given me.

That night we camped at Bubbling Spring, which once had been a geyser of considerable power. Wetherill told a story of an old Navajo who had lived there. For a long time, according to the Indian tale, the old chief resided there without complaining of this geyser that was wont to inundate his fields. But one season the unreliable waterspout made great and persistent endeavor to drown him and

[69]

his people and horses. Whereupon the old Navajo took his gun and shot repeatedly at the geyser, and thundered aloud his anger to the Great Spirit . The geyser ebbed away, and from that day never burst forth again.

Next morning under the great bulge of Navajo Mountain I calculated that we were coming to the edge of the plateau. The white bobbing pack horses disappeared and then our extra mustangs. It is no unusual thing for a man to use three mounts on this trip. Then two of our Indians disappeared. But Wetherill waited for us and so did Nas ta Bega, the Paiute who first took Wetherill down into Nonnezoshe Boco.[4] As I came up I thought we had indeed reached the end of the world.

"It's down in there," said Wetherill.

Nas ta Bega made a slow sweeping gesture. There is always something so significant and impressive about an Indian when he points anywhere. It is as if he says, "There, way beyond, over the ranges, is a place I know, and it is far." The fact was that I looked at the Paiute's dark, inscrutable face before I looked out into the void.

My gaze then seemed impelled and held by things afar, a vast yellow and purple corrugated world of distance, apparently now on a level with my eyes. I was drawn by the beauty and grandeur of that scene; and then I was transfixed, almost by fear, by the realization that I dared to venture down into this wild and upflung fastness. I kept looking afar, sweeping the three-quartered circle of horizon till my judgment of distance was confounded and my sense of proportion dwarfed one moment and magnified the next.

Wetherill was pointing and explaining, but I had not grasped all he said.

"You can see two hundred miles into Utah," he went on. "That bright rough surface, like a washboard, is wind-worn rock. Those little lines of cleavage are canyons. There are a thousand canyons down there, and only a few have we been in. That long purple ragged line is the Grand Canyon of the Colorado. And there, that blue fork in the red, that's where the San Juan comes in. And there's Escalante Canyon."

---

[4] Government publications today spell the Indian's name *Nasja Begay* and the name of the smaller canyon leading off Forbidding Canyon to Rainbow Bridge, *Nonnezoshi Biko.*

[70]

I had to adopt the Indian's method of studying unlimited spaces in the desert—to look with slow contracted eyes from near to far.

The pack train and the drivers had begun to zigzag down a long slope, bare of rock, with scant strips of green, and here and there a cedar. Half a mile down, the slope merged in what seemed a green level. But I knew it was not level. This level was a rolling plain, growing darker green, with lines of ravines and thin, undefined spaces that might be mirage. Miles and miles it swept and rolled and heaved, to lose its waves in apparent darker level. Round red rocks stood isolated. They resembled huge grazing cattle. But as I gazed, these rocks were strangely magnified. They grew and grew into mounds, castles, domes, crags, great red wind-carved buttes. One by one they drew my gaze to the wall of upflung rock. I seemed to see a thousand domes of a thousand shapes and colors, and among them a thousand blue clefts, each of which was a canyon.

Beyond this wide area of curved lines rose another wall, dwarfing the lower; dark red, horizon-long, magnificent in frowning boldness, and because of its limitless deceiving surfaces incomprehensible to the gaze of man. Away to the eastward began a winding ragged blue line, looping back upon itself, and then winding away again, growing wider and bluer. This line was San Juan Canyon. I followed that blue line all its length, a hundred miles, down toward the west where it joined a dark purple shadowy cleft. And this was the Grand Canyon of the Colorado. My eye swept along with that winding mark, farther and farther to the west, until the cleft, growing larger and closer, revealed itself as a wild and winding canyon. Still farther westward it split a vast plateau of red peaks and yellow mesas. Here the canyon was full of purple smoke. It turned, it closed, it gaped, it lost itself and showed again in that chaos of a million cliffs. And then it faded, a mere purple line, into deceiving distance.

I imagined there was no scene in all the world to equal this. The tranquillity of lesser spaces was here not manifest. This happened to be a place where so much of the desert could be seen and the effect was stupendous. Sound, movement, life seemed to have no fitness here. Ruin was there and desolation and decay. The meaning of the ages was flung at me. A man became nothing. But when I gazed across that sublime and majestic wilderness, in which the Grand

[71]

Canyon was only a dim line, I strangely lost my terror and something came to me across the shining spaces.

Then Nas ta Bega and Wetherill began the descent of the slope, and the rest of us followed. No sign of a trail showed where the base of the slope rolled out to meet the green plain. There was a level bench a mile wide, then a ravine, and then an ascent, and after that, rounded ridge and ravine, one after the other, like huge swells of a monstrous sea. Indian paintbrush vied in its scarlet hue with the deep magenta of cactus. There was no sage. Soap weed and meager grass and a bunch of cactus here and there lent the green to that barren, and it was green only at a distance.

Nas ta Bega kept on at a steady gait. The sun climbed. The wind rose and whipped dust from under the mustangs. There is seldom much talk on a ride of this nature. It is hard work and everybody for himself. Besides, it is enough just to see; and that country is conducive to silence. I looked back often, and the farther out of the plain we rode, the higher loomed the plateau we had descended; and as I faced ahead again, the lower sank the red-domed and castled horizon to the fore.

It was a wild place we were approaching. I saw piñon patches under the circled walls. I ceased to feel the dry wind in my face. We were already in the lee of a wall. I saw the rock squirrels scampering to their holes. Then the Indians disappeared between two rounded corners of cliff.

I rode round the corner into a widening space thick with cedars. It ended in a bare slope of smooth rock. Here we dismounted to begin the ascent. It was smooth and hard, though not slippery. There was not a crack. I did not see a broken piece of stone. Nas ta Bega and Wetherill climbed straight up for a while and then wound round a swell, to turn this way and that, always going up. I began to see similar mounds of rock all around me, of every shape that could be called a curve. There were yellow domes far above and small red domes far below. Ridges ran from one hill of rock to another. There were no abrupt breaks, but holes and pits and caves were everywhere, and occasionally deep down, an amphitheater green with cedar and piñon. We found no vestige of trail on those bare slopes.

Our guides led to the top of the wall, only to disclose to us another wall beyond, with a ridged, bare, and scalloped depression between. Here footing began to be precarious for both man and beast. Our mustangs were not shod and it was wonderful to see their slow, short, careful steps. They knew a great deal better than we what the danger was. In the ascent of the second slope it was necessary to zigzag up, slowly and carefully, taking advantage of every bulge and depression.

Then before us twisted and dropped and curved the most dangerous slopes I had ever seen. We had reached the height of the divide and many of the drops on this side were perpendicular and too steep for us to see the bottom.

At one bad place Wetherill and Nas ta Bega, with Joe Lee, a Mormon cowboy with us, were helping one of the pack horses named Chub. On the steepest part of this slope Chub fell and began to slide. His momentum jerked the rope from the hands of Wetherill and the Indian. But Joe Lee held on. Joe was a giant and being a Mormon he could not let go of anything he had. He began to slide with the horse, holding back with all his might.

It seemed that both man and beast must slide down to where the slope ended in a yawning precipice. Chub was snorting or screaming in terror. Our mustangs were frightened and rearing. It was not a place to have trouble with horses.

I had a moment of horrified fascination, in which Chub turned clear over. Then he slid into a little depression that, with Joe's hold on the lasso, momentarily checked his descent. Quick as thought Joe ran sidewise and down to the bulge of rock, and yelled for help. I got to him a little ahead of Wetherill and Nas ta Bega; and together we pulled Chub up out of danger. At first we thought he had been choked to death. But he came to, and got up, a bloody, skinned horse, but alive and safe. I have never seen a more magnificent effort than Joe Lee's. Those fellows are built that way. Wetherill has lost horses on those treacherous slopes, and that risk is the only thing about the trip which is not splendid.

We got over that bad place without further incident, and presently came to a long swell of naked stone that led down to a narrow green split. This one had straight walls and wound away out of sight. It was the head of a canyon.

"Nonnezoshe Boco," said the Indian.

[73]

This then was the Canyon of the Rainbow Bridge. When we got down into it we were a happy crowd. The mode of travel here was a selection of the best levels, the best places to cross the brook, the best places to climb, and it was a process of continual repetition. There was no trail ahead of us, but we certainly left one behind. And as Wetherill picked out the course and the mustangs followed him, I had all freedom to see and feel the beauty, color, wildness and changing character of Nonnezoshe Boco.

My experiences in the desert did not count much in the trip down this strange, beautiful lost canyon. All canyons are not alike. This one did not widen, though the walls grew higher. They began to lean and bulge, and the narrow strip of sky above resembled a flowing blue river. Huge caverns had been hollowed out by water or wind. And when the brook ran close under one of these overhanging places the running water made a singular indescribable sound. A crack from a hoof on a stone rang like a hollow bell and echoed from wall to wall. And the croak of a frog—the only living creature I noted in the canyon—was a weird and melancholy thing.

"We're sure gettin' deep down," said Joe Lee.

"How do you know?" I asked.

"Here are pink and yellow sego lilies. Only the white ones are found above."

I dismounted to gather some of these lilies. They were larger than the white ones of higher altitudes, of a most exquisite beauty and fragility, and of such rare pink and yellow hues as I had never seen.

"They bloom only where it's always summer," explained Joe.

That expressed their nature. They were the orchids of the summer canyons. They stood up everywhere star-like out of the green. It was impossible to prevent the mustangs treading them underfoot. And as the canyon deepened, and many little springs added their tiny volume to the brook, every grassy bench was dotted with lilies, like a green sky star-spangled. And this increasing luxuriance manifested itself in the banks of purple moss and clumps of lavender daisies and great mounds of yellow violets. The brook was lined by blossoming buck-brush; the rocky corners showed the crimson and magenta of cactus; and there were ledges of green with shining moss that sparkled with little white flowers. The hum of bees filled the fragrant, dreamy air.

But by and by, this green and colorful and verdant beauty, the almost level floor of the canyon, the banks of soft earth, the thickets and clumps of cottonwood, the shelving caverns and bulging walls— these features were gradually lost, and Nonnezoshe began to deepen in bare red and white stone steps. The walls sheered away from one another, breaking into sections and ledges, and rising higher and higher, and there began to be manifested a dark and solemn concordance with the nature that had created this old rent in the earth.

There was a stretch of miles where steep steps in hard red rock alternated with long levels of round boulders. Here, one by one, the mustangs went lame and we had to walk. And we slipped and stumbled along over these loose, treacherous stones. The hours passed; the toil increased; the progress diminished; one of the mustangs failed and was left. And all the while the dimensions of Nonnezoshe Boco magnified and its character changed. It became a thousand-foot walled canyon, leaning, broken, threatening, with great yellow slides blocking passage, with huge sections split off from the main wall, with immense dark and gloomy caverns. Strangely it had no intersecting canyons. It jealously guarded its secret. Its unusual formations of cavern and pillar and half-arch led me to expect any monstrous stone-shape left by avalanche or cataclysm.

Down and down we toiled. And now the stream bed was bare of boulders and the banks of earth. The floods that had rolled down that canyon had here borne away every loose thing. All the floor, in places, was bare red and white stone, polished, glistening, slippery, affording treacherous foothold. And the time came when Wetherill abandoned the stream bed to take the rock-strewn and cactus-covered ledges above.

The canyon widened ahead into a great ragged iron-lined amphitheater, and then apparently turned abruptly at right angles. Sunset rimmed the walls.

I had been tired for a long time and now I began to limp and lag. I wondered what on earth would make Wetherill and the Indians tired. It was with great pleasure that I observed the giant Joe Lee plodding slowly along. And when I glanced behind at my straggling party it was with both admiration for their gameness and glee for

[75]

their disheveled and weary appearance. Finally I got so that all I could do was to drag myself onward with eyes down on the rough ground. In this way I kept on until I heard Wetherill call me. He had stopped—was waiting for me. The dark and silent Indian stood beside him, looking down the canyon.

I saw past the vast jutting wall that had obstructed my view. A mile beyond, all was bright with the colors of sunset, and spanning the canyon in the graceful shape and beautiful hues of the rainbow was a magnificent natural bridge.

"Nonnezoshe," said Wetherill, simply.

This rainbow bridge was the one great natural phenomenon, the one grand spectacle which I had ever seen that did not at first give vague disappointment, a confounding of reality, a disenchantment of contrast with what the mind had conceived.

But this thing was glorious. It absolutely silenced me. My body and brain, weary and dull from the toil of travel, received a singular and revivifying freshness. I had a strange, mystic perception that this rosy-hued, tremendous arch of stone was a goal I had failed to reach in some former life, but had now found. Here was a rainbow magnified even beyond dreams, a thing not transparent and ethereal, but solidified, a work of ages, sweeping up majestically from the red walls, its iris-hued arch against the blue sky.

Then we plodded on again. Wetherill worked around to circle the huge amphitheater. The way was a steep slant, rough and loose and dragging. The rocks were as hard and jagged as lava, and cactus hindered progress. Soon the rosy and golden lights had faded. All the walls turned pale and steely and the bridge loomed dark.

We were to camp all night under the bridge. Just before we reached it Nas ta Bega halted with one of his singular motions. He was saying his prayer to this great stone god. Then he began to climb straight up the steep slope. Wetherill told me the Indian would not pass under the arch.

When we got to the bridge and unsaddled and unpacked the lame mustangs, twilight had fallen. The horses were turned loose to fare for what scant grass grew on bench and slope. Firewood was even harder to find than grass. When our simple meal had been eaten there was gloom gathering in the canyon and stars had begun to blink in the pale strip of blue above the lofty walls. The place was oppressive and we were mostly silent.

[76]

Presently I moved away into the strange dark shadow cast by the bridge. It was a weird black belt, where I imagined I was invisible, but out of which I could see. There was a slab of rock upon which I composed myself, to watch, to feel.

A stiffening of my neck made me aware that I had been continually looking up at the looming arch. I found that it never seemed the same any two moments. Near at hand it was too vast a thing for immediate comprehension. I wanted to ponder on what had formed it—to reflect upon its meaning as to age and force of nature. Yet it seemed that all I could do was to see. White stars hung along the dark curved line. The rim of the arch appeared to shine. The moon was up there somewhere. The far side of the canyon was now a blank black wall. Over its towering rim showed a pale glow. It brightened. The shades in the canyon lightened, then a white disk of moon peeped over the dark line. The bridge turned to silver.

It was then that I became aware of the presence of Nas ta Bega. Dark, silent, statuesque, with inscrutable face uplifted, with all that was spiritual of the Indian suggested by a somber and tranquil knowledge of his place there, he represented to me that which a solitary figure of human life represents in a great painting. Nonnezoshe needed life, wild life, life of its millions of years—and here stood the dark and silent Indian.

Long afterward I walked there alone, to and fro, under the bridge. The moon had long since crossed the streak of star-fired blue above, and the canyon was black in shadow. At times a current of wind, with all the strangeness of that strange country in its moan, rushed through the great stone arch. At other times there was silence such as I imagined might have dwelt deep in the center of the earth. And again an owl hooted, and the sound was nameless. It had a mocking echo. An echo of night, silence, gloom, melancholy, death, age, eternity!

The Indian lay asleep with his dark face upturned, and the other sleepers lay calm and white in the starlight. I seemed to see in them the meaning of life and the past—the illimitable train of faces that had shone under the stars. There was something nameless in that canyon, and whether or not it was what the Indian embodied in the great Nonnezoshe, or the life of the present, or the death of the ages, or the nature so magnificently manifested in those silent, dreaming, waiting walls—the truth was that there was a spirit.

I did sleep a few hours under Nonnezoshe, and when I awoke the tip of the arch was losing its cold darkness and beginning to shine. The sun had just risen high enough over some low break in the wall to reach the bridge. I watched. Slowly, in wondrous transformation, the gold and blue and rose and pink and purple blended their hues, softly, mistily, cloudily, until once more the arch was a rainbow.

I realized that long before life had evolved upon the earth this bridge had spread its grand arch from wall to wall, black and mystic at night, transparent and rosy in the sunrise, at sunset a flaming curve limned against the heavens. When the race of man had passed it would, perhaps, stand there still. It was not for many eyes to see. The tourist, the leisurely traveler, the comfort-loving motorist would never behold it. Only by toil, sweat, endurance and pain could any man ever look at Nonnezoshe. It seemed well to realize that the great things of life had to be earned. Nonnezoshe would always be alone, grand, silent, beautiful, unintelligible; and as such I bade it a mute, reverent farewell.

7

TUNA AT AVALON

Catalina Island is the birthplace of big-game angling,[1] for there on June 1, 1898, Dr. Charles Frederick Holder took the first giant tuna, a 183-pound bluefin, on rod and reel. Within a month, the Catalina Tuna Club had been formed with 24 members who had taken fish over 100 pounds, thereby entitling them to the Club's Blue Button lapel pin. The editors of *Field and Stream* were shortly to describe this pin as the "world's greatest angling insignia."

Contemporary ocean anglers, brought up with the hope that even 2,000-pound billfish will one day be taken on rod and reel, are sometimes puzzled by the hullabaloo created by Holder's first big tuna. After all, what's there to catching a 183-pound tuna on 50-pound dacron line with a Tycoon rod and Fin-Nor reel while trolling from a twin-engined Bertram with a good guide and competent mate? Not much. But to row or motor offshore in the equivalent of an oversized dory—sometimes alone—and to fish with a linen line which mildew could weaken overnight to a tenth its former strength, and to use brakeless reels and hickory rods that quickly warp to the strain of a big fish—this wasn't merely deep-sea fishing; this was heroism!

Ocean angling was still a young sport when Zane Grey first visited Catalina in August, 1914. In fact, it was just three years earlier that a Catalina guide, Captain George Chase Farnsworth, had introduced the kite outrigger as the best means to keep a trolled flying fish well away from the boat. Previously, the shadow and noise of boats passing overhead had caused most tuna to sound, so that only a small percentage of the fish available were persuaded to strike. Farnsworth's innovation enabled a boatman to run well to one side of a tuna school while keeping the angler's bait skipping invitingly in front of the fishes' noses. As ZG describes, the results are electrifying.

Zane Grey had already caught a fair variety of salt-water game fish including Mexican tarpon and New Jersey school tuna before he came to Catalina. With typical ZG moxie, he sought out Mr. Parker, the Avalon taxidermist, and began to tell him how he wanted his fish mounted. Parker quietly suggested that Grey go out and catch a few first. During the next several seasons he did—though it was five years before he earned his first Blue Button.

Gradually, the swordfishes surpassed tuna in ZG's affections. For even before science was willing to support his claim, Zane Grey knew that the largest game fish in the sea were the giant marlins. And his desire to capture the greatest among them became his lifetime ambition.

However, he never lost his affection for "horse mackerel," and the following selection describes an exciting, though ultimately disappointing, encounter during one of the best tuna seasons either ZG or the Tuna Club would ever know.

GWR

---

[1] Tarpon fishing is no longer considered "big game." The term is generally reserved for the pursuit of large blue-water fishes like the tunas, marlin, and giant sharks.

[80]

TUNA AT AVALON

The 1919 season for tuna at Avalon was the best for many years. What it might have been if the round-haul net-boats had not haunted the channel taking thousands of tons of tuna, no one could conjecture. Tuna were never before seen there in such numbers, both large and small.

But no matter how wonderful the fishing, it was spoiled by the Austrian and Japanese net-boats. These round-haul boats have nets half a mile long and several hundred feet deep. When they surround a school of tuna it is seldom that any escape. If the tuna are very large—over one hundred pounds—then a great many of them are destroyed. Sometimes the weight of a large school is so great that the netters cannot handle it, in which case they take on board all they can dispose of and let the rest sink. Some of the tons of tuna go to the canneries at San Pedro, and a good many of them go to the fertilizer plants. These market fishermen are aliens, and they break the state and federal laws every day during the season. Catalina Island has a three-mile limit, inside of which no net-boat is permitted to haul. One day this season I counted sixteen round-haul net-boats within half a mile of Avalon Bay, and some of them were loaded so heavily that they sank in the water nearly to their gunwales, and the others were hauling their nets as fast as power and muscle could do it. I counted twenty Austrians pulling on one net. It was so full of tuna that they could scarcely budge it.

No wonder I was sick with anger and disgust and bade the tuna good-by.

During the season I caught a good many tuna, more, in fact, then ever before. Captain Danielson averred that it was the best season I ever had at Catalina. This was owing to my catches of blue-button tuna. The Tuna Club of Avalon recognizes only fish that weigh over one hundred pounds. In 1919 my big tuna weighed 117 pounds, 114, 111, 109, and 109. My brother, R. C., caught one of 107 pounds. Apparently this looks like remarkably good luck. But when I think of all the bad luck I had, the good seems small in proportion.

I have no idea how many very large tuna I hooked and lost on 24-

thread[1] lines during July and August. But there must have been at least twenty-five. I had exceptionally good fortune in locating schools of large tuna. Captain Dan and I were always roaming the sea, peering for the white spouts of water on the horizon.

Tuna fishing has many poignant moments. But many as I have experienced, I had only one as painful, and as unenduringly prolonged, as this one I shall tell about.

It happened in late August. I had on board a guest, a publisher from New York, and I wanted him to hook a marlin swordfish.[2] R. C. was also with us, and last, though certainly not least, was my boy Romer, the irrepressible. Apparently the tuna season was ended. No boatman had seen tuna for days. We were convinced that the run of 1919 had passed into history. We steered off to the eastward toward San Diego and along the middle of the channel south, and finally turned west. We saw not a swordfish fin, nor a break on the surface. The sea was calm, dark blue, heaving and wonderful. The day was perfect. My friend grew tired of fishing and climbed up on deck to rest and invite his soul. There was just enough breeze blowing to ripple the water. I tired of fishing, also. R. C. was asleep. Romer was trying to fly a kite in the light wind. For a while I amused myself watching him. Then I watched the jellyfish. This season there had been a strange and remarkable run of jellyfish. The clear blue water seemed to magnify the rings and ropes and links and plaques of brilliant gelatinous matter. All of them had strings and spots of gold, of silver, of wondrous fire, in the center. The spots were the most exquisite violet, the intense color of a star seen through the telescope. The rolls clustered together, like coins, and in the center of each was the quivering electric light. The sea was full of these floating jellyfish, from tiny pieces to great coils twenty feet long. Seen deep down they had a mysterious and weird appearance; seen on the surface they were clear and transparent and beautiful. I had never seen anything like this before, nor had Captain Dan in all his years at sea.

---

[1] Approximately 72-pound test.

[2] ZG often uses the term "marlin swordfish" to distinguish striped, blue and black marlins from the true swordfish, *Xiphias gladius*. However, he sometimes does not, and you must guess the species from the context of the story.

Once I happened to look up to the westward. Far across the heaving blue on the horizon line I saw a white spout of water. I peered more keenly. Another white spout! Then another! I climbed up and stood on the gunwale. I wanted to be sure before I woke anybody. Plainly I saw more white spouts. Tuna! The sight thrilled me through. Then farther to the westward, over toward Clemente Island, I saw a white wall of water, the greatest line of tuna I had ever seen.

I hailed Captain Dan. He took one look and yelled: "There's a million of 'em! Wind in. We'll put up the kite. An' we've got to hurry!" Romer immediately became interested in the approaching tuna. They looked to be at least two miles distant, and the white wall had spread across the channel, and many white splashes showed closer to us. Suddenly I saw tuna dark and sharp in the air against the blue horizon.

"Dan, look! I believe the school is feeding!" I exclaimed.

"Feedin'? I should say so! They're drivin' the flyin' fish offshore. You're goin' to see a sight pretty quick!"

I warmed to the occasion. R. C. climbed up on top and lifted Romer after him. Captain Dan needed me to help him with kite and bait, so I could not look ahead. He let the kite up about three hundred feet, broke the kite line, and gave it to me to hold. Then he put a fresh flying fish upon my leader. This took time. When he was done, he tied my fishing line to the leader. Then, taking the kite line, he tied that at the juncture of my leader and fishing line. That done, he threw the bait overboard and told me to let out line. I let go of the reel, the kite soared, and lifted my bait so that it skipped along the surface. I let out about a hundred feet. The kite swung my bait around at right angles with the boat, and when I jerked my rod a little, the bait would leap exactly like a live flying fish. We were now ready for the tuna, and I turned my head rather breathlessly.

R. C. and Romer were yelling. My friend was also exclaiming. They had reason to be delighted. Never had my eyes been greeted and gladdened by such a sight. Ahead of the boat, only a few hundred yards distant, the air was full of flying fish. High, low, everywhere, they were in wild flight. Behind them, for a mile across the channel, came the bursting white wall of water, and all over the

[83]

ocean between us and this wall there were white boils and splashes, and hundreds of giant tuna in the air. Much as I had seen of tuna, I had never beheld this sight, surely the most wonderful to encounter on the ocean. Captain Dan had seen it but once, and not so great as this. I could hear the tumbling roar of water. I could hear the smashes and cracks where the huge fish curled on the surface, breaking water as they struck their quarry. Huge blue and green and silver flashes gleamed out of the wall of water. They were coming fast. Already the flying fish were around us, over us. They made a soft rustle in the air. We had to dodge them, but some hit the boat. They presented the most wonderful spectacle of frantic and terrified life, unable to escape the monsters of the deep. I had to feel pity for them. Their flight, usually so regular and beautiful, so sailing and soaring, was now broken and wild. It seemed they did not dare alight. But of course they had to, for a flying fish cannot really fly. He leaps out and spreads his gauze-like fins and sails. When momentum is lost, he drops the long lower lobe of his tail in the water, and by a violent wiggling of his body, gets impetus for another flight.

Then the voracious school of tuna appeared to surround us. They closed all but one quarter of the circle, and that was to the east. They had no fear of the boat. The roar of the water was so loud that it sounded like the rapids of a river. The quick sharp cracks on the surface were like gun shots. A tuna rushes his prey and literally smashes the water white. His speed, his power, his savage spirit, are indescribable. I saw dozens in the air at once, some small, mostly large, and now and then a huge one over two hundred pounds.

I forgot I was fishing. I did not think of the probability that in a moment I might have a tremendous strike. I was all eyes. But it was like trying to watch too many rings in the circus.

I saw a giant tuna swimming on his side, right under a flying fish that was in the air. I saw the tuna's great black staring eye as he shot past the boat. He made a bulge on the water, and by that bulge I followed him as he kept pace with the poor flying fish until it fell. Then—smash! The water went furiously white in a ten-foot circle. I saw another tuna knock a flying fish high into the air. The flying fish was crippled. And the tuna, so violent was his energy, went up and up fully fifteen feet, quivering and beautiful, an immense fish

[84]

all blue and silver. The flying fish fell back before the tuna, and when the tuna fell back he made a lightning swift lunge at his luckless quarry. Again I saw a tuna not twenty feet astern of our boat come out in a long low leap, cutting the water till it hissed, and he took a flying fish in the air.

"Look out!" boomed Captain Dan. "There's one after your bait! Jump it! . . . Wow! No, he missed . . . Look out, now—that tuna will go over two hundred!"

My wonderful spectacle had become alarmingly specific. The largest tuna I'd ever seen was lunging at my bait. In my excitement I jerked it away from him. But it is impossible to jerk a bait altogether away from these swift monsters. He lunged again. I saw his back, dark blue and thick, his wide tail, so imbued with power. He made a splash as big as the stern of our boat. I jerked my bait. It shot right out of the tuna's jaws. Then he went into the air as though from a catapult. The anger, the hunger, the beauty, the wild nature and terrible life expressed by that long round glistening fish made me gasp. When my bait alighted he was there. He got it. And so tremendous was the strike that he broke the line.

"Wind in! Hurry! They're all around us," yelled Dan.

In less than a minute we had another bait overboard. The turmoil around us was now at its height. Fearfully I watched my bait as the kite dragged it across the foamy water. The bait did not get forty feet away before a small tuna, verily the smallest in that vast school, hit it on the leap, hooked himself, and went down. My reel whizzed. The kite began to lower. Then the kite line broke and the kite soared up with a buoyant leap and sailed away.

The prolonged moment was upon me. I was hooked to a small tuna, but he was large enough to hold me powerless for a while. And I had to sit there and hold the bobbing rod while that vast school of magnificent fish swiftly worked away from me. How swiftly I could see! The white wall and white patches and splashes on the water, the dark darting gleam of tuna, the cloud of flying fish in the air like a swarm of frightened bees, rapidly passed on to the south, and long before I had subdued the unappreciated fish on my line they were out of sight beyond the blue horizon.

[85]

8

A RECORD FIGHT WITH A SWORDFISH

Salt-water angling records are today maintained by the International Game Fish Association in Fort Lauderdale, Florida. But their books are concerned only with the largest fish of a given species caught on a particular pound-test line and tackle.

In the early days of ocean angling, at the Long Key, Port Aransas, and Catalina Clubs—as in some tournaments today—statistics were kept for such categories as the first and last fishes of the season, the most fish caught in a single day, the greatest number of hours fished during the season with the least result (Catalina's Swaffield Trophy), the worst luck of the season (Miami's Philip Wylie Tough Luck Trophy), the quickest catch—*and the longest.*

Zane Grey and his companions swore to the truth of the following story, though some Catalina men at the time pooh-poohed it, insisting that there were probably other fish around the boat that night making the noises ZG describes, and that ZG's guide created his explanation to persuade Zane Grey that it was time to go home. In any event, despite the many hands used to play this broadbill swordfish, the tale of its fight went down as the longest of the California season.

As a record for actual hours spent on a big fish, it has since been broken. But for wonder and excitement, this story has never been beat.

GWR

A RECORD FIGHT WITH A SWORDFISH

On the very first day of our 1919 season, July 1st, my brother R. C. and I, with Captain Danielson, had the longest and hardest swordfish battle on record.

Come to think of it, there are on record really very few battles with broadbill swordfish. To be sure, many of the old gladiators of the sea have been hooked by random Catalina anglers, but swordfishermen themselves do not credit the many instances where someone happened to hook a broadbill and fought it for a few moments or perhaps longer. As a matter of fact, few novices at the game ever held a broadbill longer than a few moments. Credit has gone to the few men who deliberately go out after broadbills, and keep on going day after day for weeks and months.

Xiphias gladius is the noblest warrior of all the sea fishes. He is familiar to all sailors. He roams the Seven Seas. He was written about by Aristotle 2,300 years ago. In the annals of sea disasters there are records of his sinking ships. In the logs of many mariners have been found accounts of this swordfish attacking ships and sending them back to port for repairs. Tales of his attacks on harpooners' boats in the Atlantic are common. In these waters, where he is hunted for the market, he has often killed his pursuers. In the Pacific, off the Channel Islands, he has not killed any angler or boatman yet, but it is a safe wager that he will do so some day. Therefore, despite the wonderful nature of the sport, it is not remarkable that so few anglers have risked it. Of all the Tuna Club anglers there are only five who have won the gold-and-white broadbill swordfish button—Boschen, Adams, Johnson, Farnum, and myself.

*

July 1st seemed the most perfect of days. All Avalon days are perfect, but this day was something to make a man keen to the joy of life and the beauty of nature. A fisherman's hopes are of the future and his joys are of the present.

The fog broke up and rolled away early that morning, letting the sunshine down bright and warm. The sky shone azure blue, and the sea under it a deeper blue. Dark, glancing ripples, here and there with crests of white, waved regularly away before the west wind.

We took my boy Romer with us, and the occasion was his initial experience on the sea. I hoped to make a fisherman of him, but, alas, in his ten years of existence, he had not yet shown any remarkable tendencies toward that end. Romer's idea of fishing, like that of many grown-up men I know, was to sit on a rock or a bank or a dock—some sure, steady, safe place—and throw a lot of baited hooks into the water, and pull out fish until he had caught more than anybody else. Upon this occasion it was difficult to persuade Romer that he was merely a guest and somewhat fortunate to be that.

*

By eleven o'clock we were way up the channel, about six miles from land, directly opposite a deep cut in the rocky shore named Catalina Harbor. The west wind had softened to a light breeze; the sea was flattening out, dimpled and blue, with long, low swells running. Captain Dan was up on top, watching for swordfish fins on

[89]

the surface; Romer was in the cabin; R. C. had a keen eye on the ocean; and I was lazily holding my rod, dozing in my chair, contentedly yielding to the warm sun, the motion of the boat, and the sweet, soft scent of the sea.

Suddenly R. C. murdered this peacefulness. "Swordfish!" he bellowed.

Captain Dan's heavy feet thumped on the cabin deck above, and he yelled; Romer came running out, with his shrill treble voice at top key; R. C. stood up, alert, erect, with stiff arm pointing seaward. "Look! Are they fins or sails of a schooner? Look! If that's not a broadbill I'll eat him!"

"Broadbill all right—and a buster!" boomed Captain Dan as he threw out the clutch. "Wind in your baits and let me put on fresh flying fish."

Whereupon I came out of my trance and beheld the dark, sickle-shaped fins of a swordfish riding the slow swells some three hundred yards out. The sight gave me an inexplicable thrill. Then a bursting gush of blood warmed my sluggish veins. I hurried to wind in my bait.

All was now cheerful excitement on board the boat. Captain Dan put a new bait, a fine fat flying fish, on R. C.'s hook, throwing it overboard and heading the boat to cross in front of the swordfish, so as to drag the bait before his eyes. When we got to within a hundred yards of the fish I began to think that he was pretty big. His fins looked large, but they were partially submerged. The distance from dorsal fin to tail began to amaze me. Still I was too pleasantly excited to be sure of anything. R. C. had made some wonderful catches of marlin or roundbill swordfish the preceding years, but he had never even hooked a broadbill. Captain Dan and I were exceedingly anxious to try out his mettle on an old gladiator. R. C.'s remarkable catch of seven marlin in one day had rather made us want to see him hooked to the bottom of the ocean or to some big fish that he could not haul in right away.

I climbed up on top of the deck so that I could see better. As the boat passed the swordfish, perhaps two hundred feet distant, I could plainly see the dark, purple, rounded mass of his body, big as a barrel, it seemed, in the clear water. He was drifting lazily and did not know that there was a boat within a mile. At that moment there

[90]

never occurred to me the chances against a strike, and the further chances against hooking him if he did strike, and still further the almost impossible chance of whipping him even if he did get hooked.

When the bait reached a point about fifty feet ahead of him, he gave his tail a flirt and moved forward, to sink in a swirl of water. I believed that he meant to take R. C.'s bait. Most assuredly at least he meant to look it over.

Suddenly the line whipped up off the water. It was the motion given to a fishing line by the swordfish when he strikes the bait with his sword. No other fish in the sea gives line such a strange and thrilling motion!

"He's got it!" whispered R. C.

Then we all watched the line slip off the reel. At first it went slowly, then gradually faster. R. C.'s face wore a pleasant, satisfied smile of excitement.

"Hook him! Hook him!" boomed Captain Dan, with a deep ring in his heavy voice. It reminded me that he and I both had seen broadbills hooked before.

R. C. threw on the drag and lowered the rod while the line straightened; he squared his powerful shoulders and jerked back with all his might. Both rod and line seemed to crack. But they held. R. C. swept forward and heaved back.

"That's the way," boomed Captain Dan. "Soak him! . . . Fast an' hard now! . . . He's comin' up! See the line?"

The moment was one of great stress. I knew that R. C. had hooked a broadbill, yet I could not believe it. With strained eyes I watched the line rise and rise, until the spot where it led my sight burst into a white, crashing splash, in the midst of which a huge, obscure, purple body flashed. The swordfish did not show well, but he showed that he was hooked. He threshed around in foam, with only his sword in sight, banging at the wire leader. Then, with a heavy swirl, he sounded between four and five hundred feet, and stayed down there, slowly working seaward. We kept after him, but R. C. did not recover any line.

"Well, Red, he's comin' up," said Dan, cheerfully. "He doesn't like it down there. Now go to work on him."

I think these last words of Captain Dan's brought reality to me.

[91]

To go to work on a broadbill meant a great deal. I knew. It meant to lift and haul and pump with the rod, to lower the tip swiftly and wind the reel desperately, and to repeat that performance over and over, endlessly, until sight and muscle almost failed. When R. C. came up hard and fast the first time with his powerful sweep, I made the startling discovery that the rod he was using was my light marlin rod. I gasped with surprise and groaned inwardly with despair. How on earth did it happen that he had hooked the swordfish on that rod? The simple fact was that we had neglected to have him use the heavy rod.

To be sure, the little Murphy rod had long ago proved its wonderful quality, but it was still not enough for a broadbill. There was danger of breaking. And after a while I had to caution R. C. about this. He did not seem to let up any. Every time he heaved back with all his weight in the action, the rod described a half circle, and the line twanged like a banjo string. It was take and give. He would recover a hundred feet or so, and then the broadbill would run that much out again. He came up to thresh and roll and swish on the surface, showing only his fins and sword. He fought heavily and sluggishly. And at the end of an hour he appeared to be tiring. R. C. saved nothing of his strength then, and worked harder and harder. The big fish fought for every foot of line, but slowly he was dragged closer and closer. R. C. was hot and wet and panting now. Every time he leaned back and bent the rod double I thought he would crack it. Captain Dan's dubious face attested to the same fear. Yet both of us hated to warn him further. It was not until the swordfish was within thirty feet of the boat that either of us yielded to our dread. I was the first to see the fish. He looked a long, indistinct, purple mass. Climbing up on deck, I got a better sight of him. I could not be sure just how big he was, but I could tell that he was very large. R. C. dragged him closer inch by inch. He was swimming at right angles with the boat. His outline grew clearer. The end of the double line appeared on the surface.

"Careful, Red!" warned Captain Dan. "That's an awful strain."

"I can—bring him—to gaff," panted R. C., grimly.

"Fellows, he's bigger than you have any idea," I called from my vantage point. "Ease up or you'll break the rod."

R. C. let up on the strain and the swordfish rolled away and down

[92]

out of sight. This caution of mine might have been a blunder. R. C. always insisted afterward that he could have brought the swordfish to gaff then. For my part, I am positive he would have broken the rod. But I will say that if he had been using the heavier Murphy rod he would have brought that magnificent swordfish up to the boat. Broadbills do not wake up until they have been worked on for a few hours.

"Aw, why didn't you let Uncle Rome pull him in?" complained Romer, bitterly. "Now we'll never get him back."

It did seem that he presaged the truth. Our quarry changed his tactics. He had been slow; now he became fast. He had stayed down rather deep; now he came to the surface. First he made a long run, splashing over the swells. We had to put on full power to keep up with him, and at that he took off a good deal of line. When he slowed up he began to fight the leader. He would stick his five-foot sword out of the water and bang the leader. Then he lifted his enormous head and wagged it from side to side, so that his sword described a circle, smacking the water on his left and then on his right. Wonderful and frightful that sweep of sword! It would have cut a man in two or have pierced the planking of a boat. Evidently his efforts and failure to free himself roused him to fury. His huge tail thumped out of great white boils; when he turned sideways he made a wave like that behind a ferryboat; when he darted here and there he was as swift as a flash and he left a raised bulge, a white wake on the surface. Suddenly he electrified us by leaping. Broadbill swordfish seldom clear the water after being hooked. They leap, however, at other times. This one came out in a tremendous white splash, and when he went down with a loud crash we all saw where the foam was red with blood. Captain Dan yelled in surprise at his size. R. C. did not show any surprise and kept silent. I took out my thrilling excitement in a mad scramble for my camera. Before I could get ready the swordfish leaped again, a magnificent leap that I would give anything to have photographed. Like a leaping tuna, he shot out slick and clean. But when he dropped back he made a thunderous smash on the water.

He leaped again, almost all the way out, and was half obscured in spray. I snapped the camera on him. Then he seemed to want to perform for my benefit. He lashed a great patch of water into white

[93]

foam; he surged and went down with his wonderful broad flukes high in the air; he came up and up and up, with his black rapier straight to the sky; he fell over on his side to smack the water. Then he leaped again.

There was no use trying to hold him or fight him while he was up to such tricks. All we could do was to chase him. Half the time R. C.'s line lay slack, and often it had a wide bag in it. He did not even try to keep a tight line.

"Say! He's comin' at us!" yelled the boy. And indeed Romer was the first to become aware of possible peril.

We lost no time getting away from where he was smashing the water white. Then, at about three hundred yards, we stopped, with the stern of the boat toward him, and there we watched the conclusion of his mad rushes and leaps. In all he leaped fourteen times, several leaps of which were wholly clear of the water. But these, the greatest chances I ever had to take incomparable pictures, I missed. Too slow and overanxious! At length he settled down and with a sullen swirl ended his surface pyrotechnics.

R. C. began slowly to recover line, and for two more hours heaved like a Trojan, never resting a moment, never letting the rod down on the gunwale. But he did not get the hundred-foot mark on the line over the reel again. The swordfish had been hooked at eleven-thirty. At three-thirty R. C. had expended the best of his efforts. That was plain. He was in bad shape. Wet, hot, dirty, disheveled, he looked, indeed, as if he had been in a fight. Moreover, he began to get that greenish cast of face which portends seasickness.

"Will you take the rod?" he asked me.

I refused, but his request worried me exceedingly. I knew then that he was in worse shape than he looked. The afternoon wind was springing up, making the boat roll. It is hard enough to fight a swordfish in a smooth sea, but when the fish is underneath and the boat is rising on the waves, then the fight becomes something indescribable. I exhausted all my eloquence (and I guess, wasted it) upon R. C. Captain Dan talked and talked. R. C. saved his breath and worked wearily on the rod. His face had turned a pale green. At four-thirty he rolled and swayed at his task. "I'm all in," he said, faintly. "If I hadn't got—seasick—maybe I'd have licked him. Maybe. Take the rod!"

[94]

R. C. let the rod down on the gunwale for the first time, and while I held it firmly in the seat socket, he got up. As he went into the cabin he staggered. Captain Dan looked very gloomy.

When I straddled the rod and took the seat, I was as furious at the swordfish as I was sorry for R. C. I intended to make short work of that swordfish. Romer said, "I'll bet you can't pull him right up." It struck me then how little boys have an uncanny divination at times. I braced myself with feet against the gunwale, squared my shoulders, clamped my gloved thumbs down on the line, and heaved with all my might. Then I felt the heaviest live weight that it had ever been my fortune to have at the end of a fishing line. Ponderous, irresistible, it gave me a shock. Doubt at once assailed me. This swordfish was unbeatable. But that did not keep me from exerting myself. Fresh and strong, I began to lift and wind. It gratified me to see that I could lift him little by little. It took just thirty minutes for me to lift our quarry so that we could see the hundred-foot mark on the line. Then he anchored himself at that depth and I could not budge him. Not another foot did I gain. Worse than this, if I did not lift desperately and hold desperately he slowly sank deeper, taking more line. All the time he worked out to sea.

Two hours passed by swiftly. However laborious and painful they were, they did not drag. I toiled at that job. I spent myself in those two hours, and then, dripping wet, smarting and burning, out of breath, numb, and almost strengthless, I had to rest. Old *Xiphias* sank a couple of hundred feet, and apparently satisfied with that depth he tugged on out to sea.

At sunset the wind died away and the sea quieted down. It gave me a good deal of comfort, but I did not imagine it added anything to my chances of getting the fish. The sun set behind broken clouds of gold and silver and purple. Long rays of rare blue, fan shaped and sharply defined, spread toward the zenith. The sea seemed divided by a radiant track of golden light. The west end of Catalina Island, with its rugged mountains, took on crowns of color and glory. Clemente Island lay a dark, lonely strip of land, fading in the twilight.

By and by darkness stole over the ocean and all was obscure save in the west, where a pale afterglow marked the sunset. At seven-thirty I passed the rod to Captain Dan. He was as eager to take it as I was to give it, and he began to work on the swordfish. Big and powerful as he was, he could not subdue that swordfish. He pulled

[95]

as hard as he dared, and at every pull I said good-by to the rod. But it did not break. Many times Captain Dan got the swordfish within the hundred feet, but that was all. At nine-thirty he was tired.

"Whale of—a broadbill!" panted Dan. "What'll we do?"

"Let's both work on him," I suggested.

So, standing beside Dan, a little in front, I grasped the rod above where he held it, and heaved with him. I had rested, and aside from having pretty sore hands I was all right again. R. C. and Romer saw us from the cabin and called for us to pull the fish in or break something. Most assuredly I expected something to break. But it did not. That was the wonder of the whole fight. We both pulled in unison as hard as we could upon that rod. It bent double, but did not break.

R. C. groaned as he watched.

"Oh, if you'd only let me pull like that when I had him near the boat!"

I groaned also, and I was angry with myself and sick of the whole business. But it was too late. I think Captain Dan and I both had a sneaking hope that we would break him off, and then we could go back to Avalon. We were wet, cold, hungry. No fun, no sport any more!

The two of us working together, began to tell on the swordfish. We stopped him. We turned him. We got him coming. Still we could not tell how close we had him. The 150-foot mark had worn off the line. Then just when our hopes began to mount and we began to believe that we could whip him, the great reel went out of gear. The drag refused to stick. Dan could wind in the line, but there was no drag to hold it. He had to hold it with his thumbs. This was heartbreaking. Yet we seemed to rise to a frenzy and worked all the harder.

At eleven o'clock, in spite of our handicap, we had the swordfish coming again. It looked as if we had the best of him. Eleven and one-half hours! It did seem as if victory would crown our combined efforts. But we were both well-nigh exhausted and had to finish him quickly if we were to do it at all. The sea was dark now. A wan starlight did not help us, and we could not always tell just where our quarry was. Suddenly, to our amazement, he jerked the line from under Dan's thumbs and made a magnificent run. Then the line slacked. "He's off!" exclaimed Dan. I told him to wind. He did so, getting nearly all the line back. Then the old strain showed again on the rod. Our broadbill had only changed his tactics. He made some sounding thumps on the surface. "Say, I don't like this," said Dan. "He's runnin' wild."

I was reminded that Boschen, Adams, and myself all agreed on the theory that broadbill swordfish wake up and become fierce and dangerous after dark. This one certainly verified that theory. In the dark we could not tell where he was, whether he was close or near, whether he menaced us or not. Some of the splashes he made sounded angry and close. I expected to hear a crash at any moment. Captain Dan and I were loath to cut the line; stirred and roused as we were, it was difficult to give in. We took the chance that as long as our propeller turned the swordfish would not ram us.

But if we had only known what we were soon to learn, we might have spared ourselves further toil and dread.

Suddenly the line began to whiz off the reel. This time the fish took off several hundred feet, then stopped. The line slacked. Dan wound up the slack, and then the fish jerked out more. Still he did not run. I let go of the rod and raised myself to look out into the gloom. I could just make out the pale obscurity of heaving sea, wan and mysterious under the starlight. I heard splashes.

"Listen, Dan," I called. "What do you make of that? He's on the surface."

Captain Dan relaxed a little and listened. Then I heard more splashes, the angry swirl of water violently disturbed, the familiar swishing sound. Then followed a heavy thump. After that soft, light splashes came from the darkness here and there. I heard the rush of light bodies in the air. Then a skittering splash, right near the boat, showed us where a flying fish had ended his flight.

"Dan! Flying fish! All around us—in the air!" I cried.

We listened again, to be rewarded by practically the same sounds. Captain Dan rested the rod on the gunwale, pointing it straight out where we heard the swordfish. *Snap*! Then he wound in the slack line.

"There!" he boomed, as he dropped the rod and waved his big hands. "Do you know what that broadbill is doin' out there? He's feedin' on flyin' fish. He got hungry an' thought he'd feed up a

[97]

little. Never knew he was hooked! . . . Eleven hours an' a half—an' he goes to feedin'! . . . By gosh! if that ain't the limit!"

It was long after midnight when we reached the island. Quite a crowd of fishermen and others interested waited for us at the pier, and heard our story with disappointment and wonder. Some of our angler friends made light of the swordfish stunts, especially that one of his chasing flying fish after being fought for more than eleven hours. It did seem strange, improbable. But I had learned that there were stranger possibilities than this in connection with the life and habits of the denizens of the deep. I shall always be positive of the enormous size of this broadbill, and that, after being fought for half a day, and while still hooked, he began chasing flying fish.

DON, THE STORY OF A LION DOG

One of the ways we rate a writer is by how well he converts experience into meaningful narrative. Zane Grey was a master of this. He blended imagination and memory to produce the characters and settings for a dozen different Westerns from just two cougar hunting trips. He also wrote a number of "nonfiction" variations on these Grand Canyon adventures.

In "Roping Lions in the Grand Canyon," there is a hound named Don, the leader of the pack. But because that story is about four hunters who discover that the ecstasy of pursuit is a weaker emotion than the bitterness of defeat in a lion's death, Zane Grey would only have been wandering from his subject by describing his attachment to one of the dogs. Instead, ZG saved his memories of Don for later.

In the June, 1908, issue of *Field and Stream*, Zane Grey published his first dog story. Entitled "Tige's Lion," this tale is about a tenacious hound that tumbles over the rim of the Grand Canyon with his teeth still imbedded in the lion he's captured almost single-pawedly. This story lacks the development and detail of "Don, The Story of a Lion Dog," but it was no doubt good practice for the latter, which first appeared in the August, 1925, edition of *Harper's Magazine* and was then published in book form in 1928.

"Don" well illustrates the ability of a writer who saw and remembered and, if necessary, rewrote experience to create a great dog story. While some readers may feel cheated to know that the real Don *did* come back, ZG wrote this story to honor all those who didn't.

GWR

DON, THE STORY OF A LION DOG

It has taken me years to realize the greatness of a dog; and often as I have told the story of Don—his love of freedom and hatred of men—how I saved his life and he saved mine—it never was told as I feel it now.

I saw Don first at Flagstaff, Arizona, where arrangements had been made for me to cross the desert with Buffalo Jones and a Mormon caravan en route to Lee's Ferry on the Colorado River. Jones had brought a pack of nondescript dogs. Our purpose was to cross the river and skirt the Vermilion Cliffs, and finally work up through Buckskin Forest to the north rim of Grand Canyon, where Jones expected to lasso mountain lions and capture them alive. The most important part of our outfit, of course, was the pack of hounds. Never had I seen such a motley assembly of canines. They did not even have names. Jones gave me the privilege of finding names for them.

Among them was a hound that seemed out of place because of his superb proportions, his sleek, dark, smooth skin, his noble head, and great, solemn black eyes. He had extraordinarily long ears, thick-veined and faintly tinged with brown. Here was a dog that looked to me like a thoroughbred. My friendly overtures to him were unnoticed. Jones said he was part bloodhound and had belonged to an old Mexican don in southern California. So I named him Don.

We were ten days crossing the Painted Desert, and protracted horseback riding was then so new and hard for me that I had no enthusiasm left to scrape acquaintance with the dogs. Still, I did not forget and often felt sorry for them as they limped along, clinking their chains under the wagons. Even then I divined that horses and dogs were going to play a great part in my Western experience.

At Lee's Ferry we crossed the Colorado and I was introduced to the weird and wild canyon country, with its golden-red walls and purple depths. Here we parted with the caravan and went on with Jones's rangers, Jim and Emett, who led our outfit into such a wonderful region as I had never dreamed of. Once across the river, Jones had unchained the dogs and let them run on ahead or lag behind. Most of them lagged. Don for one, however, did not get sore feet. We entered the sage, and here Jones began to train the dogs in earnest. He carried on his saddle an old blunderbuss of a shotgun, about which I had wondered curiously. I had supposed he meant to use it to shoot small game.

Moze, our black and white dog, and the ugliest of the lot, gave chase to a jackrabbit.

"Hyar, you Moze, come back!" bawled Jones in stentorian tones. But Moze paid no attention. Jones whipped out the old shotgun and before I could utter a protest he had fired. The distance was pretty far—seventy yards or more—but Moze howled piercingly and came sneaking and limping back. It was remarkable to see him almost crawl to Jones' feet.

[101]

"Thar! That'll teach you not to chase rabbits. You're a lion dog!" shouted the old plainsman as if he were talking to a human.

At first I was so astounded and furious that I could not speak. But presently I voiced my feeling.

"Wal, it looks worse than it is," he said, with his keen gray-blue eyes on me. "I'm usin' fine birdshot an' it can't do any more than sting. You see, I've no time to train these dogs. It's necessary to make them see quick that they're not to trail or chase any varmints but lions."

There was nothing for me to do but hold my tongue, though my resentment appeared to be shared by Jim and Emett. They made excuses for the old plainsman. Jim said: "He shore can make animals do what he wants. But I never seen the dog or hoss that cared two bits for him."

We rode on through the beautiful purple sageland, gradually uphill, toward a black-fringed horizon that was Buckskin Forest. Jackrabbits, cottontails, coyotes and foxes, prairie dogs and pack rats infested the sage and engaged the attention of our assorted pack of hounds. All the dogs except Don fell victim to Jones' old blunderbuss.

"Reckon Don is too smart to let you ketch him," Jim once remarked to our leader.

"Wal, I don't know," responded Jones, dubiously. "Mabbe he just wouldn't chase this sage trash. But wait till we jump some deer. Then we'll see. He's got bloodhound in him, and I'll bet he'll run deer. All hounds will, even the best ones trained on bear and lion."

Not long after we entered the wonderful pine forest, the reckoning of Don came as Jones had predicted. Several deer bounded out of a thicket and crossed ahead of us, soon disappearing in the green blur.

"Ahuh! Now we'll see," exclaimed Jones, deliberately pulling out the old shotgun.

The hounds trotted along beside our horses, unaware of the danger ahead. Soon we reached the deer tracks. All the hounds showed excitement. Don let out a sharp yelp and shot away like a streak on the trail.

"Don, come hyar!" yelled Jones, at the same time extending his gun. Don gave no sign he had heard. Then Jones pulled the trigger and shot him. I saw the scattering of dust and pine needles all around Don. He doubled up and rolled. I feared that he might be badly injured. But he got up and turned back. It seemed strange that he did not howl. Jones drew his plunging horse to a halt and bade us all stop.

"Don, come back hyar," he called in a loud, harsh, commanding voice.

The hound obeyed, not sneakingly or cringingly. He did not put his tail between his legs. But he was frightened and no doubt pretty badly hurt. When he reached us I saw that he was trembling all over and that drops of blood dripped from his long ears. What a somber, sullen gaze in his eyes!

"See hyar," bellowed Jones. "I knowed you was a deer-chaser. Wal, now you're a lion dog."

Later that day, when I had recovered sufficiently from my disapproval, I took Jones to task about this matter of shooting the dogs. I wanted to know how he expected the hounds to learn what he required of them.

"Wal, that's easy," he replied curtly. "When we strike a lion trail I'll put them on it—let them go. They'll soon learn."

It seemed plausible, but I was so incensed that I doubted the hounds would chase anything; and I resolved that if Jones shot Don again I would force the issue and end the hunt unless assured there would be no more of such drastic training methods.

Soon after this incident we made camp on the edge of a beautiful glade where a snowbank still lingered and a stream of water trickled down into a green swale. I renewed my attempts to make friends with Don. He had been chained apart from the other dogs. He ate what I fetched him, but remained aloof. His dignity and distrust were such that I did not risk laying a hand on him then. But I resolved to win him if it were possible. His tragic eyes haunted me. There was a story in them I could not read. He always seemed to be looking afar. On this occasion I came to the conclusion that he hated Jones.

As we traveled on, the forest grew wilder and more beautiful. We rode for several days through an enchanting wilderness, gradually ascending, and one afternoon we came abruptly to a break in the forest. It was the north rim of the Grand Canyon. My astounded gaze tried to grasp an appalling abyss of purple and gold and red, a chasm too terrible and beautiful to understand all at once. The effect of that moment must have been tremendous, for I have never recovered from it. To this day the thing that fascinates me most is to stand upon a great height—canyon wall, or promontory, or peak—and gaze down into the mysterious colorful depths.

Our destination was Powell's Plateau, an isolated cape jutting out into the canyon void. Jones showed it to me—a distant gold-rimmed, black-fringed promontory, seemingly inaccessible and unscalable. The only trail leading to it was a wild-horse hunter's trail, seldom used, exceedingly dangerous. It took us two days over this canyon trail to the Saddle—a narrow strip of land dipping down from the Plateau and reaching up to the main rim. We camped under a vast looming golden wall, so wonderful that it kept me from sleeping. That night lions visited our camp. The hounds barked for hours. This was the first chance I had to hear Don. What a voice he had! Deep, ringing, wild, like the bay of a wolf.

Next morning we ascended the Saddle, from the notch of which I looked down into the chasm still asleep in purple shadows; then we climbed a narrow deer trail to the summit of the Plateau. Here indeed was the grand, wild, isolated spot of my dreams.

I wanted to make camp on the rim, but Jones laughed at me. We rode through the level, stately forest of pines until we came to a ravine on the north side of which lay a heavy bank of snow. This was very necessary, for there was no water on the Plateau. Jones rode off to scout while the rest of us pitched camp. Before we had completed our task a troop of deer appeared across the ravine, and motionless they stood watching us. There were big and little deer, blue-gray in color, sleek and graceful, so tame that to me it seemed brutal to shoot at them.

Don was the only one of the dogs that espied the deer. He stood up to gaze hard at them, but he did not bark or show any desire to chase them. Yet there seemed to me to be a strange yearning light in his dark eyes. I had never failed to approach Don whenever opportunity afforded, to continue my overtures of friendship. But now, as always, Don turned away from me. He was cold and somber. I had never seen him wag his tail or whine eagerly, as was common with most hounds.

Jones returned to camp jubilant and excited. He had found lion trails and lion tracks, and he predicted a great hunt for us.

The Plateau resembled in shape the ace of clubs. It was perhaps six miles long and three or four wide. The body of it was covered with a heavy growth of pine, and the capes that sloped somewhat toward the canyon were thick with sage and cedar. This lower part, with its numerous swales and ravines and gorges, all leading down into the jungle of splintered crags and thicketed slopes of the Grand Canyon, turned out to be a paradise for deer and lion.

In two days we had three captive lions tied to pine saplings near camp. They were two-year-olds. Don and I had treed the first lion; I had taken pictures of Jones lassoing him; I had jumped off a ledge into a cedar to escape another; I had helped Jones hold a third; I had scratches from lion claws on my chaps, and—but I keep forgetting that this is not a story about lions. Always before when I had told it I have slighted Don.

One night, a week or more after we had settled in camp, we sat round a blazing red fire and talked over the hunt of the day.

"Wal," said Jones, standing with the palms of his huge hands to the fire, "we had a poor day. If we had stuck to Don there'd have been a different story. I haven't trusted him. But now I reckon I'll have to. He'll make the greatest lion dog I ever had. Strikes me queer, too, for I never guessed it was in him. He has faults, though. He's too fast. He outruns the other hounds, an' he's goin' to be killed because of that. Some day he'll beat the pack to a mean old tom lion or a lioness with cubs, an' he'll get his everlastin'. Another fault is, he doesn't bark often. That's bad, too. You can't stick to him. He's got a grand bay, shore, but he saves his breath. Don wants to run an' trail an' fight alone. He's got more nerve than any hound I ever trained. He's too good for his own sake—an' it'll be his death."

A little later, when Jones had left the fire, Jim spoke up with his slow Texas drawl: "If Jones hadn't shot Don we'd had the best hound that ever put his nose to a track. Don is a wild, strange hound, shore enough. But it's plain he's been mistreated by men. An' Jones has just made him wuss. I wonder why Don doesn't run off from us?"

"Perhaps he thinks he'd get shot again," I ventured.

"If he ever runs away it'll not be here in the wilds," said Emett. "I take Don to be about as smart as any dog ever gets. And that's pretty close to human intelligence. People have to live lonely lives

[105]

with dogs before they understand them. I reckon I understand Don. He's either loved one master once and lost him, or else he has always hated all men."

One morning Jim galloped in, driving the horses pell-mell into camp. Any deviation from the Texan's usual leisurely manner of doing things always brought us up short with keen expectation.

"Saddle up," called Jim. "Shore there's a chase on. I seen a big red lioness up heah. She must have come down out of the tree where I hang my meat. Last night I had a haunch of venison. It's gone. . . . Say, she was a beauty. Red as a red fox."

In a very few moments we were mounted and riding up the ravine, with the eager hounds sniffing the air. Always overanxious in my excitement, I rode ahead of my comrades. The hounds trotted with me. The distance to Jim's meat tree was a short quarter of a mile. I knew well where it was and since the lion trail would be fresh, I anticipated a fine opportunity to watch Don. The other hounds had come to regard him as their leader. When we neared the meat tree, which was a low-branched oak shaded by thick, silver spruce, Don elevated his nose high in the air. He had caught a scent even at a distance. Jones had said more than once that Don had a wonderful nose. The other hounds, excited by Don, began to whine and yelp and run around with noses to the ground.

I had eyes only for Don. How imbued he was with life and fire! The hair on his neck stood up like bristles. Suddenly he let out a wild bark and bolted. He sped away from the pack and like a flash passed the oak tree, running with his head high. The hounds strung out after him and soon the woods seemed full of a baying chorus.

My horse, Black Bolly, knew the meaning of the medley and did not need to be urged. He broke into a run and swiftly carried me up out of the hollow and through a brown-aisled pine-scented strip of forest to the canyon.

I rode along the edge of one of the deep indentations on the main rim. The hounds were bawling right under me at the base of a low cliff. They had jumped the lioness. I could not see them, but that was not necessary. They were running fast towards the head of this cove, and I had hard work to hold Black Bolly to a safe gait along that rocky rim. Suddenly she shied, and then reared, so that I fell out of the saddle as much as if I'd dismounted. But I held the bridle, and then jerked my rifle from the saddle sheath. As I ran toward the rim I heard the yells of the men coming up behind. At the same instant I was startled and halted by the sight of something red and furry flashing up into a tree right in front of me. It was the red lioness. The dogs had chased her into a pine the middle branches of which were on a level with the rim.

My skin went tight and cold. The lioness looked enormous, but that was because she was so close. I could have touched her with a long fishing pole. I stood motionless for an instant, thrilling in every nerve, reveling in the beauty and wildness of that great cat. She did not see me. The hounds below engaged all her attention. But when I let out a yell, which I could not stifle, she jerked spasmodically to face me. Then I froze again. What a tigerish yellow flash of eyes and fangs! She hissed. She could have sprung from the tree to the rim and upon me in two bounds. But she leaped to a ledge below the rim, glided along that, and disappeared.

I ran ahead and with haste and violence clambered out upon a jutting point of the rim, from which I could command the situation. Jones and the others were riding and yelling back where I had left my horse. I called for them to come.

The hounds were baying along the base of the low cliff. No doubt they had seen the lioness leap out of the tree. My eyes roved everywhere. This cove was a shallow V-shaped gorge, a few hundred yards deep and as many across. Its slopes were steep, with patches of brush and rock.

All at once my quick eye caught a glimpse of something moving up the opposite slope. It was a long, red pantherish shape. The lioness! I yelled with all my might. She ran up the slope and at the base of the low wall she turned to the right. At that moment Jones strode heavily over the rough, loose rocks of the promontory toward me.

"Where's the cat?" he boomed, his gray eyes flashing. In a moment more I had pointed her out. "Ha! I see. . . . Don't like that place. The canyon boxes. She can't get out. She'll turn back."

The old hunter had been quick to grasp what had escaped me. The lioness could not find any break in the wall, and manifestly she would not go down into the gorge. She wheeled back along the base of this yellow cliff. There appeared to be a strip of bare clay or shale

[107]

rock against which background her red shape stood out clearly. She glided along, slowing her pace, and she turned her gaze across the gorge.

Then Don's deep bay rang out from the slope to our left. He had struck the trail of the lioness. I saw him running down. He leaped in long bounds. The other hounds heard him and broke for the brushy slope. In a moment they had struck the scent of their quarry and given tongue.

As they started down, Don burst out of the willow thicket at the bottom of the gorge and bounded up the opposite slope. He was five hundred yards ahead of the pack. He was swiftly climbing. He would run into the lioness.

Jones gripped my arm in his powerful hand.

"Look!" he shouted. "Look at that fool hound! . . . Runnin' uphill to get that lioness. She won't run. She's cornered. She'll meet him. She'll kill him . . . Shoot her! Shoot her!"

I scarcely needed Jones' command to stir me to save Don, but it was certain that the old plainsman's piercing voice made me tremble. I knelt and leveled my rifle. The lioness showed red against the gray—a fine target. She was gliding more and more slowly. She saw or heard Don. The gunsight wavered. I could not hold steady. But I had to hurry. My first bullet struck two yards below the beast, puffing the dust. She kept on. My second bullet hit behind her. Jones was yelling in my ear. I could see Don out of the tail of my eye. . . . Again I shot. Too high! But the lioness jumped and halted. She lashed with her tail. What a wild picture! I strained—clamped every muscle, and pulled trigger. My bullet struck right under the lioness, scattering a great puff of dust and gravel in her face. She bounded ahead a few yards and up into a cedar tree. An instant later Don flashed over the bare spot where she had waited to kill him, and in another his deep bay rang out under the cedar.

"Treed, by gosh!" yelled Jones, joyfully, pounding me on the back with his huge fist. "You saved that fool dog's life. She'd have killed him shore . . . Wal, the pack will be there pronto, an' all we've got to do is go over an' tie her up. But it was a close shave for Don."

That night in camp Don was not in the least different from his usual somber self. He took no note of my proud proprietorship or

[108]

my hovering near him while he ate the supper I provided, part of which came from my own plate. My interest and sympathy had augmented to love.

Don's attitude toward the captured and chained lions never ceased to be a source of delight and wonder to me. All the other hounds were upset by the presence of the big cats. Moze, Sounder, Tiger, Ranger would have fought these collared lions. Not so Don! For him they had ceased to exist. He would walk within ten feet of a hissing lioness without the slightest sign of having seen or heard her. He never joined in the howling chorus of the dogs. He would go to sleep close to where the lions clanked their chains, clawed the trees, whined and spat and squalled.

Several days after that incident of the red lioness we had a long and severe chase through the brushy cedar forest on the left wing of the Plateau. I did well to keep the hounds within earshot. When I arrived at the end of that run I was torn and blackened by the brush, wet with sweat, and hot as fire. Jones, lasso in hand, was walking round a large cedar tree under which the pack of hounds was clamoring. Jim and Emett were seated on a stone, wiping their red faces.

"It's a tom lion," declared Jones. "Not very big, but he looks mean. I reckon he'll mess us up some."

I climbed a cedar next to the one in which the lion had taken refuge. From the topmost fork, swaying to and fro, I stood up to photograph our quarry. He was a good-sized animal, tawny in hue, rather gray of face, and a fierce-looking brute. As the distance between us was not far, my situation was as uncomfortable as thrilling. He snarled at me and spat viciously. I was about to abandon my swinging limb when the lion turned away from me to peer down through the branches.

Jones was climbing into the cedar. Low and deep the lion growled. Jones held in one hand a long pole with a small fork at the end, upon which hung the noose of his lasso. Presently he got far enough up to reach the lion. Usually he climbed close enough to throw the rope, but evidently he regarded this beast as dangerous. He tried to slip the noose over the head of the lion. One sweep of a big paw sent pole and noose flying. Patiently Jones made ready and tried again, with similar result. Many times he tried. Finally the lion

[109]

grew careless or tired, on which instant Jones slipped the noose over its head.

Drawing the lasso tight, he threw his end over a thick branch and let it trail down to the men below. "Wait now!" he yelled and quickly backed down out of the cedar. The hounds were leaping eagerly.

"Pull him off that fork an' let him down easy so I can rope one of his paws."

It turned out, however, that the lion was hard to dislodge. I could see his muscles ridge and bulge. Dead branches cracked, the treetop waved. Jones began to roar in anger. The men replied with strained voices. I saw the lion drop from his perch and, clawing the branches, springing convulsively, he disappeared from my sight.

There followed a crash. The branch over which Jones was lowering the beast had broken. Wild yells greeted my startled ears and a perfect din of yelps and howls. Pandemonium had broken loose down there. I fell more than I descended from that tree.

As I bounded erect I saw the men scrambling out of the way of a huge furry wheel. Ten hounds and one lion comprised that brown whirling ball. Suddenly out of it a dog came hurtling. He rolled to my feet, staggered up.

It was Don. Blood was streaming from him. Swiftly I dragged him aside, out of harm's way. And I forgot the fight. My hands came away from Don wet and dripping with hot blood. It shocked me. Then I saw that his throat had been terribly torn. I thought his jugular had been severed. Don lay down and stretched out. He looked at me with those great somber eyes. Never would I forget! He was going to die right there before my eyes.

"Oh, Don! Don! What can I do?" I cried in horror.

As I sank beside him, one of my hands came in contact with snow. It had snowed that morning and there were still white patches in shady places. Like a flash I ripped off my scarf and bound it round Don's neck. Then I scraped up a double handful of snow and placed that in my bandana handkerchief. This also I bound tightly round his neck. I could do no more. My hope left me then, and I had not the courage to sit there beside him until he died.

All this while I had been aware of a bedlam near at hand. Jones, yelling at the top of his stentorian voice, seized one hound after the other by the hind legs and, jerking him from the lion, threw him down the steep slope. Jim and Emett were trying to help while at the same time they avoided close quarters with that threshing beast. At last they got the dogs off and the lion stretched out. Jones got up, shaking his shaggy head. Then he espied me and his hard face took on a look of alarm.

"Hyar—you're all—bloody," he panted plaintively, as if I had been exceedingly remiss.

Whereupon I told him briefly about Don. Then Jim and Emett approached, and we all stood looking down on the quiet dog and the patch of bloody snow.

"Wal, I reckon he's a goner," said Jones, breathing hard. "Shore I knew he'd get his everlastin'."

"Looks powerful like the lion has about got his, too," added Jim.

Emett knelt by Don and examined the bandage round his neck. "Bleeding yet," he muttered, thoughtfully. "You did all that was possible. Too bad! . . . The kindest thing we can do is to leave him here."

I did not question this, but I hated to consent. Still, to move him would only bring on hemorrhage, and to put him out of his agony would have been impossible for me. Moreover, while there was life, there was hope! Scraping up a goodly ball of snow, I rolled it close to Don so that he could lick it if he chose. Then I turned aside and could not look again. But I knew that tomorrow or the following day I would find my way back to this wild spot.

The accident to Don weighed heavily upon my mind. His eyes haunted me. I very much feared that the hunt had reached an unhappy ending for me. Next day the weather was threatening and, as I was by no means sure I could find the place where Don had been left, I had to defer that trip. We had a thrilling, hazardous, luckless chase, and I for one gave up before it ended.

Weary and dejected, I rode back. I could not get Don off my conscience. The pleasant woodland camp did not seem the same place. For the first time the hissing, spitting, chain-clinking, tail-lashing lions caused me irritation and resentment. I would have none of them. What was the capture of a lot of spiteful, vicious cats to the life of a noble dog? Slipping my saddle off, I turned Black Bolly loose.

Then I imagined I saw a beautiful black long-eared hound enter

[111]

the glade. I rubbed my eyes. Indeed there was a dog coming. Don! I shouted my joy and awe. Running like a boy, I knelt by him, saying I knew not what. Don wagged his tail! He licked my hand! These actions seemed as marvelous as his return. He looked sick and weak, but he was all right. The handkerchief was gone from his neck but the scarf remained, and it was stuck tight where his throat had been lacerated.

Later Emett examined Don and said we had made a mistake about the jugular vein being severed. Don's injury had been serious, however, and without the prompt aid I had so fortunately given he would soon have bled to death. Jones shook his head: "Reckon Don's time hadn't come. Hope that will teach him sense."

A subtle change had come over Don in his relation to me. I did not grasp it so clearly then. Thought and memory afterward brought the realization to me. But there was a light in his eyes for me which had never been there before.

One day Jones and I treed three lions. The largest leaped and ran down into the canyon. The hounds followed. Jones strode after them, leaving me alone with nothing but a camera to keep those two lions up that tree. I had left horse and gun far up the slope. I protested; I yelled after him, "What'll I do if they start down?"

He turned to gaze up at me. His grim face flashed in the sunlight.

"Grab a club an' chase them back," he replied.

Then I was left alone with two ferocious looking lions in a piñon tree scarcely thirty feet high. While they heard the baying of the hounds they paid no attention to me, but after that ceased they got ugly. Then I hid behind a bush and barked like a dog. It worked beautifully. The lions grew quiet. I barked and yelped and bayed until I lost my voice. Then they got ugly again! They started down. With stones and clubs I kept them up there, while all the time I was wearing to collapse. When at last I was about to give up in terror and despair I heard Don's bay, faint and far away. The lions had heard it before I had. How they strained! I could see the beating of their hearts through their lean sides. My own heart leaped. Don's bay floated up, wild and mournful. He was coming. Jones had put him on the back trail of the lion that had leaped from the tree.

Deeper and clearer came the bays. How strange that Don should

vary from his habit of seldom baying! There was something uncanny in this change. Soon I saw him far down the rocky slope. He
was climbing fast. On and up he came, ringing out that wild bay. It
must have curdled the blood of those palpitating lions. It seemed
the herald of that bawling pack of hounds.

Don saw me before he reached the piñon in which were the lions.
He bounded right past it and up to me with the wildest demeanor.
He leaped up and placed his forepaws on my breast. And as I leaned
down, excited and amazed, he licked my face. Then he whirled back
to the tree, where he stood up and fiercely bayed the lions. While I
sank down to rest, overcome, the familiar baying chorus of the
hounds floated up from below. As usual they were far behind the
fleet Don, but they were coming.

Another day I was heading for camp, with Don trotting behind.
When we reached the notch of a huge cove that opened down into
the main canyon the hound let out his deep bay and bounded down
a break in the low wall. I dismounted and called. Only another
deep bay answered me. Don had scented a lion or crossed one's trail.
Suddenly several sharp deep yelps came from below, a crashing of
brush, a rattling of stones. Don had jumped a lion.

Quickly I threw off sombrero and coat and chaps. I retained my
left glove. Then, with camera over my shoulder and revolver in my
belt, I plunged down the break in the crag. Reaching a dry stream
bed, I saw in the sand the tracks of a big lion, and beside them
smaller tracks that were Don's. And as I ran I yelled at the top of
my lungs, hoping to help Don tree the lion. What I was afraid of
was that the beast might wait for Don and kill him.

Finally I came to an open place near the main jump-off into the
canyon, and here I saw a tawny shape in a cedar tree. It belonged to
a big tom lion. He swayed the branch and leaped to a ledge, and
from that down to another, and then vanished round a corner of
wall.

Don could not follow those high steps. Neither could I. We
worked along the ledge, under cedars, and over huge slabs of rock
toward the corner where our quarry had disappeared. We were
close to the great abyss. I could almost feel it. Then the glaring
light of a void struck my eyes like some tangible thing.

At last I worked out from the shade of rocks and trees and, turn-

[113]

ing the abrupt jut of wall, I found a few feet of stone ledge between me and the appalling chasm. How blue, how fathomless! Despite my pursuit of a lion I was suddenly shocked into awe and fear.

Then Don returned to me. The hair on his neck was bristling. He had come from the right, from round the corner of wall where the ledge ran, and where surely the lion had gone. My blood was up and I meant to track that beast to his lair and photograph him if possible. So I strode on to the ledge and round the point of wall. Soon I espied huge cat tracks in the dust, close to the base. A well-defined lion trail showed there. And ahead I saw the ledge—widening somewhat and far from level—stretch before me to another corner.

Don acted queerly. He followed me, close at my heels. He whined. He growled. I did not stop to think then what he wanted to do. But it must have been that he wanted to go back. The heat of youth and the wildness of adventure had gripped me, and fear and caution were not in me.

Nevertheless, my sensibilities were remarkably acute. When Don got in front of me there was something that compelled me to go slowly. Soon, in any event, I should have been forced to do that. The ledge narrowed. Then it widened again to a large bench with cavernous walls overhanging it. I passed this safe zone to turn on to a narrowing edge of rock that disappeared round another corner. When I came to this point I must have been possessed, for I flattened myself against the wall and worked round it.

Again the way appeared easier. But what made Don go so cautiously? I heard his growls; still, no longer did I look at him. I felt this pursuit was nearing an end. At the next turn I halted short, suddenly quivering. The ledge ended—and there lay the lion, licking a bloody paw.

Tumultuous indeed were my emotions, yet on that instant I did not seem conscious of fear. Jones had told me never, in close quarters, to take my eyes off a lion. I forgot. In the wild excitement of a chance for an incomparable picture, I forgot. A few seconds were wasted over the attempt to focus my camera.

Then I heard quick thuds. Don growled. With a start I jerked up to see the lion had leaped or run half the distance. He was coming. His eyes blazed purple fire. They seemed to paralyze me, yet I began to back along the ledge. Whipping out my revolver I tried to

[114]

aim. But my nerves had undergone such a shock that I could not aim. The gun wobbled. I dared not risk shooting. If I wounded the lion it was certain he would knock me off that narrow ledge.

So I kept on backing, step by step. Don did likewise. He stayed between me and the lion. Therein lay the greatness of that hound. How easily he could have dodged by me to escape the ledge! But he did not do it.

A precious opportunity presented itself when I reached the widest part of the bench. Here I had a chance and I recognized it. Then, when the overhanging wall bumped my shoulder, I realized too late. I had come to the narrowing part of the ledge. Not reason but fright kept me from turning to run. Perhaps that might have been the best way out of the predicament. I backed along the strip of stone that was only a foot wide. A few more blind steps might mean death. My nerve was gone. Collapse seemed inevitable. I had a camera in one hand and a revolver in the other.

That purple-eyed beast did not halt. My distorted imagination gave him a thousand shapes and actions. Bitter, despairing thoughts flashed through my mind. Jones had said mountain lions were cowards, but not when cornered—never when there was no avenue of escape!

Then Don's haunches backed into my knees. I dared not look down, but I felt the hound against me. He was shaking, yet he snarled fiercely. The feel of Don there, the sense of his courage, caused my cold blood to flow. In another second he would be pawed off the ledge or he would grapple with this hissing lion. That meant destruction for both, for they would roll off the ledge.

I had to save Don. That mounting thought was my salvation. Physically, he could not have saved me or himself, but this grand spirit somehow pierced to my manhood.

Leaning against the wall, I lifted the revolver and steadied my arm with my left hand, which still held the camera. I aimed between the purple eyes. That second was eternity. The gun crashed. The blaze of one of those terrible eyes went out.

Up leaped the lion, beating the wall with heavy thudding paws. Then he seemed to propel himself outward, off the ledge into space —a tawny figure that careened majestically over and over, down—down—down to vanish in the blue depths.

Don whined. I stared at the abyss, slowly becoming unlocked

[115]

from the grip of terror. I staggered a few steps forward to a wider part of the ledge and there I sank down, unable to stand longer. Don crept to me, put his head in my lap.

I listened. I strained my ears. How endlessly long seemed that lion in falling! But all was magnified. At last puffed up a sliding roar, swelling and dying until again the terrific silence of the canyon enfolded me.

Presently Don sat up and gazed into the depths. How strange to see him peer down! Then he turned his sleek dark head to look at me. What did I see through the somber sadness of his eyes? He whined and licked my hand. It seemed to me Don and I were more than man and dog. He moved away then round the narrow ledge, and I had to summon energy to follow. I turned my back on that awful chasm and held my breath while I slipped round the perilous place. Don waited there for me, then trotted on. Not until I had gotten safely off that ledge did I draw a full breath. Then I toiled up the steep rough slope to the rim. Don was waiting beside my horse. Between us we drank the rest of the water in my canteen, and when we reached camp, night had fallen. A bright fire and a good supper broke the gloom of my mind. My story held those rugged Westerners spellbound. Don stayed close to me, followed me of his own accord, and slept beside me in my tent.

There came a frosty morning when the sun rose red over the ramparts of colored rock. We had a lion running before the misty shadows dispersed from the canyon depths.

The hounds chased him through the sage and cedar into the wild brakes of the north wing of the Plateau. This lion must have been a mean old tom, for he did not soon go down the slopes.

The particular section he at last took refuge in was impassable for man. The hounds gave him a grueling chase, then one by one they crawled up, sore and thirsty. All but Don! He did not come. Jones rolled out his mighty voice, which pealed back in mocking hollow echoes. Don did not come. At noonday Jones and the men left for camp with the hounds.

I remained. I had a vigil there on the lofty rim, along where I could peer down the yellow-green slope and beyond to the sinister depths. It was a still day. The silence was overpowering. When Don's haunting bay floated up it shocked me. At long intervals I heard it, fainter and fainter. Then no more!

Still I waited and watched and listened. Afternoon waned. My horse neighed piercingly from the cedars. The sinking sun began to fire the Pink Cliffs of Utah, and then the hundred miles of immense chasm over which my charmed gaze held dominion. How lonely, how terrifying that stupendous rent in the earth! Lion and hound had no fear. But the thinking, feeling man was afraid. What did they mean—this exquisite hued and monstrous canyon—the setting sun—the wildness of a lion, the grand spirit of a dog—and the wondering sadness of a man?

I rode home without Don. Half the night I lay awake waiting, hoping. But he did not return by dawn, nor through the day. He never came back.

10

THE GREAT RIVER OF THE GULF

A charter boatman, W. D. "Bill" Hatch, is generally credited with developing the drop-back technique of hooking sailfish about 1915. Before this period Florida ocean angling consisted of trolling the inshore reefs for king mackerel. The Gulf Stream was viewed with trepidation by many charter skippers, and the few sailfish that were taken were accidental catches that came over the reefs from deeper water. Sailfish were mostly regarded as nuisances that rapped and mangled baits meant for "better" fish. Infrequently a sailfish would charge and swallow a bait or even snag itself while trying to stun the trolled baitfish. Then a bewildered but fortunate angler would have some taste of the speed and acrobatic qualities of these great gamesters.

Bill Hatch discovered that if you released the reel's drag so the bait drifted back to the sailfish after he thought he'd stunned it with his bill, the fish would usually turn and pick it up. Of course, Captain Hatch may have had a little help in his discovery by patrons who had seen the "drop-back" inherent in the Catalina kite fishing described in Chapter 7 which had already been used for Pacific marlin before 1915. In any event, as soon as it was learned that sailfish could be taken with consistency, king-mackerel fishing rapidly faded as "big-game" sport.

All this happened up the Florida coast off Palm Beach and Miami. But in the winter of 1916 Zane Grey persuaded Captain Sam "Horse-Mackerel" Johnson of Seabright, New Jersey, to go to Long Key with him to concentrate on sailfish. The results were spectacular, and Sam's confidence while fishing the Gulf Stream soon tempted other Keys boatmen farther offshore.

In following years Zane Grey used—and trained—other boatmen. By 1920, sailfish, wahoo, and dolphin had all but eclipsed the Keys' former devotion to mackerel, grouper, and barracuda. In these early days before pollution and commercial longlining (introduced by the Japanese, who relish marlin and sailfish flesh in proportion to our own ignorance of its fine flavor), Zane Grey's Long Key companions thought they had discovered a cornucopia sport-fishery that nothing would ever change. Only ZG, with his experience of commercial netting and live-bait fishing along the California coast, tempered this vision with a warning.

GWR

THE GREAT RIVER OF THE GULF

It may be something of a poetic fallacy to call the Gulf Stream a river of the South, a flowing stream within the sea, but to me that is just what it is. As a matter of fact it is a current of blue water fifty miles or more wide, and it moves appreciably faster than the green ocean water that it divides.

This dark blue river is a thing of beauty and mystery. It circles the Gulf of Mexico,[1] flows up the straits between the Bahama Islands and Florida, and, gradually working away from the coast, it passes north, carrying to colder shores some of the beneficent warmth of the South.

Off Long Key, Florida, on approaching the Gulf Stream from the reef, there can be seen a chafing of the waters, a long line of low whitecaps and blue water encroaching upon the green. The air becomes more balmy, and, once in the Stream, the several degrees of higher temperature can be appreciated. The current flows north and seems to be quite swift, though to the best of my calculations it moves only several miles an hour. The prevailing winds are the northeast trades, and blowing quarterly against this current they usually kick up a choppy sea. Short, billowy, white-crested swells, rough on boat and angler!

On a fine day, with just the right breeze, the Gulf Stream presents a changing, beautiful panorama of blue and white rolling waters. It breathes of the tropics, blowing fragrance from far-off palm-bordered shores, and laden with the lonely atmosphere of coral reefs. It does not seem like the sea, except in motion. It apparently has nothing in common with the green-blanched, restless Atlantic main. It flows from under the Equator, with the message of unplumbed tropic seas. Its depth and current, its mystery and charm, its burden of marine life, will ever be a fascinating study for naturalists.

The winter of 1924 was noted all over the South and West as being one of unusually bad weather. At Long Key for days there had been unsettled weather, southwest winds, and northwesters, and finally the genuine *del norte*. One day was very cold. Then for two days the wind lulled at noon, and the afternoons grew calm and warm. At last the wind made a little shift toward northeast.

I went out to the Gulf Stream one morning; cool, invigorating, with the sun not too bright, and the sea just ridged with white. We headed for Half Moon Reef, and trolled across it hoping to catch a

---

[1] ZG's description of the Gulf Stream is more or less accurate. Though oceanographers more properly refer to it as the Florida or Caribbean Current, a loop current does originate in the Gulf of Mexico and joins the main stream coming from the Caribbean off the Florida Keys.

mackerel for bait. But we were not so fortunate. We went on into the Stream.

It did not seem as blue as usual, which was owing, no doubt, to the reflection of sky. The sea grew somewhat rough, then gradually went down with the breeze. I trolled a cut bait of mullet, not overly fresh, and it was a long time until I had a strike. I saw the sailfish. He looked big and bronze. He let go, then came back, took the bait with a swoop, and shot away. I let him run. I was using 6/9 tackle,[2] and handled it accordingly. I hooked this fish. He ran a long way without leaping. When he circled, we ran to meet him. Then he swerved toward us, and I could not get in the slack, though I wound the reel with might and main. We could not locate him, and at last when I saw the line going under the boat, it was too late. He leaped on the other side, a big sailfish, with his sail spread. The line had a lot of slack and it floated up on the swells before I could reel in, and it fouled on the boat. We tried to poke it loose, but finally had to break it and pull up the other part with a gaff and break that. Then we tied the ends together. The sailfish was still on. I worked him toward the boat, to find that he was keeping company with several others. Here the hook pulled out. All our trouble had been in vain. The other sailfish disappeared.

Presently I espied the sharp spear-pointed tails of sailfish riding the swells. We ran close to discover a large school. They always work south against the Gulf Stream current. I never saw a sailfish swimming or leaping any way except against the current. We crossed in front of them, and I had a strike. I hooked this one, and he came out at once, throwing the hook. My bad start was holding on. We chased the school and got in front of them again. I could see the slim smooth bronze backs cutting the water, and the sickle tails coming out of the swells. Soon I had three or four after my bait; and one got away with it. We lost this school before we could get out another bait.

In the succeeding hours I sighted three more large schools. And I hooked five more fish, only one of which I got to the boat. We

---

[2] The first number is the weight of the rod tip in ounces; the second, the number of threads in the line testing at approximately three pounds per thread. Hence, his line had a breaking strength of about 27 pounds.

fooled around a good deal with several, trying to make them leap for pictures. Otherwise I might have caught one or two more. Late in the afternoon I hooked a large wahoo, and lost it, too.

This was one of the bad luck days, common to every angler of wide experience. It seemed inexplicable, considering that the other boats all caught sailfish, some of them a number. One woman who had never before caught a sailfish got one weighing 74¼ pounds, a remarkable fish, eight feet, two inches long. A still larger one was caught, measuring eight feet, six inches,[3] which is the longest recorded here. Some of the boatmen reported dozens of schools of sailfish up toward Alligator Reef. Here and there one of these schools refused to notice a bait, but most of them were hungry. This date was about the first quarter of the moon in February.

We had a long spell of bad weather—northwesters, northers, northeasters, all the same as far as we were concerned. There came a day when at sunrise the sea was gently rippled, and there was scarcely any wind. I saw the first dull red gleam of the sun as it rose above the level horizon into a bank of purple cloud. This bank was a long line of trade wind clouds, flat above its base, broken and columnar above. Soon these lofty edges began to take on the freshness of bright color—gold. Far up in the sky floated a sea of wispy particles of cloud, like blown feathers. They turned to silver. Soon there was a beautiful sunrise of gold and silver, without one vestige of the morning red.

Nevertheless, the wind came with the sunrise.

Not to be daunted, R. C. and I were the first to leave the dock, and in half an hour were bumping the heavy green seas of Hawk Channel. All the time the wind grew stronger. By the time we reached the Gulf Stream there was a rough sea running. We continued out into the dark blue tumbling waters and began to troll.

R. C. called my attention to sailfish swooping down the incline of a giant wave, under our lines, and between us and the baits. Then,

---

[3] This is a huge specimen by contemporary standards, but Atlantic sailfish do grow extremely fast. A sailfish hatched in June will measure about four and a half feet in November, and at two years of age will be seven feet long and weigh approximately 43 pounds. A four-year-old may reach eight feet or more in length, but since fishing pressure has been so intense along the South Florida coast in recent decades, few this size are caught any more. Most of the sportfishery is provided by fish between six months and two years of age.

[123]

as we were heaved higher and higher, I saw a fish larger than any I had seen and of more vivid color, with the telltale purple that spelled marlin swordfish. Like a flash it was gone.

The wind increased, and the sea likewise. I had not visited the Gulf Stream in such a surging turmoil. The water splashed over us and the motion was so violent that we had to hold on. It became work, and most unpleasant work. So soon I gave the word to head for Long Key Camp.

There followed days with cold westerly and northwest winds, and then the wind got back into the east.

Nevertheless, we ventured out to the reef. There was a tumultuous sea running, both high and shifting. The Gulf Stream was an impassable river for us this day. We got within two hundred yards of it—near enough to see the tremendous crosscurrent and to hear the roar of contending tides. It was a beautiful wild sight, dark blue, white-crested, chafing along against the bright green waters.

Sailfish showed in the transparent billows, long, slim, sharp, bronze fish, riding the swells and shooting down the curving slopes of the waves. We maneuvered the boat so that we got ahead of some of them, and drew our baits in front of their very bills. They would follow the baits awhile, then shoot on forward, to come even with the boat and to pass it, not ten feet distant. This afforded a wonderful opportunity to see the sailfish close at hand, free, indifferent to bait or boat. They had marvelous control over their native element, as much at home there as a frigate bird in the air.

We tried a number of fish without getting a strike, and then decided it was one of their off days. Sometimes they will not touch any kind of bait, and at others they will bite anything.

The boat tossed like a cork upon the waves and the tips of the crests curled over into the cockpit, wetting us thoroughly. It was not possible to sit in the fishing seats without holding on; and at that the sudden jars and shocks, the tilting to one side, then to the other, were most uncomfortable and alarming.

Yet the great green billows, so exquisitely bright in the sunlight, fascinated me and made me reluctant to start back to camp. Not often did we encounter a sea like that. It showed something of the unrest and hidden power of the ocean. The cloud shadows sailed like dark ships across the heaving plain of green. Now we were down in the trough, and next moment lifted high upon a wave. Everywhere over the waves shone the little colored Portuguese men-of-war riding out the gale as if perfectly at home. How delicate these globules! Yet the whole might of the stormy main seemed powerless to destroy them. Many were accompanied by the tiny butterfly fish; and to see them together in that wild ocean was something beyond understanding. Both creatures seemed intended for shallow tranquil waters. Perhaps they blew across the Gulf Stream from the Cuban shoals. But my belief was that they came into being right there in the blue Stream.

At last we turned campward, and had the exhilarating movement occasioned by a following sea. We were lifted high and higher, driven forward and down, to the music of thunderous waves that threatened to engulf the boat, yet always passed on under us.

*

As far as Long Key was concerned, and elsewhere, so far as I know, I was the first angler to take sailfish on light tackle.[4] This was in 1916. Theretofore sailfish had been mostly caught while the angler was fishing for other surface fish.

My first tackle was a nine-ounce rod and fifteen-thread line. I used a wire leader and two hooks, and for bait half a mullet, or, better, a whole ballyhoo or whitefish. We trolled at moderate speed, and when a sailfish took hold we let him run—sometimes, when he was wary, a long way—before hooking him. Sometimes when one tapped the bait we let it drift back to him, and if he took it and let go we gave him more line, until he took it for sure. I used to jerk the bait away from a finicky biter just to aggravate him. This method brought results, though even then I realized it was not the right one. But at the time I could not improve upon it.

Sailfishing today has grown to be an art. The experts, a few, use a six-ounce tip and nine-thread line, which is a little light for heavy fish.[5] One hook is used, a number eight, fastened on thin wire with

---

[4] The term "light" is officially interpreted to mean 6/9 or 3/6 tackle. Here ZG merely means tackle lighter than the 24-thread normally used in blue-water trolling.

[5] *Tales of Southern Rivers*, from which this selection is taken, was published in 1924. Today most "experts" rarely use anything heavier than 20-pound test tackle.

an end left free to hold the head of the cut bait. In trolling the speed is easily six or seven miles an hour, which is going pretty fast. Even then, sometimes a sailfish will refuse a bait. Cut bait of mullet is commonly used, but the best is a piece of bonita or mackerel belly. All the boatmen cut bait; but only the boatmen native to Florida, and used to cutting fish with a sharp knife, can do the trick with a most finished art. The proof is that a perfectly cut bait will attract a sailfish that will refuse one poorly cut.

The small hook hangs perfectly and is scarcely felt. The method of procedure is, when the sailfish strikes, to let him run a few yards, then give him the rod hard. As to fighting a sailfish, I prefer to chase him when he is running and work on him, pump and wind, when he is sounding. This does not appear to be the general method in vogue at Long Key. All the boatmen, at least those I observed, ran round and round with the sailfish. In most instances fish caught by members of the club were not gaffed, but held by the bill and detached from the hook and released.

Teasers—baits or lures trolled behind the boat to attract sailfish— were first used by Avalon boatmen in marlin fishing. I tried it at Long Key years ago, and pronounced it a failure because mackerel, barracuda,[6] and other fish snapped off the cut-bait teasers as fast as they could be put out. The Tarporeno wooden plug lure minus the hooks has taken the place of the destructible fish bait, and seems to work as well.

Sailfishing on light tackle comes very close to being the finest sport of the trolling game. And since the discovery of small marlin swordfish at Miami and Long Key, such angling has an added fascination.

*

Everything is emphasized by contrast. The day I had selected to fish from Sandy Key lighthouse, on the edge of the Gulf Stream off Key West, to Sombrero Reef, turned out to be surprisingly ideal. Good weather was necessary for fishing fifty miles of Gulf Stream, and this was almost too good to be true. After the everlasting gales and northers and winds, what a relief and joy to have a calm day!

---

[6] In the early days of deep-sea reporting, another spelling for this fish—*barracouta*—was generally used. But Zane Grey favored barra*cuda* and his preference stuck.

The sea was smooth, rippled by a slight breeze; and as we ran out toward the Stream, jack crevalle were cracking the green water in pursuit of ballyhoo. The gulls and pelicans were hovering aloft, swooping down now and then to pounce upon a disabled fish. Far out over the glistening emerald sea showed the dark bulk of oil steamers on their way to Tampico.

Long before we reached the Gulf Stream I saw the dark line of blue water sharply defined against the green. There was now no ruffled current, as on windy days. The cloudy violet water merged irregularly into the green, raggedly and mistily, with streamers and ribbons, and thick bulks of solid color, and thin broken wandering lines. A low, heaving swell, just a perceptible movement of the water, made me think of the Pacific. It added immeasurably to the thrill of the moment, to the prospect of the day.

Then in the green water just outside the Stream we saw two sailfish leap, a large one and a small one. Both came sliding out on their sides, in the graceful action characteristic of these fish. It looked like play to me. When sailfish leap to shake off the remoras, they come out high and rather convulsively, and make several leaps, sometimes as many as nine or ten in succession.

We turned and ran ahead of where they had showed, and trolled out baits over the spot and all around it, to no avail. Then we headed into the Gulf Stream. I climbed out on the bow, leaving R. C. to do the trolling, and took a position facing north, so that I could command the water level ahead. It seemed rather remarkable that I could actually have a comfortable seat on a launch in the Gulf Stream. But it was a most pleasant fact.

Several flying fish shot up from our bow and skimmed in different directions. They were larger than any I had seen in the Stream farther north. I noted that as they came out their wings curved upwards, and as long as the lower lobes of their tails were propelling them towards the final sail, these wings fluttered, somewhat resembling wings of birds. Then when the flying fish cleared the water, their wings straightened stiff and held that position until they lowered their tails for more propulsion. They could cover a long stretch of water. It was conceivable for me that a flying fish might, in the process of evolution, really come to fly.

R. C. called out. I felt the boat slow to a released clutch, and,

[127]

hurrying aft, I found R. C. jerking the light tackle hard, in the act of hooking a sailfish. I made a dive for the cameras and, placing them in good position on the seats, I took up one and stood beside my brother.

"He's a lunker," said R. C. as the line whizzed off. "There were two, and the bigger struck at the teaser . . . Captain, I guess you'd better chase this fish."

He came up a goodly distance out, and leaped with the peculiar jerky action common to this species. Once he shot aloft, very high, waving his spread sail, and, turning a complete somersault, he plunged back. This was the kind of picture I always wanted to get of a leaping sailfish, but on this particular leap I was winding up the camera. After nine or ten jumps he sounded, and worked away, swimming hard and fast. We chased him, headed him off, and R. C. endeavored to turn back so he would run in the direction we wished to take. This appeared no easy matter. R. C. bent the little Murphy rod to an alarming extent.

Presently a yellow shape showed indistinctly in the violet water. I caught the motion. Shark! And he assuredly accomplished what R. C. could not—he started that sailfish north. Such a run! It was all of nine hundred feet. And we were hard put to keep up with him. Evidently he eluded the shark, for he slowed down and kept plugging away, much to our satisfaction. R. C. pumped and wound while we ran up on him. I was expecting a second series of leaps, if this sailfish acted normally, and, sure enough, was not disappointed.

He came out shining like a green-white and silvered bird with purple wings. And his next leap was a wiggling supple exhibition that reminded me of jazz music. Suddenly he became enraged, and threshed on the surface, and skittered toward us half out of water. This came as close to the marlin's famous feat of walking on his tail as the less powerful sailfish could attain. He was not strong enough to raise himself all the way out and then go wagging across the sea in white boiling foam. But he gave a marvelous display of frantic motion of every kind, while all the while one-fourth of his body remained in the water. This might have lasted ten seconds or longer. I had no way to judge. It was a frenzied and strenuous energy, and took his stamina. I could see him growing weaker as both effort and distance of each separate motion lessened. Finally he made a last supreme effort, describing a parabolic dive, and then soused back for good.

R. C. seemed disposed to take it easy. So finally I said: "Time is passing. We can't hang around here all day to watch this sailfish swim. I'd like to look for some more fish."

"Uhuh! And hook me onto them!" declared R. C. good-naturedly. But he proceeded to "wrap the hickory into him," as Captain Sid was wont to say, and brought the sailfish up to the boat.

One good look at this fish at close range convinced me I had been right about his being large. He was certainly the largest R. C. had ever hooked. So I advised careful handling, and in due time we pulled him into the boat, a beautiful specimen of iridescent colors. We estimated him at seventy pounds, but he could have weighed more, perhaps eighty. Owing to the many mistakes we had made in guessing the weight of fish, we had learned to underestimate.

I took up my rod and, standing in the cockpit, I fished while at the same time I kept a keen lookout. That was the pleasure of roaming the sea. Indeed, seldom in twelve winter seasons off Long Key had we ever had such comfortable water, so that we could enjoy looking for sea creatures.

I saw a purple and pink jellyfish, a globular ethereal creature, moving with its own life as well as the current of the Stream. It passed on, faded, and vanished. All I could remember was the rare color, the strange delicacy and abnormality of structure, the sucking bellows-like action that evidently propelled it, and the undoubtable fact of life. I had never before seen any other living thing like it and the chances were I never would again. Here is the fact that makes the ocean so supremely above other mediums of nature in fascinating possibilities, in unsolvable mysteries, in endless experiences.

From time to time I espied a loggerhead turtle on the surface. It was always fun to run down on them. They were exceedingly wary for such ungainly creatures. Every little while they lifted their huge blunt hawk-like heads to peer around. When they had their heads submerged it was easy to glide right down upon them. Then they made frantic efforts to escape the looming monster above. Once started into motion, they disappeared very rapidly in the blue depths.

Next to attract our attention were tiny flying fish. They flitted up

[129]

like steely locust and glinted in the sunlight and darted away a few yards, to fall back. They had no control over direction. Once I saw one close to the boat and high enough to be silhouetted against the sky. He was scarcely two inches long. I discerned wings and tail, tiny black eyes in a blunt little head. Except for that eye he appeared steely white in color. He popped out of a wave and blew with the gentle breeze.

Captain Knowles called our attention to sailfish leaping ahead. We looked eagerly, one on each side of the boat. I saw two sailfish come out at once in their long side leaps, some hundred yards ahead. One of them kept on leaping until he had seven jumps to his credit. Far beyond that point another leaped. Then he saw white splashes here and there.

"School of sailfish! Good night!" exclaimed R. C.

Presently I saw a number of sharp dark tails piercing the surface and moving swiftly.

"Cross ahead of them, Cappy," I directed the boatman.

We let out line as the boat sheered, and soon saw the gleaming bronze figures of sailfish coming in great numbers. A school of any kind of game fish is always an inspiring sight. Sailfish in this school appeared to be as thick as fence pickets. Soon there were a dozen behind our baits.

"Pick out a big one," yelled R. C., maneuvering his bait. This was fun, even if it was impossible. The only thing we could do was to wind our baits away from a small fish, but this only made that fish, and all the others, rush the baits harder. We both had strikes at once. R. C. hooked his quickly. I missed mine. He came back at the bait, took it again, let go, recovered it, and ran swiftly. I pulled it away from him. The third time he snatched it, made furious by the teasing. I let him go far, then hooked him.

Just then R. C.'s fish leaped high and crossed my line. We performed acrobatics to change positions and to pass my rod under his. The lines, speeding off the reels all the time, came straight. My sailfish took to pyrotechnics more in the air than in the water. R. C.'s ran off deep.

Meanwhile the boatman had been throwing the wheel over hard, so as to get in a position to chase our fish. We soon found ourselves surrounded by sailfish. They passed the boat on each side in an endless stream.

"Hey! Look at that son-of-a-gun biting my line!" yelled my brother.

It was indeed plain to see. A sailfish, not more than seventy feet out, had his mouth open like a scissors and was biting at the line. We had seen this before, but never so close. It was highly diverting for me, and I gayly instructed R. C. to pull the line away from the tricky fish. R. C. swore. Then he shouted for me to attend to my own troubles. It developed that I had some. Two sailfish, some fifteen feet apart, were operating on my line.

"Say, if you sailfish had any sense you'd saw the line off with your bills, instead of trying to bite it off," I remarked.

However what might have been, the fact was that the nearer sailfish quit, and the second fooled with my line until he cut it. I reeled in and began hurriedly to rig on another leader.

"Oh boy! Look at 'em jump!" R. C. exclaimed.

We appeared to be in the midst of the school. R. C.'s victim had excited some of the others and they were threshing, sliding, breaking on the surface. His fish was small, but he was a jumper. When he turned toward us, that was too much for me and I abandoned my tackle for a camera. But I was just too late for a magnificent chance at a number of sailfish in the air at once, all around R. C.'s fish. It sounded, and the others did not leap again. I waited eagerly.

"Put out a bait," advised Captain Knowles.

By the time I was ready, R. C. had his sailfish in. He instructed the boatman to release it. So it chanced we got both our baits out together, and had strikes without ever trolling. And we both hooked fish. That was the beginning of a most remarkable experience. Things happened so swiftly that I cannot recall them in sequence. But I remember some of the startling incidents. We caught those two sailfish and still the school kept passing us on each side. Sometimes a dozen or more would loom up in back of the boat, slender and sharp, swimming with fins invisible, heading south. No sooner had we put baits overboard again than we had another double-header. By the time we had whipped these two the school had passed on. It was a temptation to follow them, but, as we had many miles of Gulf Stream to travel, we could not spare the time.

We went on. The sun was getting high now, and about one o'clock we passed American Shoal lighthouse. It appeared a lonely place, standing on iron girders out of the sea. By and by we ran into another school of sailfish. R. C. jocularly exclaimed that this was sailfish day. He got one and I lost one out of this school. It took him quite a while to bring in a rather heavy and nonleaping fish. All the time the ripple on the sea imperceptibly darkened and deepened. Still, for the Atlantic it was a placid sea. We had expected to catch dolphin, kingfish, bonito, and cero [mackerel], but nothing of the kind happened. At times we were a mile out in the Stream, though for the most part we ran right along the edge.

About two o'clock I sighted another school of sailfish, evidently more playful than the others, probably owing to the slightly ruffled water. Sailfish like rough sea. They love to ride the swells, as do marlin swordfish.

This school occupied us more than an hour, me with the camera and R. C. on the rod. I could hardly claim that the school took that length of time in passing, but we were that long in their midst. Anyway, we got three sailfish out of the school, two of which were lightly hooked and which we let go.

As far as the dimensions of a school of sailfish is concerned, this one was the largest I ever saw. But Captain Knowles said he had seen many larger ones, one notably that took hours to pass and extended on all sides as far as he could see. There must be millions of sailfish; and always there should be splendid sailfishing. Unless some market use is discovered!

[132]

11

THE BONEFISH BRIGADE

Until he discovered giant marlin, the bonefish was Zane Grey's pet salt-water gamester. And *Albula vulpes* owes much of its popularity and glamor to what ZG wrote about the species in the 1910's when this fish was just getting started as one of the great light-tackle fish of the inshore waters.

Listen to these enthusiastic words written by Zane Grey in 1919 for his *Tales of Fishes*:

> If I spent another month bonefishing, I would become obsessed and perhaps lose my enthusiasm for other kinds of fish.
> *Why?*
> My reasons range from the exceedingly graceful beauty of a bonefish to the fact that he is the wisest, shyest, wariest, strangest fish I ever studied; and I am not excepting the great Xiphias gladius—the broadbill swordfish. As for the speed of a bonefish, I claim no salmon, no barracuda, no other fish celebrated for swiftness of motion, is in his class. As for the strength of a bonefish, I actually hesitate to give my impressions. As for his cunning, it is utterly baffling. As for his biting, it is almost imperceptible. As for his tactics, they are beyond conjecture.

The year *Tales of Fishes* appeared, Zane Grey was President of the Long Key (Florida) Fishing Camp whose nearby shoals and flats teemed with bonefish. At the same time ZG was Vice-President of the Catalina Tuna Club, a far grander and more prestigious organization. But Zane Grey preferred his Long Key association—possibly because there're no bonefish around Catalina!

Another reason for his preference was that Zane Grey was one of Long Key's early members (the Camp was founded in 1906) while at Catalina he was a Johnny-Come-Lately who had little influence in shaping the Club's angling regulations—some of which ZG found objectionable. He eventually resigned from the Tuna Club over a dispute about the type of the tackle to be used on broadbill swordfish (ZG favored a heavier line than was permitted by Club rules), while his connection with the Long Key Camp only ceased after the hurricane of '35 drowned its facilities under 15 feet of water.

In the following selection, which first appeared in the *Izaak Walton League Monthly* and became ZG's Christmas greeting for 1922, Zane Grey teases himself and the rest of the Long Key fraternity about their obsession with bonefish. The names of the players were thinly disguised to protect no one. "Lucky Stickem," for instance, was actually Frank Stick, well-known outdoor artist who came to New York from the midwest after the turn of the century to provide illustrations for *Century*, *Harper's* and *Field and Stream*. In 1920 he collaborated with another young protégé of Zane Grey's, Van Campen Heilner, to produce one of the first books of surf fishing, *The Call of the Surf*.

In 1936, when a mature Heilner produced the definitive study of ocean angling called simply *Salt Water Fishing*, Zane Grey wrote in the foreword: Heilner's book "is a fulfillment of my ambition for him and my tireless criticism in those old Long Key days. It is sad to think that Long Key, doomed by a hurricane, is gone forever. But the memory of that long white winding lonely shore of coral sand, and the green surf, and the blue Gulf Stream will live in memory"—and in such stories as "The Bonefish Brigade."

GWR

THE BONEFISH BRIGADE

In February, 1922, I returned to my old haunts at Long Key, Florida, to find that absence had only endeared the coral islet to me, and that the interval of study, writing, and the charm of new places had brought me only greater appreciation of old associations.

It is now ten or twelve years since R. C. and I accidentally dropped into Long Key Fishing Camp. We had been en route for Tampico to fish for tarpon, and when the captain of the Ward Liner told us of yellow fever in Mexico, we disembarked at Nassau and eventually wound up at Long Key.

How well I remember being puzzled by a number of anglers quite out of my ken! They were bonefishermen. At that time this vague classification did not mean anything in my young angling life. I really did not give them credit for rationality. Somebody designated them as "bonefish bugs." It is not my intention to dwell upon the years required to inoculate R. C. and me with this peculiar and irresistible mania.

It will suffice to give a few impressions of what I nicknamed the Bonefish Brigade. Even at that early day they had been coming to Florida every winter in pursuit of their strange and illusive game. They generally appeared along in February, six or eight or even ten in number; and they fell at once into what seemed to me most unproductive and mysterious ways.

First they would convene on the porch of their cottage facing the sea, and there they would loll and lounge, with their pale, tired and pleasant faces up to the sun. They always had an interest in other anglers and their luck, but they were strangely reticent about their own pursuits. Indeed I can see now how they dwelt upon the

[135]

heights of angling bliss, down from which they condescended to look upon less fortunate mortals.

Usually after a day or two of rest three or four of these gentlemen would don the most disreputable clothes, and armed with an old bag and a bucket they would sally forth on some errand most strikingly and obviously important. It puzzled me. I used to watch them wonderingly and half with pity and amusement. But the ragged old clothes bothered me. I had to respect that circumstance. R. C. and I had imagined the prerogative of wearing comfortable old togs as ours alone. And the bag and bucket made me suspicious. Could it be possible that this gang, among whose number were Standard Oil magnates and other kinds of millionaires, was going to catch bait? The idea was preposterous. I dismissed it from mind. But when they came back wet, tired, dirty and happy, with the bag and bucket full of something manifestly precious, I had a shock. Actually these men had been after bait! R. C. shared my amaze and discomfiture; and thereafter we spied upon these men who had our secret of harking back to boyhood.

Fishermanz, the chief of this brigade, would carry a camp chair out on the beach, and a rod big enough to catch tarpon, and a tin can and a hammer, and a mysterious article about the size of a pancake, only much thicker and heavier. This he would hold on his knees and crack something on it with his hammer. Then, as a small boy throws an apple from a pointed springy stick, Fishermanz would swing his big rod and cast bait and sinker far out into a foot of shallow water. That done, he would recline in the camp chair, the rod over his knees, the line between his fingers, and there he would stay. I repeat the word *stay*! I used to wonder if he was watching the incoming tide. Much as I studied him that first visit of mine at Long Key, I never saw him get even a bite. He seemed to dream and that made me jealous. I can stand a man to be a better angler than I am—which is not hard to be—but as for the dreamer end of it I claim distinction. Fishermanz did this thing every day, getting a little later each day, until my dense brain began to associate his vigil somehow with the maneuvers of the tide.

Bumfellar was Fishermanz's constant companion, except when they fished. R. C. and I thought this the queerest thing. Manifestly when they fished along the beach they got as far apart as possible. I believe each of them was afraid the other might catch a bonefish. Bumfellar's way was to anchor a skiff some fifty feet offshore and sit in it all day, motionless as an Indian fisherman, which is to be as motionless as a rock.

Loosfish was the most interesting one of this remarkable group. He was the eldest, a slight, serious-faced man, quite frail, and a very courteous and friendly and fine old gentleman, except upon his return from fishing. Then he was energetic, violent, and exceedingly profane. I gathered that, according to his own statements, he could not do anything but lose fish.

He would don a big sun hat, and armed with considerable paraphernalia, he would walk up the beach to a secluded spot, and there act very much like a big dog that turns round and round, finally to settle down for a sleep. Loosfish, however, was certainly wide awake. To my dismay I passed near him twice, once on the beach, where naturally I had to walk, as there was only the narrow strip of coral; and again in a canoe. With the canoe I imagined it much more considerate of me to paddle quite close to the beach, so as not to scare any bonefish. But on the first occasion Loosfish glared so savagely at me that I feared I had done something terrible; and upon the second he spoke in cold cutting language, the content of which I dare not give to the printed page. Really I was ashamed of myself for spying upon these estimable gentlemen, and meekly went upon my way. Nevertheless I did not cease my industry as to what and why and when and where.

One of the brigade was a very short, stout, red-faced man, most wonderfully cheerful, who singularly enough went by the name Rounddelay, for at lying around he had all the others of the brigade beaten to a frazzle.

I always felt sorry for Rounddelay. His gang led him the life of a dog. All because he did not, or could not, or would not fish, yet insisted on going with them! He was the most cheerful man I ever met. When after a day on the sea you encountered him it was to find him most inquisitive, eager as a boy to hear of your luck, and if that had been good he was glad. A most unusual type round a fishing camp! A man to console you! An individual immeasurably above these poor boobs of fishermen who imagine they had the best of you!

[137]

It would never do for me to forget Rushenwait, the funniest member of the brigade. He was a great talker, and that was one reason why the brigade made him fish by himself. I took advantage of his weakness and asked him how to catch bonefish. He told me. And I was soon in a state of mental aberration. But I always believed I profited by his concluding remarks: "Den you set dere an' waid for a bide which when it comes you doon know only by de feel an' you must jerg ver queeck."

Crownshanks was scarcely a member of this historic aggregation, yet it is necessary to mention him because he was always there, always on the beach, omnipresent. His forte was walking along the beach. He had very long legs and he could use them; and as a walker along the shore and a collector of trash cast up by the sea he had only one peer, and that was myself.

The tragedy of Crownshanks was that he would assuredly have been a great bonefisherman but for an unfortunate accident upon his very first trial at this tremendous game. Unwittingly he put on two hooks and two baits and hooked two bonefish. At the same time on the one line! Now one bonefish is quite master of most any situation. But two husky bonefish at once! I hesitate to express myself. The two that Crownshanks hooked ran off, as is the unkind disposition of this species, and they split round a snag of mangrove. That is to say one bonefish went one way and the other went another way. Yet, but, nevertheless, and marvelously, Crownshanks caught those two bonefish. It ruined his career. As I stated, he might have been great. But this was too much. He never went bonefishing again. He would listen to the woes and exultings of the brigade, but he could never again see that any of them had hopes of mastering the intricacies of bonefishing. Crownshanks might have had a career, but he became only the best tarpon and sailfish catcher of his day—always releasing his fish alive. To be sure, this is no distinction as compared to what he might have become in the bonefish world, but it will serve to show that he was not altogether an utter failure.

In passing I must mention one of Crownshanks' gifts. It amounted to genius. It was a most fascinating thing to watch. He always had a cigarette in his mouth—no, not exactly that, for the end of the cigarette was pasted on the under edge of his left central incisor tooth.

It hung there. It performed miraculous feats. It never fell. That was
the mystery to me. Crownshanks never smoked it, that was sure. I
do not know whether he ever had more than one cigarette or not, but
he did not need more. Now this genial and intellectual gentleman
would discourse with you for hours on any subject, though he preferred fishology, and he was equally well versed in business, politics,
religion, literature, socialism, metaphysics, psychology, psycho-
analysis, altruism and prizefighting. But I was always so bewitched
and bewildered by the sight of his everlasting cigarette—by my irresistible gamble on whether it would stick there longer or not—that
I could never concentrate on what he was talking about.

Well, the years went by, and R. C. and I, by dint of dogged
persistence and boyish enthusiasm, and development of skill, at
length mastered the mystery of bonefishing.

I have never been able to tell why it seems the fullest, the most
difficult, the strangest and most thrilling, the lonesomest and most
all-satisfying of all kinds of angling. Many salmon fishermen claim
that to take the silver king of the Restigouche on the fly is the
highest type and greatest of all fishing. Many make this claim for
the wonderful steelhead of Oregon and Washington. But bonefishing has all the finesse, the delicacy, the skill, the incomprehensible
vagaries, the test of endurance that salmon fishing has. And more!
For in bonefishing there is more of a return to boyish emotions
than in salmon fishing. Perhaps that is the secret.

Every winter R. C. and I went back to Long Key, to grow more
and more like members of the Bonefish Brigade, which I think was
a happy and profitable development for us.

Then, owing to outdoor interests in California, we missed going
to Long Key for several years. In February, 1922, I went back to
renew the unforgotten associations that had haunted me, and I took
my friend Lone Angler Wilborn with me. He was famous for a
good deal more than his feat of taking tuna and marlin swordfish
without the help of boatman or engineer. Wilborn was an expert
with fly, and all kinds of light tackle. Needless to say I had lauded
bonefish to the skies, and I anticipated more fun and sport than I
had ever had before. I had them, but not quite as anticipated.

The Bonefish Brigade appeared on schedule, and I was reminded
of the passing of years. They were the same in spirit, but the wear of

[139]

labor and the pallor of the city were upon them. So imperceptibly we pass on through life. It is a blessing that lonely places and sunshine and fishing can restore some semblance of our earlier and more youthful selves.

Fishermanz lay all that first day in his camp chair, his pale face up to the sun, with a slow smile of contentment stealing away the shadows. Bumfellar had grown thinner and Rounddelay had grown thicker. Both had been ill. Long Key was a haven of rest. Rushenwait rushed around to show his new tackle to everybody and to talk. He fished out a photograph of me taken ten years before, posed ridiculously with a queer fish called African pompano. Crownshanks started out at once to walk with the same old inevitable cigarette pasted to his tooth. Then there were new members of the brigade, one of whom was a little spider-shaped man with the look of a fish-hawk, known as Thompsonias. I knew he would catch fish, and I could not see why they had to fetch him along.

We began to fish, and things happened. I cannot chronicle in this story the extraordinary exhibitions given by my friend Lone Angler. I must reserve them for separate treatment and more space. And I will leave to him and R. C. the pleasant task of retaliating.

There appeared to be an unusual number of bonefish on the shoals and some larger than we had ever caught. I caught several running up to eight pounds, which was an unprecedented performance for me and made me exultant. What it did to Fishermanz and his crew I am too generous to state. Then that dark horse Thompsonias appeared in a one-piece bathing suit. He looked like a California bathing girl minus the shape. He was a long-legged spider wearing an abbreviated union suit and a pair of sneakers. Every morning Thompsonias appeared in this rig, and carrying tackle and bag he would disappear up the beach, to return at sunset with at least two bonefish. Sometimes more!

This fellow got on my nerves. I could not fish for worrying about him. I think he had a seine hidden up the beach. He was Fishermanz's bosom friend and I expected Fishermanz to murder him. The way he brought bonefish back to camp was uncanny. I think he never took off that bathing suit. His spider shape changed from white to red and from red to brown. I tried to keep track of him, but as we didn't have any hydroplanes, I had to give that up. As a pedestrian he was in a class by himself. We did not mind that or how long he absented himself from camp. What hurt us was the inconsiderate way he packed bonefish back until in two weeks he had thirty-four. This was heartrending. But unfortunately they were all small, and we knew he was slaving to catch one to beat our record of nine pounds.

Next, to our dismay, there appeared on the scene a newcomer by the name of Lucky Stickem. He had been felicitously named. Of all the lucky fishermen I ever had the bad luck to meet, Stickem was the luckiest. He frankly said that he only fished for exercise, as the fact of fish crawling out and lying down at his feet made it needless for him to work hard. As a matter of fact I never saw him even exercise. By profession he was a fine artist and by disposition a splendid fellow. But I could only appreciate his sterling qualities by approaching him when he was not fishing.

For tackle he had a dinky little bass rod and reel, and a few hundred feet of long-used number six line. When I saw this outfit I felt relieved, because it would be funny what a bonefish would do to that.

I got back one night to be almost overwhelmed by the stunning fact that Stickem had caught two bonefish weighing respectively $9\frac{1}{4}$ and $8\frac{3}{4}$ pounds. He had been seen fighting them—running around in the shallow water, tearing here and there as a fish took line—in a most undignified manner. But he caught them! I knew Fishermanz was ill that night.

Stickem wore his honors easily, as if he had not done much. And he had the effrontery and the unmitigated audacity and the magnificent sportsmanship to tell us he had used a new bait. There was none of our kind of bait, and so he had caught common blue crabs, cut them in half, torn off one side of the shell, and stuck a half on his hook. All we had considered blue crabs good for was to pinch. Stickem revolutionized our bait problem and utterly ruined a perfectly good illusion. Next day everybody except myself took to hunting for blue crabs.

Three days later Lone Angler and I were in my canoe anchored on the coral shoal at the upper end of Long Key—my favorite place for bonefishing. It was a lonely spot, gray shoal near at hand, green sea leading out to blue water, long lines of cocoanut palms leaning with the wind, white strip of coral beach, and the dense wall of mangroves.

The restfulness and peacefulness coincident with bonefishing are much of its charms. Of course there is no rest or peace if you hook a bonefish—rather toil and torture—but as these incidents are infrequent an angler can be happy.

Lone Angler had not yet caught a bonefish. He had performed miraculously at casting, and he said he had imagined he had a bite. When his hook came in minus the bait, he always assured me the crabs had eaten it off.

I was sinking into what may be termed bonefish oblivion—a combination of suspense, dream, and sleep—when I had a tremendous strike. It sort of paralyzed me.

"Hey! Didn't your rod jerk?" yelled Lone Angler.

"Quiet!" I hissed, tensely.

I waited until I could not wait anymore, perhaps a matter of a couple of endless seconds. The second tug is the one I wait for and strike on. But as this second tug did not come I was unable to refrain from jerking.

Sharp and hard I came up on a live weight. There was a quivering of my tight line. My rod bent double. The old thrill went over me, deep and wonderful sensation. Then the shallow water opened with a sodden thump and mud colored the spray. I had hooked a heavy bonefish.

His opening run was not electrifying for its speed, but the very slowness and heaviness of it made me shake. I stood up while Lone Angler balanced the canoe.

This fish ran off five hundred feet and stayed out there. If he had not splashed and thumped on the surface I would have been certain I had fouled my line—an accident that causes loss of so many bonefish. But this fellow hung out there and jerked his head. I could not move him an inch. I pulled until I heard the rod crack and the line sing. If he started another run I knew it would be good-by.

By dint of risky and hard pulling, I got his head turned and he began the famous circle performed by this gamefish. As he swam round the boat I pumped and reeled as hard as I dared, gradually working him closer, so that on the first circle I had him within a hundred feet. I strained my eyes to see him, but could not. But I

[142]

began to be afraid I had a larger bonefish than I had ever hooked before. This meant nothing but disaster.

Lone Angler's amazement and enthusiasm inspired me, and gave me as many thrills as the fish. I had a good bamboo rod and nine-thread line, yet I could not do much with this bonefish. Suddenly he boiled the water and started off again, inshore. I saw a blackish checkered form. He hit the little mounds of coral marl, making muddy patches in the water. Then finding it too shallow, he sheered off for the open sea. His run grew harder and longer than the first, though no swifter. I gave him up. I had a sinking sensation in my stomach. Would I never stop one of these big fellows?

"Stop him or lose him!" shouted Wilborn, excitedly. "You can't risk all that line."

"I'm not risking line. He's taking it," I retorted. Yet I did shut down on the reel and burned a blister on my thumb. The line held and he turned at right angles, beginning a wide, sweeping circle that slowly narrowed its radius. I got him perhaps seventy feet from the canoe, and from that point he began a tugging, sullen fight to tear loose the hook. He did not make any more long runs.

Still not sure of the size of this fish, I handled him with more hurry and force than I should have used. But I was a long time in whipping him, and when at last I caught a glimpse of him I nearly fell out of the canoe. From that instant I handled him with ridiculous delicacy, much to Lone Angler's amusement.

I could not keep the bonefish from circling in close to the canoe and the anchors. He was too heavy to lead. I had to hold tight and let him swim. He came to within ten feet of us and then circled. In two feet of crystal clear water he looked as long as the canoe to me. And he was thick, round, heavy. He was covered with mud. His black eyes appeared sharp, staring, wild. I stood in the center of the canoe and moved my rod round with him. Wilborn had pulled up one anchor. But there was the other and I could not risk reaching for it or letting him pass me in the canoe. I should have stepped out into the water and led the bonefish ashore, but I never thought of that.

He must have circled us at least twenty times before he showed signs of weariness. I lifted him carefully, but every time Wilborn leaned out with the net he plunged and went down.

[143]

This part of the battle, with the fish in plain sight, and the risks so great, made me as weak as if I had been fighting a swordfish. I knew he was the biggest one I had ever gotten close to capture. It would not have been such a strain if I had not been able to see him so clearly. He rolled over. He stuck his big head out of the water and gaped. He gave the line sullen heavy jerks. But he grew slower and slower, and after what seemed an interminable time of stress, I lifted him high enough for Wilborn to slip the net under him.

When he lay in the canoe, gasping, a gleaming silver and opal, with lavender tinted fins and tail, a most beautiful creature of the sea, and so long and thick that I could scarcely believe my eyes, I almost succumbed and let him go free.

But that night at the camp he weighed ten pounds, two ounces, and was the Long Key record. The way I condescended to tell Lucky Stickem how to catch bonefish, and the way I tortured poor Fishermanz, who had been yearning to catch such a bonefish for 25 years, was a shameful thing. But such fun! After all, anglers are the most simple-minded of men. I could scarcely realize my good fortune, and I was scared stiff for fear someone would beat my record, yet I strutted around nonchalantly and sympathized with the fellows who did not know how to fish.

One day I fished alone, and had both good and bad luck, as I caught three small bonefish and lost several large ones.

As I was going down the walk toward the lodge, Mrs. Wilborn appeared suddenly from behind a thick clump of palms. She looked vastly important. My heart began to sink. But her smile saved one from awful conclusions.

"They've put up a job on you," she whispered. "Play up to it now!"

Then she vanished. I plodded along pondering this subtle hint. Job! What could it be? Play up to it now! That meant clearly I must be game to meet some situation.

When I turned the corner of the walk to face the gang on the lodge porch, I was greeted by a lusty yell and many calls, from which I gathered that catastrophe had befallen me.

Wilborn came off the porch to meet me. He wore his old bright smile and his eyes were keen. Too keen! I caught a twinkle that I might have missed but for his good wife's bidding me be prepared. I was reminded of his tricks when we played on the varsity in college.

[144]

The sly fox! But I gave no sign. I was as innocent as he affected to be.

"Hard luck, Chief," he said, with his hand going to my shoulder. "Your record's broken. Fishermanz has trimmed you! Go in and see!"

Right there I blessed Mrs. Wilborn for having intuition to understand my sensitive feelings. For even with the assurance of a monstrous deceit to be perpetrated upon me I experienced an inward quaking.

"Is that so?" And I stepped into the lodge.

Upon a large platter lay what seemed the most wonderful bonefish I had ever seen. I got up on a chair so to see the better. And I looked down. It took all my willpower to concentrate upon Mrs. Wilborn's hint. She must have meant that this bonefish did not truly beat my record though the brigade had made it appear so.

10 pounds 5 ounces
Mr. Fishermanz
Long Key Record

So ran the words on a large white placard. I had a queer sensation. Surely this fish was bigger than mine. Of course it was! Then my conscience twinged me for doubting Mrs. W.'s loyalty. What a terrible ordeal that would have been for me if she had not told me!

The Bonefish Brigade filed in, accompanied by Lone Angler Wilborn and Lucky Stickem. What a bunch of destructive wretches they were! They crowded around me and the table, solicitous, sympathizing, crooked as rail fences in their pretended commiseration for me. The truth was they were most curiously bent on seeing how I would take my defeat. It was a diabolical trick that owed its origin to the fertile brain of Lone Angler. His wife had divined that. The Bonefish Brigade never had an idea in their lives except to sit down in the sun and wait for a bite. If they had anticipated extreme joy in seeing me utterly crushed—the villains—they were to be sadly disappointed.

I expanded. I gazed with rapt admiration. I stared at that bonefish in delight.

"What a magnificent fish!" I burst out. "Why, he makes mine

[145]

look little . . . Three ounces to the good? Surely he looks three pounds!"

Then I got down off the chair and faced Fishermanz with the mien of a vanquished champion true to the traditions of sportsmanship.

"I congratulate you," I said, heartily, as I wrung his hand. "There's no angler in the world so worthy of this record as you are. My fish was only a lucky catch. It only inspired you to greater effort. Believe me, Fishermanz, I would be happy if your new record was one I could never beat."

The funny thing about this oration of mine was that it was true.

The brigade to a man looked crestfallen. Thanks to my gentle monitor I had played up to their bent and had fooled them. The moment passed to my credit and we went back upon the porch. The bonefish was brought outside. Long Angler insisted that I take a photograph of it and the brigade. After that was done he took the fish and, walking over to me, held it out. That sly little twinkle gleamed in his eyes.

"Say, Chief, feel that," he said, with his hand on the plump belly of the bonefish. He tried to appear tremendously concerned.

I felt some hard lumps inside the fish, and remarked that they must be some of Stickem's hard-shelled crabs.

"Don't you want to weigh this fish yourself?" he queried, anxiously. "Fishermanz was very careful to see yours weighed."

"Weigh it myself? No indeed," I replied loftily. "His word is enough for me."

Whereupon Lone Angler turned the bonefish upside down, and jogged it vigorously, as if to dislodge something from its insides. Suddenly out plumped half a dozen heavy lead sinkers!

12

TONTO BASIN

Zane Grey was a proud parent, and, as the expression goes, he wanted to give his sons all the advantages he hadn't had. So whereas sunfish and suckers represented ZG's first taste of fishing, casting for steelhead and trolling for marlin were among Romer's and Loren's first experiences. But enough of the child remained in papa Grey so he was not crestfallen when the boys showed a preference for chasing minnows in the shallows or fishing with handlines off the docks to watching daddy wield an uncomfortably heavy rod in combat with gigantic fish.

Though Zane Grey regularly returned to New York on business and continued to visit Pennsylvania and Florida for fishing, by 1918 his permanent home was in Altadena, California, with another house overlooking the Tuna Club and harbor at Catalina. His eldest boy, Romer, was nine years of age and old enough, it was finally decided, to sample bear hunting in Arizona.

But it wasn't bear alone that interested Romer. Squirrel, deer, and especially turkey were his favorite game. In the early days of this century, turkey were viewed primarily as fresh camp food by serious bear hunters. However, Romer's enthusiasm for these birds quickly affected his father's point of view, and soon the two of them (with Uncle R. C. tagging along) were creeping over rocks and under fallen timbers hunting turkey the way Zane Grey himself had once stalked smaller birds in Ohio when he was a boy. And that part of ZG's nature which guilted about killing-in-hunting yielded to old boyhood feelings, and he saw the excitement of camping in the Tonto Basin through the eyes of a nine-year-old. The following excerpts represent, perhaps, the happiest hunting trip ZG ever made.

GWR

TONTO BASIN

The start of a camping trip, the getting of a big outfit together and packed and on the move, is always a difficult and laborsome job. Nevertheless, for me the preparation and the actual getting under way have always been matters of thrilling interest. This start of my hunt in Arizona, September 24, 1918, was particularly momentous because I had brought my boy Romer with me for his first trip into the wilds.

It may be that the boy was too young for such an undertaking. His mother feared he would be injured; his teachers presaged his utter ruin; his old nurse, with whom he waged war until he was free of her, averred that the best it could do for him would be to show what kind of stuff he was made of. His uncle R. C. was stoutly in favor of taking him. I believe the balance fell in Romer's favor when I remembered my own boyhood. As a youngster of three I had babbled of "bars an' buffers," and woven fantastic and marvelous tales of fiction about my imagined adventures—a habit, alas! I have never yet outgrown.

Anyway, we only made six miles' travel on this September 24th, and Romer was with us.

Indeed he was omnipresent. His keen, eager joy communicated itself to me. Once he rode up alongside me and said: "Dad, this's great, but I'd rather do like Buck Duane."[1] The boy had read all of my books, in spite of parents and teachers, and he knew them by heart, and invariably liked the outlaws and gunmen best of all.

We made camp at sunset, with a flare of gold along the west, and the peaks rising rosy and clear to the north. We camped in a cut-over pine forest, where stumps and looped tops and burned deadfalls made an aspect of blackened desolation. From a distance, however, the scene was superb. At sunset there was a faint wind which soon died away.

My old guide on so many trips across the Painted Desert was in charge of the outfit.[2] He was a wiry, gray, old pioneer, over seventy years, hollow-cheeked and bronzed, with blue-gray eyes still keen with fire. He was no longer robust, but he was tireless and willing. When he told a story he always began: "In the early days—" His son, Lee, had charge of the horses, of which we had fourteen, two teams and ten saddle horses. Lee was a typical Westerner of many occupations—cowboy, rider, rancher, cattleman. He was small, thin, supple, quick, tough and strong. He had a bronzed face, always chapped, a hooked nose, gray-blue eyes like his father's, sharp and keen.

Darkness had enveloped us at supper time. I was tired out, but the red-embered camp fire, the cool air, the smell of wood smoke, and the white stars kept me awake awhile. Romer had to be put to

---

[1] Buckley Duane, hero of *The Lone Star Ranger*, published in January, 1915.

[2] Al Doyle—who had also accompanied Zane Grey and John Wetherill on their expedition to Rainbow Bridge described in "Nonnezoshe."

bed. He was wild with excitement. We had had a sleeping bag made for him so that once snugly in it, with the flaps buckled, he could not kick off the blankets. When we got him into it, he quieted down and took exceeding interest in his first bed in the open. He did not, however, go quickly to sleep. Presently he called R. C. over and whispered: "Say, Uncle Rome, I coiled a lasso an' put it under Nielsen's[3] bed. When he's asleep, you go pull it. He's a tenderfoot like Dad was. He'll think it's a rattlesnake." This trick Romer must have remembered from reading *The Last of the Plainsmen*, where I related what Buffalo Jones' cowboys did to me. Once Romer got that secret off his mind he fell asleep.

Next day at dawn the forest was full of the soughing of wind in the pines—a wind that presaged storm. No stars showed. Romer-boy piled out at six o'clock. I had to follow him. The sky was dark and cloudy. Only a faint light showed in the east and it was just light enough to see when we ate breakfast. Owing to strayed horses we did not get started till after nine o'clock.

Five miles through the woods, gradually descending, led us into an open plain where there was a grass-bordered pond full of ducks. Here appeared an opportunity to get some meat. R. C. tried with shotgun and I with rifle, all to no avail. These ducks were shy. Romer seemed to evince some disdain at our failure, but he did not voice his feelings. We found some wild-turkey tracks, and a few feathers, which put our hopes high.

Crossing the open ground we again entered the forest, which gradually grew thicker as we got down to a lower altitude. Oak trees began to show in swales. And then we soon began to see squirrels,

---

[3] Sievert Nielsen was one of Zane Grey's most interesting companions. Born in Norway, Nielsen ran away to sea at an early age. One day in a Mexican port, he jumped ship and became a prospector. He wrote ZG after reading *Desert Gold* and, assuming that the lost treasure described in this book was real, asked Grey for more details, promising to split the treasure fifty-fifty when and if it was recovered. Grey was intrigued by the letter and asked Nielsen to visit him in Catalina. When the man showed up, ZG was surprised to find him a bright and well-read young man. After a couple of fishing trips, Nielsen was made a permanent part of the Zane Grey retinue, accompanying the famous writer on many outdoor expeditions. But in 1924 while ZG was in New York on business, Nielsen mysteriously disappeared. Grey made every effort to locate him, but finally had to settle for the substantial rumor that he had been killed in a brawl in Tijuana, Mexico.

big, plump, gray fellows, with bushy tails almost silver. They appeared wilder than we would have suspected, at that distance from the settlements. Romer was eager to hunt them, and with his usual persistence, succeeded at length in persuading his uncle to do so.

To that end we rode out far ahead of the wagon and horses. Lee had a yellow dog he called Pups, a close-haired, keen-faced, muscular canine to which I had taken a dislike. To be fair to Pups, I had no reason except that he barked all the time. Now this dog of Lee's would run ahead of us, trail squirrels, chase them and tree them, whereupon he would bark vociferously. Sometimes up in the bushy top we would fail to spy the squirrel, but we had no doubt one was there. Romer wasted many and many a cartridge of the .22 Winchester trying to hit a squirrel. He had practiced a good deal, and was a fairly good shot for a youngster, but hitting a little gray ball of fur high on a tree, or waving at the tip of a branch, was no easy matter.

"Son," I said, "you don't take after your Dad."

And his uncle tried the lad's temper by teasing him about Wetzel. Now Wetzel, the great Indian killer of frontier days, was Romer's favorite hero.

"Gimme the .20 gauge," finally cried Romer, in desperation, with his eyes flashing.

Whereupon his uncle handed him the shotgun, with a word of caution as to the trigger. This particular squirrel was pretty high up, presenting no easy target. Romer stood almost directly under it, raised the gun nearly straight up, waved and wobbled and hesitated, and finally fired. Down sailed the squirrel to hit with a plump. That was Romer's first successful hunting experience. How proud he was of that gray squirrel! I suffered a pang to see the boy so radiant, so full of fire at the killing of a beautiful creature of the woods. Then again I remembered my own first sensations. Boys are bloodthirsty little savages. In their hunting, playing, even their reading, some element of brute instinct dominates them. They are worthy descendants of progenitors who had to fight and kill to live.

"Some shot, I'll say!" declared Romer to his uncle, loftily. And he said to me half a dozen times, "Say, Dad, wasn't it a grand peg?"

But toward the end of that afternoon his enthusiasm waned for

[151]

shooting, for anything, especially riding. He kept asking when the wagon was going to stop. Once he yelled out, "Here's a peach of a place to camp." Then I asked him, "Romer, are you tired?" "Naw! But what's the use ridin' till dark?" At length he had to give up and be put on the wagon. The moment was tragic for him. Soon, however, he brightened at something Doyle told him, and began to ply the old pioneer with rapid-fire questions.

We pitched camp in an open flat, gray and red with short grass, and sheltered by towering pines on one side. Under these we set up our tents. The mat of pine needles was half a foot thick, soft and springy and fragrant. The woods appeared full of slanting rays of golden sunlight.

This day we had supper over before sunset. Romer showed no effects from his long, hard ride. He interfered with the work of our camp cook, Isbel, and I had a hard time to manage him. He wanted to be eternally active. He teased and begged to go hunting—then he compromised on target practice. R. C. and I, however, were too tired, and we preferred to rest beside the camp fire.

"Look here, kid," said R. C., "save something for tomorrow."

In disgust Romer replied, "Well, I suppose if a flock of antelope came along here you wouldn't move. . . . You an' Dad are great hunters, I don't think!"

After the lad had gone over to the other men, R. C. turned to me and said, "Does he remind you of us where we were little?"

To which I replied with emotion, "In him I live over again!"

This evening, despite my fatigue, I was the last one to stay up. My seat was most comfortable, consisting of thick folds of blankets against a log. How the wind mourned in the trees! How the camp fire sparkled, glowed red and white! Sometimes it seemed full of blazing opals. Always it held faces. And stories—more stories than I can ever tell! Once I was stirred and inspired by the beautiful effect of the pine trees in outline against the starry sky when the camp fire blazed up. The color of the foliage seemed indescribably blue-green, something never seen by day. Every line shone bright, graceful, curved, rounded, and all thrown with sharp relief against the sky. How magical, exquisitely delicate and fanciful! The great trunks were soft serrated brown, and the gnarled branches stood out in perfect proportions.

[152]

Next morning early, while Romer slept, and the men had just begun to stir, I went apart from the camp out into the woods. All seemed solemn and still and cool, with the aisles of the forest brown and green and gold. I heard an owl, perhaps belated in his nocturnal habit. I wandered around among big, gray rocks and windfalls and clumps of young oak and majestic pines. More than one saucy red squirrel chattered at me. When I returned to camp my comrades were at breakfast. Romer appeared vastly relieved to see that I had not taken a gun with me.

We got an early start and rode for hours through a beautiful shady forest, where a fragrant breeze in our faces made riding pleasant. Large oaks and patches of sumac appeared on the rocky slopes. We descended a good deal in this morning's travel, and the air grew appreciably warmer. The smell of pine was thick and fragrant; the sound of wind was sweet and soothing. Everywhere pine needles dropped, shining in the sunlight like thin slants of rain.

Only once or twice did I see Romer in all these morning hours; then he was out in front with the cowboy Isbel, riding his black pony over all the logs and washes he could find. I could see his feet sticking straight out almost even with his saddle. He did not appear to need stirrups. My fears gradually lessened.

During the afternoon the ride grew hot, and very dusty. We came to a long, open valley where the dust lay several inches deep. It had been an unusually dry summer and fall—a fact that presaged poor luck for our hunting—and the washes and stream beds were bleached white. We came to two water holes, tanks the Arizonians called them, and they were vile mud holes with green scum on the water. The horses drank, but I would have had to be far gone from thirst before I would have slaked mine there. We faced west with the hot sun beating on us and the dust rising in clouds. No wonder that ride was interminably long.

At last we descended a canyon, and decided to camp in a level spot where several ravines met, in one of which a tiny stream of clear water oozed out of the gravel. The inclosure was rocky-sloped, full of caves and covered with pines; and the best I could say for it was that in case of storm the camp would be well protected. We shoveled out a deep hole in the gravel, so that it would fill up with water. Romer had evidently enjoyed himself this day. When I asked

[153]

Isbel about him, the cowboy's hard face gleamed with a smile: "Shore thet kid's all right. He'll make a cowpuncher!" His remark pleased me. In view of Romer's determination to emulate the worst bandit I ever wrote about, I was tremendously glad to think of him as a cowboy. But as for myself I was tired, and the ride had been rather unprofitable, and this campsite did not inspire me. It was neither wild nor beautiful nor comfortable. I went early to bed and slept like a log.

*

The sun was high and hot when we rode off. The pleasant and dusty stretches alternated. About one o'clock we halted on the edge of a deep wooded ravine to take our usual noonday rest. I scouted along the edge in the hope of seeing game of some kind. Presently I heard the cluck-cluck of turkeys. Slipping along to an open place, I peered down, to be thrilled by the sight of four good-sized turkeys. They were walking along the open strip of dry stream-bed at the bottom of the ravine. One was chasing grasshoppers. They were fairly close. I took aim at one, and though I could have hit him, I suddenly remembered Romer and R. C. So I slipped back and called them.

Hurriedly and stealthily we returned to the point where I had seen the turkeys. Romer had a pale face and wonderfully bright eyes. Even though he didn't have a gun, his actions resembled those of a stalking Indian. The turkeys were farther down, but still in plain sight. I told R. C. to take the boy and slip down, and run and hide and run till they got close enough for a shot. I would keep to the edge of the ravine.

Some moments later I saw R. C. and the boy running and stooping and creeping along the bottom of the ravine. Then I ran myself to reach a point opposite the turkeys, so in case they flew uphill I might get a shot. But I did not see them, and nothing happened. I lost sight of the turkeys. Hurrying back to where I had tied my horse I mounted him and loped ahead and came out upon the ravine some distance above. Here I hunted around for a little while. Once I heard the report of a rifle. Finally, R. C. and Romer came wagging up the hill, both red and wet and tired. R. C. carried a small turkey, about the size of a chicken. He told me, between pants, that they chased the four large turkeys, and were just about

[154]

to get a shot when up jumped a hen turkey with a flock of young ones. They ran every way. He got one. Then he told me, between more pants and some laughs, that Romer had chased the little turkeys all over the ravine, almost catching several. Romer said for himself: "I almost pulled feathers out of their tails. Gee! If I'd had a gun!"

We resumed our journey. About the middle of the afternoon Doyle called my attention to an opening in the forest through which I could see the yellow-walled rim of the mesa, and the great blue void below. Arizona! That explained the black forests, the red and yellow cliffs of rock, the gray cedars, the heights and depths.

Long ride indeed was it down off the mesa. The road was winding, rough, full of loose rocks, and dusty. We were all tired out trying to keep up with the wagon. Romer, however, averred time and again that he was not tired. Still I saw him often shift his seat from one side of the saddle to the other.

At last we descended to a comparative level and came to a little hamlet. Like all Mormon villages it had quaint log cabins, low stone houses, an irrigation ditch running at the side of the road, orchards, and many rosy-cheeked children. We lingered there long enough to rest a little and drink our fill of the cold granite water. I would travel out of my way to get a drink of water that came from granite rock.

About five o'clock we left for the Natural Bridge.[4] Romer invited or rather taunted me to a race. When it ended in his victory I found that I had jolted my rifle out of its saddle sheath. I went back some distance to look for it, but did so in vain. Isbel said he would ride back in the morning and find it.

The country here appeared to be on a vast scale. But that was only because we had gotten out where we could see all around. Arizona is all on a grand, vast scale. Mountain ranges stood up to the south and east. North loomed up the lofty, steep rim of the Mogollon Mesa, with its cliffs of yellow and red, and its black line of timber. Westward lay fold on fold of low cedar-covered hills. The valley appeared a kind of magnificent bowl, rough and wild, with the

---

[4] This Arizona bridge is not to be confused with Utah's Rainbow Bridge many miles to the north and previously described in "Nonnezoshe."

distance lost in blue haze. The vegetation was dense and rather low. I saw both prickly-pear and mescal cactus, cedars, manzanita brush, scrub oak, and juniper trees.

We crossed the plateau leading to the valley where the Natural Bridge was located. A winding road descended the east side of this valley. A rancher lived down there. Green of alfalfa and orchard and walnut trees contrasted vividly with a bare, gray slope on one side, and a red, rugged mountain on the other. A deep gorge showed dark and wild. At length, just after sunset, we reached the ranch, and rode through orchards of peach and pear and apple trees, all colored with fruit, and down through grassy meadows to a walnut grove where we pitched camp. By the time we had supper it was dark. Wonderful stars, thick, dreamy hum of insects, murmur of swift water, a rosy and golden afterglow on the notch of the mountain range to the west—these were inducements to stay up, but I was so tired I had to go to bed, where my eyelids fell tight, as if pleasantly weighted.

After the long, hard rides and the barren campsites, what delight to awaken in this beautiful valley with the morning cool and breezy and bright, with smell of new-mown hay from the green and purple alfalfa fields, and the sunlight gilding the jagged crags above! Romer made a beeline for the peach trees. He beat his daddy by only a few yards. The kind rancher had visited us the night before and he had told us to help ourselves to fruit, melons, alfalfa. Needless to say, I made my breakfast on peaches!

Then I trailed the swift, murmuring stream that ran through the rancher's land to its source on the dark green slope where there opened up a big hole bordered by watercress, long grass, and fragrant mint. This spring was one of perfectly clear water, six feet deep, boiling up to bulge on the surface. A grass of dark color and bunches of light green plant grew under the surface. Bees and blue dragonflies hummed around and frogs as green as the grass blinked with jewelled eyes from the wet margins. The spring had a large volume that spilled over its borders with low, hollow gurgle, with fresh, cool splash. The water was soft, tasting of limestone. Here was the secret of the verdure and fragrance and color and beauty and life of the oasis.

Part of the rancher's cultivated land, to the extent of several acres, was level with the top of the Natural Bridge. A meadow of alfalfa and a fine vineyard, in the air, like the hanging gardens of Babylon! Opposite a winding trail led deep down on the lower side of this wonderful natural span. It showed the cliffs of limestone, porous, craggy, broken, chalky. At the bottom the gorge was full of tremendous boulders, water-worn ledges, sycamore and juniper trees, red and yellow flowers, and dark, beautiful green pools. I espied tiny gray frogs, reminding me of those I found in the gulches of the Grand Canyon. Many huge black beetles lined the wet borders of the pools, and a species of fish that resembled mullet lay in the shadow of the rocks.

From underneath, the Natural Bridge showed to advantage, and if not magnificent like the grand Nonnezoshe of Utah, it was at least striking and beautiful. It had a rounded ceiling colored gray, yellow, green, bronze, purple, white, making a crude and scalloped mosaic. Water dripped from it like a rain of heavy scattered drops. The left side was dryest and large, dark caves opened up, one above the other, the upper being so high that it was dangerous to attempt reaching it. The right side was slippery and wet. All rocks were thickly encrusted with lime salt. Doyle told us that any object left under the ceaseless drip, drip of the lime water would soon become encrusted, and heavy as stone. The upper opening of the arch was much higher and smaller than the lower. Any noise gave forth strange and sepulchral echoes. Romer certainly made the welkin ring. A streak of sunlight shone through a small hole in the thinnest part of the roof. Doyle pointed out the high cave where Indians had once lived, showing the markings of their fire. Also he told a story of Apaches being driven into the highest cave, from which they had never escaped. This tale was manifestly to Romer's liking and I had to use force to keep him from risking his neck. I tried to interest Romer in some bat nests in crevices high up, but the boy wanted to roll stones and fish for the mullet. When we climbed out and were once more on a level, I asked him what he thought of the place. "Some hole—I'll say!" he panted.

At five o'clock we came to the end of the road. It led to a forest glade, overlooking the stream we had followed, and that was as far as our wagon could go. The glade shone red with sumac, and surrounded by tall pines, with a rocky and shady glen below, it ap-

[157]

peared a delightful place to camp. As I was about to unsaddle my horses I heard the cluck-cluck of turkeys. Pulling out my borrowed rifle,[5] and calling Romer, I ran to the edge of the glade. The shady, swift stream ran fifty feet or so below me. Across it I saw into the woods where shade and gray rocks and colored brush mingled. Again I heard the turkeys cluck. "Look hard, son," I whispered. "They're close." R. C. came slipping along below us, with his rifle ready. Suddenly Romer stiffened, then pointed. "There! Dad! There!" I saw two gobblers wade into the brook not more than a hundred and fifty feet away. Drawing down with fine aim, I fired. The bullet splashed water all over the turkeys. One with loud whirr of wings flew away. The other leaped across the brook and ran— swift as a deer—right up the slope. As I tried to get the sight on him, I heard other turkeys fly, and the crack-crack of R. C.'s gun. I shot twice at my running turkey, and all I did was to scatter the dirt over him, and make him run faster. R. C. had not done any better shooting. Romer, wonderful to relate, was so excited that he forgot to make fun of our marksmanship. We scouted around some, but the turkeys had gone. By promising to take Romer hunting after supper I contrived to get him back to the glade where we had made camp.

*

After we had unpacked and while the men were pitching the tents and getting supper, I took Romer on a hunt up the creek. I was pleased to see good-sized trout in the deeper pools. A little way above camp the creek forked. As the right-hand branch appeared to be larger and more attractive, we followed its course. Soon the bustle of camp life and the sound of the horses were left far behind. Romer slipped along beside me stealthily as an Indian, all eyes and ears.

We had not traveled thus for a quarter of a mile when my quick ear caught the cluck-cluck of turkeys. "Listen," I whispered, halting. Romer became like a statue, his dark eyes dilating, his nostrils quivering, his whole body strung. A turkey called again; then another answered. Romer started, and nodded his head vehemently.

---

[5] Isbel never found the rifle ZG lost in the race with Romer, so a cowboy named Copple loaned Zane Grey his.

"Come on now, right behind me," I whispered. "Step where I step and do what I do. Don't break any twigs."

Cautiously we glided up the creek, listening now and then to get the direction, until we came to an open place where we could see some distance up a ridge. The turkey clucks came from across the creek somewhere up this open aisle of the forest. I crawled ahead several rods to a more advantageous point, much pleased to note that Romer kept noiselessly at my heels. Then from behind a stone we peeped out. Almost at once a turkey flew down from a tree into the open lane. "Look Dad!" whispered Romer, wildly. I had to hold him down. "That's a hen turkey," I said. "See, it's small and dull-colored. The gobblers are big, shiny, and they have red on their heads."

Another hen turkey flew down from a rather low height. Then I made out grapevines, and I saw several animated dark patches among them. As I looked, three turkeys flopped down to the ground. One was a gobbler of considerable size, with beautiful white and bronze feathers. Rather suspiciously he looked down our way. This distance was not more than a hundred yards. I aimed at him, feeling as I did so how Romer quivered beside me, but I had no confidence in Copple's rifle. The sights were wrong for me. The stock did not fit me. So, hoping for a closer and better shot, I let this opportunity pass. Of course I should have taken it. The gobbler clucked and began to trot up the ridge, with the others after him. They were not frightened, but they appeared suspicious. When they disappeared in the woods, Romer and I got up and hurried in pursuit. "Gee! Why didn't you peg that gobbler?" broke out Romer, breathlessly. "Wasn't he a peach?"

When we reached the top of the ridge we advanced very cautiously again. Another open place led to a steep, rocky hillside with cedars and pines growing somewhat separated. I was disappointed in not seeing the turkeys. Then in our anxiety and eagerness we hurried on, not noiselessly by any means. All of a sudden there was a rustle, and then a great whirr of wings. Three turkeys flew like grouse away into the woods. Next I saw the white gobbler running up the rocky hillside. At first he was in the open. Aiming as best I could, I waited for him to stop or hesitate. But he did neither. "Peg him, Dad!" yelled Romer. The lad was right. My best chance I had

[159]

again forfeited. To hit a running wild turkey with a rifle bullet was a feat I had not done so often as to inspire conceit. The gobbler was wise, too. For that matter all grown gobblers are as wise as old bucks, except in the spring mating season, when it is a crime to hunt them. This one, just as I got a bead on him, always ran behind a rock or tree or shrub. Finally in desperation I took a snap shot at him, hitting under him, making him jump. Then in rapid succession I fired four more times. I had the satisfaction of seeing where my bullets struck up the dust, even though they did go wide of the mark. After my last shot the gobbler disappeared.

"Well, Dad, you sure throwed the dirt over him!" declared Romer.

*

Next morning a hunter named Haught from a neighboring camp asked me if I would like to ride through the woods and get a shot at a deer. Romer coaxed so to go that I finally consented.

We rode down the canyon, and presently came to a wide grassy park inclosed by high green-clad slopes, the features of which appeared to be that the timber on the west slope was mostly pine, and on the east slope it was mostly spruce. I could arrive at no certain reason for this, but I thought it must be owing to the snow lying somewhat longer on the east slope. The stream here was running with quite a little volume of water. Our horses were grazing in this park. I saw fresh elk tracks made the day before. Elk were quite abundant through this forest, Haught informed me, and were protected by law.

A couple of miles down this trail the canyon narrowed, losing its park-like dimensions. The farther we traveled the more water there was in the stream, and more elk, deer, and turkey tracks in the sand. Every half mile or so we would come to the mouth of a small intersecting canyon, and at length we rode up one of these, presently to climb out on top. At this distance from the rim the forest was more open than in the vicinity of our camp, affording better riding and hunting. Still the thickets of aspen and young pine were so frequent that seldom could I see ahead more than several hundred yards.

Haught led the way, I rode next, and Romer kept beside me where it was possible to do so. There was, however, no trail. How

[160]

difficult to keep the lad quiet! I expected of course that Haught would dismount, and take me to hunt on foot. After a while I gathered he did not hunt deer except on horseback. He explained that cowboys rounded up cattle in this forest in the spring and fall, and deer were not frightened at sound or sight of a horse.

We rode across a grove of widely separated, stately pines, at the far end of which stood a thicket of young pines and other brush. As we neared this, Haught suddenly reined in, and in quick and noiseless action he dismounted. Then he jerked his rifle from his saddle sheath, took a couple of forward steps, and leveled it. I was so struck with the rugged and significant picture he made that I did not dismount, and did not see any game until after he fired. Then as I tumbled off and got out my rifle I heard Romer gasping and crying out. A gray streak with a bobbing white end flashed away out of sight to the left. Next I saw a deer bounding through the thicket. Haught fired again. The deer ran so fast that I could not get my sights anywhere near him. Haught thudded through an opening, and an instant later, when both he and the deer had disappeared, he shot the third time. Presently he returned.

"Never could shoot with them open sights nohow," he said. "Shore I missed that yearlin' buck when he was standin'. Why didn't you smoke him up?"

"Dad, why didn't you peg him?" asked Romer, with intense regret. "Why, I could have knocked him!"

Then it was incumbent upon me to confess that the action had appeared to be a little swift. "Wal," said Haught, "when you see one, you want to pile off quick."

As we rode on, Romer asked me if ever in my life I had seen anything run so fast as that deer. We entered another big grove with thin patches of thicket here and there. Haught said these were good places for deer to lie down, relying on their noses to scent danger from windward, and on their eyes in the other direction. We circled to go round thickets, descending somewhat into a swale. Here Haught got off a little to the right. Romer and I rode up a gentle slope toward a thin line of little pines, through which I could see into the pines beyond. Suddenly up jumped three big gray bucks. Literally I fell off my horse, bounced up, and pulled out my rifle. One buck was loping in a thicket. I could see his broad,

[161]

gray body behind the slender trees. I aimed—followed him—got a bead on him—and was just about to pull the trigger when he vanished. Plunging forward I yelled to Haught. Then Romer cried in his shrill treble: "Dad, here's a big buck—hurry!" Turning I ran back. In wild excitement Romer was pointing. I was just in time to see a gray rump disappear in the green. Just then Haught shot, and after that he halloed. Romer and I went through the thicket, working to our left, and presently came out into the open forest. Haught was leading his horse. To Romer's eager query he replied: "Shore, I piled him up. Two-year-old blacktail buck."

Sure enough he had shot straight this time. The buck lay motionless under a pine, with one point of his antlers imbedded deep in the ground. A sleek, gray, graceful deer, he was just beginning to get his winter coat. His color was indeed a bluish gray. Haught hung him up to a branch, spread his hind legs, and cut him down the middle. The hunter's dexterity with a knife made me wonder how many deer he had dressed in his life in the open. We lifted the deer upon the saddle of Haught's horse and securely tied it there with a lasso; then with the hunter on foot, leading the way, we rode through the forest up the main ridge between Beaver and Turkey Canyons.

*

After supper that evening R. C. heard a turkey call up on the hill east of camp. Then I heard it, and Romer also. We ran out a ways into the open to listen the better. R. C.'s ears were exceptionally keen. He could hear a squirrel jump a long distance in the forest. In this case he distinctly heard three turkeys fly up into trees. I heard one. Romer declared he heard a flock. Then R. C. located a big bronze and white gobbler on a lower limb of a huge pine. Presently I, too, saw it. Whereupon we took shotgun and rifle, and sallied forth sure of fetching back to camp some wild turkey. Romer tagged at our heels.

Hurrying to the slope we climbed up at least three-quarters of the way, as swiftly as possible. And that was work enough to make me wet and hot. The sun had set and twilight was upon us, so that we had to hurry if we were to be successful. Locating the big gobbler turned out to be a task. We had to climb over brush and around rocks, up a steep slope, rather open; and we had to do it

[162]

without being seen or making noise. Romer, despite his eagerness, did very well indeed. At last I spotted our quarry, and the sight was thrilling! A wild turkey gobbler to me, who've hunted them enough to learn how sagacious and cunning and difficult to stalk they are, always seems as provocative of excitement as larger game. This big fellow hopped up from limb to limb of the huge dead pine, and he bobbed around as if undecided, and tried each limb for a place to roost. Then he hopped farther up until we lost sight of him in the gnarled network of branches.

R. C. wanted me to slip on alone, but I preferred to have him and Romer go, too. So we moved stealthily upward until we reached the level. Then progress was easier. I went to the left with the rifle; and R. C. with the .20 gauge, and Romer, went around to the right. How rapidly it was growing dark! Low down in the forest I could not distinguish objects. We circled that big pine tree, and I made rather a wide detour, perhaps eighty yards from it. At last I got the upper part of the dead pine silhouetted against the western sky. Moving to and fro, I finally made out a large black lump way out upon a spreading branch. Could that be the gobbler? I studied that dark enlarged part of the limb with great intentness, and I had about decided that it was only a knot when I saw a long neck shoot out. That lump was the wise old turkey all right. He was almost in the top of the tree and far out from the trunk. No wildcat or lynx could ever surprise him there! I reflected upon the instinct that governed him to protect his life so cunningly. Safe he was from all but man and gun!

When I came to aim at him with the rifle I found that I could see only a blur of sights. Other branches and the tip of a very high pine adjoining made a dark background. I changed my position, working around to where the background was all open sky. It proved to be better. By putting the sights against this open sky I could faintly see the front sight through the blurred ring. This done I moved the rifle over until I had the sight aligned against the dark shape. Straining my eyes I held hard—then fired. The big dark lump on the branch changed shape, and fell, to alight with a sounding thump. I heard Romer running, but could not see him. Then his voice pealed out: "I got him, Dad. You made a grand peg!"

Not only had Romer gotten him, but he insisted on packing him

[163]

back to camp. The gobbler was the largest I ever killed, not indeed a huge 35-pounder, but a fat, heavy turkey, and quite a load for a boy. Romer packed him down that steep slope in the dark without a slip, for which performance I allowed him to stay up awhile around the camp fire.

Haught came over from his camp that night and visited us. Much as I loved to sit alone beside a red-embered fire at night in the forest, or on the desert, I also liked upon occasions to have company. We talked and talked. Old-timer Doyle told more than one of his "in the early days" stories. Then Haught told us some bear stories.

Romer's enjoyment of this storytelling hour around the glowing camp fire was equalled by his reluctance to go to bed. "Aw, Dad, please let me hear one more," he pleaded. His shining eyes would have weakened a sterner discipline than mine. And Haught seemed inspired by them.

"Wal now, listen to this hyar," he began again, with a twinkle in his eye. "Thar was an old fellar had a ranch in Chevelon Canyon, an' he was always bein' pestered by mountain lions. His name was Bill Tinker. Now Bill was no sort of a hunter, fact was he was afeerd of lions an' bears, but he shore did git riled when any critters rustled around his cabin. One day in the fall he comes home an' seen a big she-lion sneakin' around. He grabbed a club, an' throwed it, and yelled to scare the critter away. Wal, he had an old water barrel layin' around, an' darned if the lion didn't run in thet barrel an' hide. Bill run quick an' flopped the barrel end up, so he had the lion trapped. He had to set on the barrel to hold it down. Shore that lion raised old Jasper under the barrel. Bill was plumb scared. Then he seen the lion's tail stick out through the bung-hole. Bill bent over an' shore quick tied a knot in thet long tail. Then he run fer his cabin. When he got to the door he looked back to see the lion tearin' down the hill fer the woods with the barrel bumpin' behind her. Bill said he never seen her again till next spring, an' she had the barrel still on her tail. But what was stranger'n thet Bill swore she had four cubs with her an' each of them had a keg on its tail."

We all roared with laughter except Romer. His interest had been so all-absorbing, his excitement so great, and his faith in the storyteller so reverential that at first he could not grasp the trick at the end of the story. His face was radiant, his eyes were dark and dilated. When the truth dawned upon him, amazement and disappointment changed his mobile face, and then came mirth. He shouted as if to the treetops. Long after he was in bed I heard him laughing to himself.

I was awakened a little after daylight by the lad trying to get into his boots. His boots were rather tight, and somehow, even in a dry forest, he always contrived to get them wet, so that in the morning it was a herculean task for him to pull them on. This occasion appeared more strenuous than usual. "Son, what's the idea?" I inquired. "It's just daylight—not time to get up." He desisted from his labors long enough to pant: "Uncle Rome's—gone after turkeys. Edd's[6] going to—call them with—a caller—made out of a turkey's wing bone." And I said, "But they've gone now." Whereupon he subsided: "Darned old boots! I heard Edd and Uncle Rome. I'd been ready if I could have got into my darned old boots . . . See here, Dad, I'm gonna wear moccasins."

As we were sitting around the camp fire, eating breakfast, R. C. and Edd returned; and R. C. carried a turkey gobbler the very size and color of the one I had shot the night before. R. C.'s face wore the keen, pleased expression characteristic of it when he had just had some unusual and satisfying experience.

"Sure was great," he said, warming his hands at the fire. "We went up on the hill where you killed your gobbler last night. Got there just in the gray light of dawn. We were careful not to make any noise. Edd said if there were any more turkeys they would come down at daylight. So we waited until it was light enough to see. Edd had picked out a thicket of little pines for us to hide in, and in front of us was a glade with a big fallen tree lying across it. The woods was all gray and quiet. I don't know when I've felt so good. Then Edd got out his turkey bone and began to call. At once turkeys answered from all around in the trees. Next I heard a swish of wings, then a thump. Then more swishes. The turkeys were flying down from their roosts. It seemed to me there were a hundred of them! We could hear them pattering over the ground. Edd whis-

---

[6] Another wrangler in ZG's retinue.

pered: 'They're down. Now we got to do some real callin'.' I felt how tense, and cautious he was. When he called again, there was some little difference. I don't know what, unless it was his call sounded more like a real turkey. They answered. They were gathering in front of us and coming into the glade. Edd stopped calling. Then he whispered: 'Ready now. Look out!' . . . Sure I was looking all right. This was my first experience calling turkeys and I simply shook all over. Suddenly I saw a turkey head stick up over the log. Then!—up hopped a beautiful gobbler. He walked along the log, looked and peered, and stretched his neck. He sure was suspicious! Edd gave me a punch, which I took to be a warning to shoot quick. I wanted to watch the gobbler, and I wanted to see the others, too. But this was my chance. Quickly I rose and took a shot. A cloud of feathers puffed off him. He gave a great bounce, flapping his wings. I heard a roaring whirr of other turkeys. With my eye on my gobbler I seemed to see the air full of big, black, flying things. My gobbler came down, bounced up again, got going—when with the second barrel I knocked him cold. Then I stood there watching the flock whirring every way into the forest. Must have been thirty-five or forty of them, all gobblers! It was a great sight. And right here I declared myself—wild turkey is the game for me."

Romer listened to this narrative with mingled feelings of delight and despair. "Uncle Rome, wild turkey's the game for me, too . . . and by gosh, I'll fix those boots of mine!"

13

FISHING VIRGIN WATERS

Zane Grey was fascinated by giant fishes, and when the outdoor press began publishing reports of huge bluefin tuna being hooked off Nova Scotia, ZG lost some of his enthusiasm for their smaller cousins at Catalina. He initiated correspondence with a former British Army officer and remittance man living in Liverpool, Nova Scotia, who had fought between fifty and sixty of the giants, and succeeded in landing one, a 710-pounder. Their letter writing led to a long-distance friendship and finally to a visit by Zane Grey to Nova Scotia in the summer of 1924.

Of course, ZG didn't abandon swordfishing off Catalina and cross a sweltering continent merely to meet Captain Laurie Mitchell. He also went to fish. He therefore had two Nova Scotian skiffs—one 20 feet long, the other 18 feet—custom built and waiting for him, and he had one of his Florida boatmen, Robert King, build a 25-foot mullet-fishing launch in Fort Myers, Florida. ZG then packed the boat, King, and another Florida boatman, Sid Boerstler, north to Liverpool. Coming from California, ZG brought R. C., son Romer, and an Arizona cowboy, Jess R. Smith. The party must have startled some of Nova Scotia's older fishermen, but Zane Grey's presence and fresh ideas bore fruit. Several huge tuna were landed, including a new world's record.

In an affidavit dated August 22, 1924, and postmarked East Jordan, Nova Scotia, Captain Laurie D. Mitchell writes:

> This is to certify that I was one of the eight men who saw Mr. Zane Grey's 758-pound tuna fought, landed, and weighed. It broke my record tuna weight, 710 pounds, which I have held for some years.

Impressed by Mitchell's generosity, Zane Grey invited the Captain on ZG's next fishing trip—an expedition that grew directly out of Grey's stay in Nova Scotia. While visiting the docks one day in Liverpool, Grey saw a beautiful three-masted schooner and decided she'd be the perfect ship in which to sail to new fishing waters. He bought her for $17,000, put aboard his Florida boatmen, plus some Nova Scotian recruits, and asked Captain Mitchell to join them.

"Where are you going?" the Captain asked.

ZG hesitated just a moment. Perhaps he considered the approaching Canadian winter. "The South Seas," he replied.

Mitchell accepted, and the trip became the first of many expeditions to exotic lands the Captain was to make with his new friend and sponsor, Zane Grey. The story of their first cruise is told in *Tales of Fishing Virgin Seas*, published in 1925, from which the following excerpts are taken.

GWR

FISHING VIRGIN WATERS

A fisherman has many dreams, and from boyhood one of mine was to own a beautiful white ship with sails like wings, and to sail into lonely tropic seas.

Sometimes dreams, even those of a fisherman, come true. In August, 1924, I bought a big three-masted schooner that, of the many vessels along the south shore of Nova Scotia, appeared to be the finest, and the most wonderful bargain. She had been built near Lunenburg five years before, and was one of the stanchest ships sailing from that seafaring port. The four skippers who had been master of her were loud in praise of her seaworthiness and speed. She had to her credit a record run from New York to Halifax, and that without a cargo. She had been twice across the Atlantic. Fortunately for me she had never been used as a rumrunner, as had practically all the ships I inspected. I would not have taken a bootlegger's vessel as a gift.[1]

Her length was one hundred and ninety feet over all, with beam of thirty-five feet, and she drew eleven feet, six inches of water. I changed the name *Marshal Foch* to that of *Fisherman*, and left my boatman, Captain Sid Boerstler, in charge to make the extensive changes we had planned. The work employed a large force of men for over three months.

Before I left Nova Scotia I selected a sailing master for the ship, and did so perhaps without as much caution as should have been exercised. Captain Sid had the engineers come on from Avalon, and he chose the crew from the Nova Scotia herring fleet, and the first and second mates from the Gloucester swordfish schooner fishermen.

The *Fisherman* left Lunenburg, Nova Scotia, early in December, 1924, and soon ran into the terrific gales then raging the Atlantic. The run to Santiago, Cuba, took twelve days. The next run was to Jamaica. From here the master set a course for Colon, Panama, and on the second morning out, despite the protests of his officers, endeavored to run between some dangerous reefs and went

---

[1] ZG is not merely expressing appropriate feelings for the benefit of his Prohibition Era readers; he, in fact, never smoked nor drank liquor in his life.

aground. While trying to work the ship off, canoes full of half-savage natives living on the islands in that part of the Caribbean Sea came out to loot the ship. Fortunately she was backed off with apparently little damage. At that, Captain Sid said he had his rifle ready. At Colon the ship was put in dry dock, where it turned out she had stripped her keel. I was notified by cable to discharge the master and put Captain Sid in his place. Both the first and second officers were good navigators, a circumstance Captain Sid had wisely met. They reached Balboa, the Pacific end of the Panama Canal, on January 17th, two days before I sailed from Los Angeles on the S. S. *Manchuria*.

I found my ship *Fisherman* something to explore, and more satisfactory than I had dared hope. The after-cabin had been built to extend over the forward hatch, and it contained eight staterooms and salon. Galley and crew quarters were new. Below deck there was a combination salon and dining room, four bathrooms, a dark room for photography, tackle room, storerooms, a large refrigerator plant, half a dozen staterooms; and back of these the engine room, which had been Captain Sid's particular care and pride. It contained two Fairbanks-Morse driving engines, an engine to generate electricity for the lights and fans, another for the compressed air that forced water over the ship, an emergency engine to use in case of accident to the electric generator, and automatic pumps and devices. The tanks were all built of steel, and fitted into the sides of the vessel. There were tanks for five thousand gallons of crude oil and one for cylinder oil; tanks for five thousand gallons of water and twenty-five hundred gallons of gasoline. In the forecastle was an engine to hoist sails and anchors; there were lathes, tool bench, forge, and carpenter shop.

The *Fisherman* carried three launches, one swung over the stern, lashed fast, the other two in cradles on the main deck between the main and mizzen masts. These were launches upon which there had been spent much thought and work. They were intended to be an improvement upon the little boat we had sent to Nova Scotia and which had proved so successful with the giant tuna. They were thirty-two and twenty-five feet, respectively, round bottomed, long and slim, and solid as a rock. The keels had been built particularly heavy so that iron bolts holding rings would furnish means by which they could be swung up on deck of the *Fisherman*. Both boats had two New Jersey motors and two propellers, and various other features we had found good in different style models. This time with the California, Florida, and New Jersey features we combined several of Nova Scotia.

For catching fish and battling the monsters of tropic seas we had every kind of tackle that money could buy and ingenuity devise.

*

Next morning we were out of Panama Bay, headed southwest over the lonely lanes of the Pacific. We did not see a steamship or a sailboat. Before the sun set that night I began to appreciate the vast waste of the ocean.

Next day we had a strong breeze that ruffled up a white sea, and we went bowling along at eight knots, without the engines. It took hours for me to grow accustomed to the motion of a sailing ship. How slow and stately she rose and fell, and rolled! The great tall spars with their huge sails seemed to reach the skies. I walked the deck and sat here and there, always looking. It was a lonely sea. That night a wisp of a moon shone out of the dark blue. Later the stars appeared new or out of place for me.

On the following morning I was awakened by heavy sousing splashes outside my stateroom window. I looked out in time to see a big leathery blackfish leap high and plunge back. Then yells from R. C. and Romer called me hurriedly on deck. A school of blackfish had accompanied the ship for hours, so the mate said. They played around and ahead of us, sometimes leaping, and riding the swells close to the ship. They were not the balloon-nosed blackfish common to Catalina waters in summer. They were smaller fish,[2] and more agile, sometimes leaping fully thirty feet.

The sea grew calmer as the day advanced, until it was almost smooth. The water began to grow beautifully blue, and its temperature was 85 degrees. That amazed me. It was too warm to enjoy a shower bath.

The sunset was beyond words to describe. Golden fire, edged about by purple clouds! Then the tropic dusk fell quickly and the silver moon shone straight above the dark sails and the spear-tipped

---

[2] Not true fish, of course—probably pilot whales, a species of the family *Delphinidae* belonging to the mammalian order *Cetacea*.

[171]

spars. The motion of the ship was stately and beautiful, and the soft ripple of water, the creak of the booms, the flap of canvas, were strange to me. I stayed on deck for hours. It was something staggering to realize where I was, and to look out across the dim, pale, mysterious sea. The worries and troubles incident to this long-planned-for trip began to slough off my mind and to leave me with gradually mounting sensations of awe and wonder and joy. I was going down the grand old Pacific; and there was promise of adventure, beauty, discovery.

*

The day was clear and hot, with very little breeze. The sea was calm, yet great ground swells rolled in from the sea, making the ship keel over so far that it was hard to keep upright.

We ran around beyond Wreck Bay [at Cocos Island] to fish near the waterfall, and take pictures against that beautiful background. White cloud-ships sailed the azure sky, and cast moving shadows along the vivid green slopes.

R. C. and I began to troll with cut bait a little way offshore under the looming mountain. We forgot the beauty of the scene. The green-purple sea was alive with fish, and the air with birds, both of which made frantic efforts to steal the baits from our hooks. In truth the swift frigate birds were more adept at snatching our baits than the yellowtail, crevalle, turbot, and other fish, including sharks, were in getting them. But the birds were absolutely fearless, and the fish showed some little caution. I actually saw a frigate bird snatch my bait right out of the jaws of a fish. For a second both had hold of it.

Whenever I did hook a fish the birds soon soared upward again, to wheel along the green cliffs. Here the water was not more than thirty feet deep and the bottom could be seen distinctly. It was a veritable marine garden, with dark gray shadows of sharks moving over the opal-hued rocks. If I failed to haul in a fish very quickly he became fodder for the sharks.

After a time we grew sick of this carnage and ran west a mile, and out into the sea where a ragged rock stood up lonesomely, begirt by white wreaths of surf. Here the water was very deep, and a dark purple in hue. When we ran in close to the rock, within fifty feet, which was pretty risky, we could see the gold and amber rocks, and myriads of fish.

[172]

R. C. put a bait over. A swarm of blue-sided, purple-striped crevalle appeared, and among them gleamed the long beautifully slim and striped shapes of yellowtail. They appeared to run from fifteen pounds up, to thirty for the crevalle and twice that, perhaps, for the yellowtail. What a wonderful aquarium! R. C. hooked a fish at once, and the fight was on. We had decided light tackle was foolish and cruel, as we could not hope to land even one fish. With heavy tackle we hoped to work very hard and beat the sharks. R. C. brought a crevalle to the boat in record time. Behind it flashed a bronze-backed shark with black silver-tipped fins and tail, and he rushed so fast that he splashed water all over Bob, who had bent to lift R. C.'s crevalle out. The shark thumped the boat. He was about ten feet long and might have weighed three hundred pounds. He acted very much as if he had been cheated out of his dinner.

"Well, the peevish son-of-a-gun!" R. C. exclaimed. "What do you know about that?"

"I know I'm going to put the hickory on some of these sea hogs," I replied, grimly.

That was when we took to the tuna tackle. I trolled a bait about twenty feet. A school of beautiful turbot, velvet dark in color with blue stripes, churned the water back of my bait. Blue gleams, green flashes! Then a broad bar of bronze! Smash! A shark hit that bait as clean and hard as any tarpon or marlin I ever saw. He made a long run and cut my line.

"Doggone!" I complained. "That was one of my airplane leaders.[3] This is getting expensive."

The next hour was so full of fish that I could never tell actually what did happen. We had hold of some big crevalle, and at least one enormous yellowtail, perhaps seventy-five pounds. But the instant we hooked one, great swift gray and green shadows appeared out of obscurity. We never got a fish near the boat. Such angling got on my nerves. It was a marvelous sight to peer down into that exquisitely clear water and see fish as thickly laid as fence pickets, and the deeper down the larger they showed. All kinds of fish lived together down there. We saw yellowtail and amberjack swim among the sharks as if they were all friendly. But the instant we hooked a poor luckless fish he was set upon by these voracious monsters and

---

[3] Braided wire cable.

[173]

devoured. They fought like wolves. Whenever the blood of a fish discolored the water these sharks seemed to grow frantic. They appeared on all sides, as if by magic.

By and by we had sharks of all sizes swimming round under our boat. One appeared to be about twelve feet long or more, and big as a barrel. There were only two kinds, the yellow sharp-nosed species, and the bronze shark with black fins, silver edged. He was almost as grand as a swordfish.

While trying to get the big fellow to take a bait I hooked and whipped three of this bunch, the largest one being about two hundred and fifty pounds. It did not take me long to whip them, once I got a hook into their hideous jaws. The largest, however, did not get to my bait.

An interesting and gruesome sight was presented when Bob, after dismembering one I had caught, tumbled the bloody carcass back into the water. It sank. A cloud of blood spread like smoke. Then I watched a performance that beggared description. Sharks came thick upon the scene from everywhere. Some far down seemed as long as our boat. They massed around the carcass of their slain comrade, and a terrible battle ensued. Such swift action, such ferocity, such unparalleled instinct to kill and eat! But this was a tropic sea, with water at 85 degrees, where life is so intensely developed. Slowly that yellow clashing, churning mass of sharks faded into the green depths.

R. C. looked at me; I looked at him. We both had the same realization. Fishing for game fish, to which he and I had so long devoted ourselves, was almost an impossibility in these tropic seas. The fish were there, more abundant by far than our wildest dreams had pictured, but they could not be fought in a sportsmanlike way and landed.

Strife in this hot ocean was intensely magnified, in proportion to the enormous number of fish. Nature had developed them to be swifter, fiercer, stronger than fish in northern seas. It struck me strangely that there had not been any sign of fish feeding on the surface, such as was so familiar to our eyes in Florida, California, and Nova Scotia waters. Yet here there were a million times more fish, little and big! The upper stratum of water was hot, and all species of fish remained below it, until something unusual brought them up. Tremendous contending strife went on below the beautiful blue surface of the Pacific. It seemed appallingly deceitful. The beauty was there to see, but not the joy of life.

*

A few West Indian Negroes lived on Pedro Gonzales Island, and we lost no time in scraping acquaintance. The men whom we met were agreeable and willing. They eked out what seemed a miserable existence there, farming a little, and living mostly by the sea. They were pearl fishermen. This season was not good for the diving for pearls, the water being too cold. In March, when the rainy season began, the water grew warm, the nesting birds all left the islands, and the fish came in. It was then the Negroes dove for the oyster pearls. One of them, George Samuels by name, an intelligent, honest-appearing man, told me he knew of six divers having been devoured by sharks. Whenever sharks came near the diving ground the Negroes abandoned it as soon as possible. How strange so many people, including fishermen and sailors, have no patience with the theory that sharks kill men! It is not a theory. It is a terrible fact. These sharks were huge in size and could take a man in one bite. Samuels also informed me that the sharks were exceedingly fond of young pelicans. This was a great surprise to me. I had imagined ducks and gulls and other salt-water fowl wholly free of peril from sharks.

Samuels gave us interesting information about big fish. Swordfish were plentiful in these waters, and according to him they were very "cross" and often attacked a boat. He knew of boats having been rammed. Another fish, "three and four yards long, with a beak, and a fin all the way down its back," was also very aggressive. This species must be either a sailfish or a marlin swordfish. No specimen had ever been taken around the Perlas Islands. At this particular season Samuels assured us the big fish were out at sea.

He guided us, in three boats, round to the windward side of the island. It was very different and infinitely more fascinating, possessing all the colorful foliage, and in addition a wild, rugged, storm-beaten and reef-strung coast, and many times more birds. Countless thousands of these sea fowl dotted the sea and studded the sky. Coves indented the shore line; curved strips of golden beach afforded beautiful contrast to rugged gray cliffs with forest mantles

[175]

of rich green and pale pink. Suddenly my eye was startled by a perfectly scarlet tree, full-foliaged and sturdy, that stood up above its fellows of green and pink. Then I espied several more. They rose out of the jungle, almost too rare and lovely to be credible.

Among the reefs and rocky islands offshore Samuels directed us to fish. Captain Mitchell was the first angler to meet with luck. He had a battle with a worthy antagonist that turned out to be a big red snapper. Johnny,[4] who was in the boat with Captain Mitchell, hooked a fish that gave him all he could do to hold it, let alone drag it in. And at about the same time Romer, in my boat, hung on to another. R. C. with Chester,[5] in the third boat, were busy taking motion pictures of the diving, screaming, wheeling sea birds all around us. I left the fishing for the others. This wild coast was too wonderful to miss.

Romer caught his fish, a fine snapper upward of twenty pounds, while Johnny made little progress with his. We watched nearby until the long fight was over and Johnny had taken a fifty-pound amberjack.

We came at length to a place that, the moment my eyes fell upon it, struck me with the singular thrilling appreciation and realization that it must be recorded in my memory book for rare fishing spots. And the charm of living over my experience of them never dies.

The outermost island of this group was a long, low, black ledge absolutely covered with pelicans. Perhaps this rock island was half an acre in extent and rose twenty feet or so above the sea. It marked the end of the reef, and around it the current heaved with swelling power and resonant music. There was a tide-rip that set in from the open sea, and which met the offshore current just around the corner of this island. I could see amber and yellow rock running out some rods, under the green water. Over this submerged ledge the left-hand current poured to meet presently the incoming tide-rip. The result was a foaming maelstrom, and in the boiling water below shone a great crimson patch a hundred feet long and half as wide. Fish! Red snapper! There were thousands of them. And when we ran into that current the crimson patch disintegrated and appeared

---

[4] Johnny Shields, one of Romer's friends from Avalon, Catalina.

[5] Chester Wortley, a Hollywood cameraman.

to string out after our boats. The red snapper followed us. Each angler was playing a fish at the same time, while hundreds of great red-golden fish, hungry and fierce, almost charged the boats! They ran in weight from ten to forty, perhaps fifty pounds. They were gamy, hard-fighting fish, and when first out of the water seemed the most gorgeously flaming creatures I had ever seen come from the sea. While the boys were having such splendid sport I happily remembered that we could use some fresh food fish, and that the natives would also welcome some.

When the swell rolled in, slow and grand, and heaved up on the island to the very feet of the comical pelicans, it made a roar that shook my heart and made me turn fearfully. But it had only expended its force on the rock barrier and had foamed back to slide down that long golden ledge, like a millrace, and mingle with the white foam and green current so beautifully spotted with flashing red fish.

I saw one great amberjack, between seventy-five and a hundred pounds, strike at Romer's spoon and miss it. I saw a huge silver shield-shaped fish that must go nameless. These are myriads of small green-colored yellow-barred fish, very shy and swift. I caught a gleam of a golden dolphin.

Over our heads, while the anglers trolled and struck and pulled, and the boatmen handled wheels and levers, the screaming wild fowl sailed to and fro. The deep, low, melodious roar of the surge was never still. What fascinated me most, as I stood high on the bow, was the millrace pouring over the amber ledge to meet that incoming tide-rip. The two formed a corner apart from the tranquil sea beyond, a foaming, eddying, dimpling, rippling triangular pool full of red flashing shadows of fish.

It was a wonderful place and I had to force myself to leave it, though I had not laid my hand on a rod. Some privileges should be respected. And as we ran away from that white-wreathed and bird-haunted rock, I knew another marvelous fishing place had been added to my gallery of pictures. Such possessions as that are infinitely precious. In the years to come, when perhaps I cannot fish anymore—though imagination halts here—I shall have that gray pelican-dotted rock to recall, and the swell and thundering surge, and golden ledge and swarm of red fish. The places that we cannot return to, if they are enchanting, may not be best beloved, but they are most regretted.

*

On March 22nd, all morning the sea was a dark, glooming, heaving expanse, gray under the soft clouds. It was such delightful weather that I almost did not care whether or not I saw any fish. But I had two strikes, and missed both. I got a jump out of each fish, which Chester photographed, before they threw the hook.

That was the extent of my connection with sailfish this memorable day. To R. C. belonged the credit of making it memorable. I had Captain Sid run my boat close to R. C. all the morning; and that was how I happened to be witness to his extraordinary experience.

We saw a sailfish leap near Black Rock,[6] and we ran to troll our baits round the spot. R. C. raised this fish, hooked him, and got a high tumbling leap out of him before they parted.

An hour later, some miles out, we heard a yell that turned us quickly. A long ragged purple fin was shooting behind R. C.'s bait, which was perhaps fifty feet in the rear of the boat. R. C. duplicated my performance of missing three times, and he beat it with a fourth miss. The fifth time, however, with three hundred feet of line out, he finally hung this sailfish solidly. With all that line out, there was bound to be a circus. I ran round in my boat, camera in hands, while this game fish leaped thirty-three times. When he was brought to the boat we were all out of breath, especially Chester, who had photographed every leap.

Not a great while after that Sid's yell made me wheel in time to see another sailfish on R. C.'s line. My camera caught the third jump, and my eye began to appreciate the extraordinary length of this fish. We danced round R. C. in our little boats while his sailfish cleared the water some twenty-odd times. After he quit jumping, it appeared he took a good deal of hard punishment. We ran close to see the finish. The sailfish came up tail first, apparently entangled in the leader, something that R. C. and I abominate. I saw the broken leader standing out of its mouth. We were to learn presently that the swivel on the leader had cut into the tail, and stuck there,

---

[6] ZG's group is now in Zihuatanejo Bay, Guerrero, Mexico.

after the leader broke. I not only gasped at R. C.'s announcement of the facts of the case, but also, at the wonderful length and slim beauty of this sailfish. He was black with light bars and a purple fin.

But that was not all! In less than thirty minutes R. C. had another big fin behind his bait. He had to tease this fish to bite, and only hooked it after many slackings back of the bait.

White spurts of spray! A lean wagging, wild birdlike, fish shape in the air!

Suddenly close to R. C.'s boat there was an enormous splash, and a heavy sailfish, wiggling and waving, cleaved the air. At the same instant the sailfish on R. C.'s hook leaped splendidly, so close to our boat that Sid had to throw the wheel hard to port. What was our utter amazement then to see, in another leap near R. C.'s boat, that he had *two* sailfish on his line.

Just what was actually transpiring I could not understand; still I knew it was actual and incomparable.

I lost track of the sailfish on R. C.'s hook, and kept my eye keen for the one tangled up in his line. It leaped repeatedly, so quickly that I was never quite ready. My boat rocked and the excitement was intense. This sailfish quieted down quickly, as far as surface work was concerned, and went to plugging deep. However, in perhaps a quarter of an hour more, R. C. brought it to the boat. Bob[7] got hold of the tangled line, drew the fish close, and grasped its bill. There was some threshing, and flying spray.

The minds of all of us then reverted to the sailfish that had been on R. C.'s hook. It was gone. So was the leader.

We ran close and R. C. said: "Did you ever see the beat of that? Never again can I jolly myself with hard-luck stuff! . . . This blooming sailfish ran past the boat, right at my line, *and began to bite it.* Then the sailfish on my hook made a quick leap, twitching my line over the bill of this one. I saw it happen. He made a lunge, came out, turned over, and twisted up in my line."

Remarkable as were all the facts of this capture, it was my opinion that the fact of the sailfish biting at R. C.'s line was the most wonderful. We had seen the same act performed by sailfish in the Gulf Stream.

---

[7] Florida boatman, Bob King.

R. C.'s first fish measured nine feet and two inches, and weighed one hundred and nine pounds; the second, nine feet, ten inches long, and weighed one hundred and thirteen pounds; and the third fish, nine feet, three inches, overall, tipped the scales at one hundred and eighteen pounds. If the long slim specimen had been fat instead of lean he would have reached two hundred.

Fishermen, no matter what supreme good fortune befalls them, cannot be absolutely satisfied. It is their fundamental weakness.

An hour or more after R. C. captured his sailfish I stood up in the cockpit to ease my cramped legs. The sea was blue with a slow swell. I heard a solid splash, and looked down to note that some kind of a fish had smashed at the teaser. He did so, until it was not more than two feet from the stern, right in the boil of water from the propellers. I saw a flash. Then the teaser disappeared. I thought a sailfish had taken it. I reeled my bait in until the swivel on the leader was up to the tip of my rod. A moving dark color appeared under the bait. Suddenly it was taken by a powerful fish, almost without a splash. I let the line play out, then set the drag, and struck. I came up on a tremendous weight.

The fish broke water with a roar, and I was almost paralyzed by sight of an enormous marlin swordfish, the largest by far I had ever seen.

It leaped four times, and took line so swiftly I ordered Sid to speed up with both engines. The other boat followed us, and I saw that Chester was beside his camera. We were all excited.

The marlin shot out like the ricochet of a cannonball over the water. He hit on his side and skittered with terrific speed across the sea, parallel with our boat and about a hundred feet distant. His back was turned toward us, and I saw his immense girth, fully as large in the middle as a barrel. His length must have exceeded twelve feet. Right there I estimated his weight, too, and was positive it reached six hundred pounds. He went clear round us, in the air all the time, beating the water with his tail. The sound was amazing. When he went down it was in front of our bow and the bag of my line extended far astern.

But we straightened it out and got behind him to give chase. He started another exhibition of leaping, running his leaps up to thirty. I had more opportunity to study his size. He looked three feet deep at the shoulders. He had a short thick bill. His back was black, which probably identified him as a black marlin. Broad bars of purple shone from his silver sides. The breadth of his tail made me gasp.

When he sounded for good and the fight began I realized that I had hooked the most wonderful marlin I had ever seen on light tackle—medium rod and fifteen-thread line.[8] It made me sick. It was a terrible catastrophe. There was no hope to defeat such a monster on that rig. The feeling was so strong that it spoiled what otherwise might have been thrilling. But I had no more thrills. I was bitter at myself for such asininity. I complained aloud and to myself.

Nevertheless, I settled down to the hardest battle I ever had on light tackle and I did so because that was playing the game, and I might afford more opportunity for pictures.

I fought incessantly and unreservedly for over four hours, during which the fish took us miles out to sea, and never showed again. I labored under a double strain, that of intense sense of what power to put on the tackle, and that from the muscular exertion I put forth. My arms, and especially my hands, caused me excruciating pain.

Then I found that I could get the double line over the reel. It was staggering. I did it again and again. Thus hope to capture that magnificent fish was born in my breast, and despite all my judgment and common sense it grew all the time. I felt that something might happen. Most of the time we had to chase the fish. But gradually he tired. After four hours and a quarter he stayed close. We saw him often. When I got the double line over the reel and held on for all it would stand we could see him—a huge purple fish shape, appalling to the gaze. Every time my heart came to my throat.

Then I got the leader up to where Heisler[9] could grasp it. He pulled. Slowly the great marlin sheered away and upward, coming to the surface, rolling out, his black back, his barred side, and wonderful purple fins bright in the sunlight. I recognized the chance and yelled for Heisler to haul the fish closer. But Sid, in his excitement, countermanded my order. Heisler hesitated for the several seconds when the fish rolled there. We had time to get him close

---

[8] Approximately 45-pound test.

[9] One of the crew from Nova Scotia.

and gaff him. But the golden opportunity was lost. The fish sounded.

A dozen times after that I worked desperately, and got the leader to Heisler and then to Sid. But neither could hold the fish. Yet it was plain he was almost exhausted. This quarter of an hour expended my strength. Finally I strained every last ounce of muscle I had for the last time to get the leader up to Heisler's eager hands. Then the double line broke. I saw the gigantic purple fish shape fade and sink.

Whereupon I fell down in the cockpit and lay there, all in an instant utterly prostrated. When I recovered somewhat and sat up I found I was suffering in many ways—nausea, dizziness, excessive heat and labored breathing, stinging swollen hands and a terrible oppression in my breast. My arms were numb.

It was a long two hours' run back to the bay.

In the afternoon I watched Romer hook and fight a silver fish near the shore. It leaped high and often. I could see that he was having a hard time of it, but he got the fish, and when he returned, was wild with excitement about a new kind of fish and a terrific fighter. We classified the fish as the *gallo*, or rooster-fish.[10] It was indigo blue on the back, silver underneath, very admirably shaped, with long strong body, forked tail, and big head, neither sharp nor blunt. The dorsal fin somewhat resembled the comb of a rooster, at least enough to give it that name. But I thought the name a poor one for so beautiful and wonderful a fish. The natives told us that *gallo* reached a length of five feet, and that information was about the last straw for this bewildering day.

*

On our last morning at Zihuatanejo we spent several hours trolling a couple of miles off Morro Rocks. The sea was beautiful, and heaved in colossal swells that lifted us to the skies and then let us down, down, in the trough. These swells were so long and slow, however, that riding them was a delight. Sometimes R. C.'s boat, with its red umbrella, soared far above me on the crest of a mountain wave, and again it would sink out of my sight, not to reappear for long.

---

[10] This is one of the first references to roosterfish in angling literature.

Dolphin played on the surface around us, and swam along beside us, and sported before our bows. Mating turtles in couples scarce took the trouble of paddling out of our way. Boobies and terns swooped over us, with hoarse and plaintive cries. Here and there a sailfish slid out to go high and shine in the sun, then plump back with the sheeted splashes we have come to know so well.

Romer fished with me, and after eight days holding a rod through all the long hot hours without hooking a sailfish he was prone to discontent and the use of wild and whirling words.

We raised four sailfish between seven and eleven o'clock. Each and every one of them was a wary, swift, suspicious fish, and this, in conjunction with an inexplicable stupidity and slowness on my part, was accountable for the fact that the first, second, and third sailfish showed us a clean pair of heels, or fins, and got away.

But when the fourth, a big shadowy purple fish, sailed at my bait, and rushed away with it, I got my rod into Romer's hands before the first leap. That, when it came, showed the sailfish to more than average the others. He ran off a lot of line, making us chase him, leaping and tumbling all the time, giving Romer a good deal of trouble, as well as joy. The boy acquitted himself creditably, and in half an hour had the sailfish up to the boat, within reach of a gaff. But as we did not want to risk pulling the fish then, we let it run off on a free line, to be rewarded by several slow and final leaps, close to R. C.'s boat. Then the hook came out. Romer was tragic at first, but soon got over that, and was satisfied with the pictures and the fact that we could have gaffed the sailfish.

*

One morning as we ran out off the Cape[11] we espied a long dark line of leaping fish on the horizon. It was an inspiring sight, and we headed full speed toward it.

The sun was not more than an hour high, not overbright, and the sea was smooth, fresh, cool, with a glimmering sun track to the eastward. The fish looked black against the sky, mere dots at first, but gradually growing larger as we sped on. The even, regular motion of the line inclined me to the opinion that the fish were porpoises. They might well enough have been blackfish or dolphin.

---

[11] Now they're at Cabo San Lucas, Baja California Sur.

[183]

I stood up on deck and watched closely. When we were within two miles I decided the marching white and black wall was an enormous school of porpoises—by far the greatest number I had ever seen together. The school had fully a mile front. They were traveling northwest, and if they did not change their course or increase their speed, would run right into us.

There were thousands of porpoises, of all sizes, apparently, and half of them appeared to be in the air when the other half was down. Occasionally a huge black-and-silver porpoise would leap high above the others and fall back, making a high splash. They did not leap like dolphin. The latter have a spiral motion, and these porpoises made a forward dive on their regular leap. The rhythmic motion and the flash of black, gold, silver above the white spray made a singularly beautiful sight.

Then a few seconds later there suddenly came a sounding roar of water, quite distinct and different from anything I had ever heard. It was a sound of a multitude of sharp strong fish cutting water. The thousands of porpoises seemed actuated by a single idea. As one fish they leaped, faster and farther. Glittering, flying, disappearing, rank and file, whole columns like soldiers coming out together in a graceful parabolic curve, they thrilled the spectator as much as a great herd of caribou in the snow, or a rumbling herd of African buffalo crashing through the high grass.

We gave chase, and for several miles I could not see that we gained perceptibly. Our boats at top speed made about fourteen miles an hour. Gradually the porpoises slowed down, and we began to gain. Soon they were settling down to their regular gait and their playful water gymnastics. I saw porpoises leap twenty feet into the air, and farther than that on a straightaway forward dive. Usually it was a big fellow well in the lead that did the high leaping. A child could have seen that it was a playful jump.

What action, life, rhythm! How the black backs and silver sides flashed! The roar, while yet a quarter of a mile distant, was so loud that we had to shout to hear each other.

In a few moments we were surrounded by splashing, puffing, leaping gray bodies. Tiny baby porpoises leaped alongside huge plump ones, presumably their mothers. The roar of splitting water filled my ears. Sometimes a row of twenty would leap right in front of me. I would be looking down upon their glistening backs. The slapping of flat tails mingled with the roar.

They drew away from us, and sheering east, headed into the track of the sun. To our right came the other half of the school, soon to join those we had followed. Then we were afforded a scene of extraordinary beauty and life. The sunlight now was strong, the sea like a sheet of burnished silver, and the porpoises became black as ebony. What vigor, what strange freedom, what glittering incessant action! Above the white splashes showered millions of sparkling drops, bright as diamonds. Thus the maelstrom distanced us and swept on into the glare of the sun.

*

The sea was dark blue, calm, and hot under the noonday sun. I was trying to keep from falling into a doze when Sid roused me:

"They're yellin' for us. Somethin' doin'."

At the same time he opened both throttles. I got up to face forward, with zest and the old curious thrill. R. C.'s boat was perhaps a quarter of a mile from us. R. C. was standing in the stern and instead of a rod he held his camera. Next instant I espied a high sharp black fin not far behind his boat. He yelled and waved for us to come.

"It's a basking shark, like we saw the other day," shouted Sid.

I thought so, too, but when we got within a hundred feet and I had a close view of that enormous fish I changed my mind. Still, it had the shape of a shark tail.

"What do you know about this?" yelled R. C. "Some fish! He's bigger than the boat. Doesn't seem to mind us."

Sid ran my boat closer. I saw white spots on the huge fins. It was not a fin, but the lobe of an enormous tail. I saw a silvery green mass, long and wide, with projections. Then in another moment the green changed to a dark beautiful blue, dotted and streaked all over by a brilliant silver. The dorsal fin was low and stubby, the pectorals huge, apparently fan-shaped, almost resembling the wings of a colossal bat. The fish had a wide flat head, like that of a catfish, and he was close to sixty feet long. I recognized him as one of the rarest creatures in the sea—the *Rhineodon typus*, or whale shark. I had always wondered if I would ever have the luck to see one. Dr. Gudger of New York Natural History Museum had sent me his

[185]

fascinating booklet, containing all that was scientifically known about it.

In 1829, a Dr. Smith of South Africa harpooned a large shark of unusual appearance, and assisted by a number of men finally captured it. Dr. Smith named it *Rhineodon typus*. The skin was sent to the Paris Museum.

In 1850 Dr. Buist described a gigantic shark native to Karachi in northwest India, forty to sixty feet in length. This no doubt was the *Rhineodon typus*. In 1865 Dr. Gill described an enormous spotted shark of the Gulf of California, called by the natives "Tiburone ballenas," or "whale shark." A specimen about twenty feet long sent to the Smithsonian Institution.

In 1902 an eighteen-foot *Rhineodon* floated ashore at Ormond, Florida. From that year writers made frequent mention of the Rhineodon, and it became evident that the great shark had a wide distribution. Around the Seychelles Islands, north of Madagascar, this species was common. In the Indian Ocean it is called "chagrin."

In 1912, Captain Thompson, a local boatman of Miami, Florida, captured a *Rhineodon* thirty-eight feet long. This fish was exhibited as an unknown sea monster, and was finally identified by Dr. Gudger. In 1924, my boatman, Captain Newton Knowles, with whom I have fished for years around Long Key, Florida, harpooned and killed a *Rhineodon* somewhat smaller than Thompson's.

Knowles told me there were two sharks together, and that the one he harpooned was much the smaller. An interesting statement was that the bridge-tender on the viaduct below Knight's Key informed Knowles he saw a number of these huge sharks every June. They came across the shoals from Florida Bay, and were working out into the Gulf Stream. Knowles said the shallow water made the capture of his fish a comparatively easy matter.

I remembered all this in a flash, while I was afraid the fish would take fright and sound, but it paid not the slightest attention to either boat. We moved along very slowly, with the fish between us and a little ahead.

"What the devil is it?" called Bob King, leaning over the gunwale.

"*Rhineodon typus*," I replied, with the satisfaction of being able to classify what none of us had ever seen.

We had one enormous gaff, and thought to get that in the shark. So, tying it to a heavy rope, we ran almost up on top of the fish.

That afforded clearer view. The size was tremendous. From its dorsal fin to its head the length exceeded that of our boat, and it was wider than our beam. Lazily, with ponderous, slow weave of tail, it moved along, six or eight feet under the surface. Its dark blue color changed to a velvety brown, and the silver spots turned white. There was an exquisite purple along the edge of the broad pectoral fins. Altogether its colossal size, its singular beauty, its indifference to the boats, its suggestion of incredible power, made it the most wonderful fish I had ever seen.

"Good night!" called R. C., facetiously, as Heisler prepared to throw the gaff over the fish. "We'll pick up your remains in a minute."

I was standing on deck, beside Heisler, who wielded the heavy gaff. Up to that instant I had not thought of danger. The fish was harmless. But I realized that one blow from its tail could smash and sink us. What a strange cold prickle of my skin. I was all tight, breathless, staring, and as Heisler threw the gaff I suddenly sat down and held on to the hatch. Still I could see. The gaff sank over the side of the shark. Heisler pulled with all his might. It slipped off. The fish did not appear to be aware of our ambitious and evil intent. Bob was yelling, I know not what. R. C. and Chester had the cameras on us, and I was sure they were gleefully expecting to see us go flying into the air, with the debris of the boat. Heisler threw the gaff again. It would not stick. Twice more he failed to get a hold.

"Leave me have that gaff," yelled Bob. "I got six hundred feet of rope."

We gave it over to him. Then we ran alongside, just a little behind. R. C. took the wheel of his boat, while Chester stood up on deck, at the camera.

Bob got out on the bow with the gaff. He had put it on the pole, and evidently did not intend to throw it loose on the rope, as Heisler had done. Bob motioned for R. C. to run the boat to suit him, and they drew up close to that weaving black tail. Bob lunged to gaff that tail. He got hold, but not securely. I stood breathlessly, pointing my camera, expecting to see something most startling. The fish did not change speed or position. His tail stuck six feet above the water. Bob took more time, waiting till the tail was right under him. Then he gaffed it. I saw the iron go through.

Next instant the tail disappeared in a waterspout. Then followed a thunderous crash that stopped my heart. But it was a sound of churning water. The shark had not hit the boat. I had been frightened out of securing a remarkable picture. The turmoil at the bow subsided. Then I saw Bob paying out rope, and huge bulges and swirls ahead of the boat. R. C. put on full speed, and so did Sid. We chased the *Rhineodon typus*. It was not a long chase, yet I felt I had never experienced one in any way similar. I could hardly believe what I saw. And I was convinced it would be over quickly. But that fish came up before long and swam on the surface as before. The gaff hook stuck there in the high black tail. We ran alongside and hailed that crew with excitement equal to their own.

Bob got Chester to hold the rope, while he went below. I divined at once that he meant to rig up some kind of an iron. Bob had a reputation in Florida for catching huge rays, sharks, manatees, alligators; and I knew he was bent on outdoing the feats of Thompson and Knowles. Chester had been left a Herculean task. But he was valiant. And when he lost rope, R. C. would run the boat ahead so that he recovered it. Sometimes the black tail would slap against the bow.

Presently Bob appeared with some kind of a spear rigged from a file that had been bound on a gaff pole. He attached a rope to the spear. Then with businesslike promptness he plunged the thing into the fish. He shoved down on it with all his might. The shark made a roaring hole in the sea, almost large enough to swamp the boat. Then he sounded, R. C.'s boat ran to the edge of the maelstrom and stopped. Quickly the water smoothed out, hissing and seething. Both ropes went slipping over the gunwale until several hundred feet were gone. Gradually then the shark slowed until he stopped. With that Bob signaled us to come alongside.

"Go back to the ship an' fetch ropes, barrels, harpoons, guns," he called. "We'll ketch this Rhinoceros tappus!"

I tried to persuade Bob that we had no equipment equal to the job.

"Shore we can ketch him," he replied, with a keen flash of his blue eyes.

"But the water is deep," I protested. "Those few that have been caught were found in shallow water."

"This bird will come up," averred Bob. "We'll get a couple more holds, then when he comes to the surface break his back with bullets. Bring your heavy guns."

"But there's danger—leaving you here alone," I replied, hesitating.

"Give you my word we'll keep away from him," said Bob.

At that assurance I consented and we headed toward the bay at a speed never before equaled by the little boat. The stern sunk down level with the water and the bow stood high. How the engines roared! It was impossible for me not to revel in the whole proceeding, however preposterous it was.

Upon reaching the ship we created a great deal of excitement by our hurry, and what seemed mysterious conduct.

"Get Romer, Johnny, Captain Mitchell," I yelled, and rushed to my cabin for guns and shells, more films, a heavy coat, and a flashlight. Heisler was to get the other things Bob wanted. When I emerged Romer and Johnny met me, wild with excitement and curiosity.

"We're hooked on to a *Rhineodon typus* sixty feet long," I said, in answer to their queries.

"What on earth's that?" shouted Romer. "Where? How? When? Is it a sea serpent?"

"Get your coats. Hustle," was all the satisfaction I gave them.

In a few moments we were again aboard the little boat. Captain Mitchell forgot his hat. Everybody left on board cheered from the rail. We shot off to the eastward between two sheets of spray. Then I had time to tell the boys what a *Rhineodon typus* was and how we had come to get tangled up with one. If anything this information only served to make them wilder.

We expected any moment to see R. C.'s boat coming back. But we were mistaken, and when finally I sighted it, a dot on the horizon, it appeared to be stationary. They were still fast to the fish. We were 35 minutes getting back to R. C.'s boat. They waved and yelled a welcome. I believed R. C. looked relieved. The shark was on the surface, tail and dorsal out, and it was towing the boat.

We gaily hailed R. C. and his men, and running close put Captain Mitchell aboard his boat.

"Jab a couple of irons into this Rhinoceros," said Bob, and he instructed Heisler just where and how to hit the shark.

[189]

We ran ahead, alongside our quarry, now with dorsal out of the water. I picked up a rifle. With calmer eye I judged the *Rhineodon* to exceed fifty feet in length, at the most conservative estimate. But if he had shrunk a little in size he still retained his strange beauty. We drew close, with the bow at his head. Heisler lunged down with the pole. It was as if he had struck a rock. The iron came back bent. While Heisler hammered it straight, the huge fish swam on unconcernedly. Soon Heisler was ready for another try. We had grown somewhat hardened to the presence of the *Rhineodon* and therefore less fearful. We ran right alongside it, so that I had the most wonderful sight of this marine monster. Heisler repeated his harpooning performance, with all the violence of which he was capable. Crash went the mighty tail. We were deluged with water. Everybody on both boats appeared to be yelling hoarse instructions. I heard the impact of the fish against the boat. "Hold on!" yelled Heisler. I thought he meant for the boys to stay with him at the rope. But when the boat began to rise out of the water I knew differently. Then with the lifting motion came a tremendous scraping on the bottom of the boat. The shark had swerved under us. The boys fell with Heisler, all hanging to the rope. I came within an inch of going overboard, but managed desperately to cling to a ring-bolt until the launch righted. Then the threshing, thumping tail appeared above water on our port side. What a narrow escape! The iron pulled out, the rope slackened; and that enabled us to run from in front of Bob, who was swearing lustily. When we got in good position again, Bob called for Heisler to come aboard his launch. Still the *Rhineodon* stayed on the surface. Bob was soon ready, and we followed close beside his boat. The shark was moving faster now, though still high in the water. While Heisler, Chester, and Mitchell held the ropes, Bob plunged the iron deep back of the dorsal. Roar of beaten water, flooded bobbing boats, blinded fishermen! That was surely the most terrific moment in all my fishing experience. My blood ran cold, my heart seemed to freeze, then burst. I had one knee locked on the engine hatch, and my other leg hung overboard. The rifle had fallen, luckily to catch along the rail. When I extricated myself I was relieved to see that the *Rhineodon* had sounded, and was taking line with remarkable swiftness compared to his former movements. Bob had two ropes and Heisler had one. Chester and Mitchell were very busy getting out other ropes.

At about six hundred feet the shark stopped, and swam on at that depth, towing the boat for miles an hour. Presently, at Bob's word, the four men began to haul in on the ropes. It was a slow, laborsome task. The ropes had to be coiled in tubs as they came in. The afternoon was still and hot. Red-faced, and dripping sweat, the men worked incessantly. It took an hour to pull the *Rhineodon* to the surface. He towed the boat a couple of miles inshore, and then to the westward. Then he sounded. The men had a harder job to haul him up. They were wringing wet, and Bob, who had labored longest, was a sight to behold.

To make a long story short, they fought that fish until nearly sunset, during which it sounded five times, going deeper every time, the last being over twelve hundred feet.

When they got him up again Bob yelled to me, "Come aboard this boat with your big rifle." We ran up to them and I went aboard, together with Romer and Johnny. While I watched for a chance to shoot, the boys pitched in to help. But the *Rhineodon* did not come to the surface enough for me to disable it, even with the big fifty caliber.

Sunset came. Our quarry suddenly sounded. Different lengths of rope, tied together, marked how many feet he descended. Six hundred! Twelve hundred! Fifteen! Two of the tubs went overboard to sink. Heisler made a Herculean effort to save his tub, but it could not be done. As the end of the rope left his hands he kicked the tub overboard. Someone else had the white line to which the tub rope was attached.

Down, slower and slower, but surely inevitably down, the great shark sounded. The boys, with Chester and Mitchell, strove frantically to save the new rope from following the others. In vain! Foot by foot it slipped through their wet, grimy gloved hands. Bob had his rope under the cleat on the bow. He too was in desperate straits, but not vanquished.

Here I put aside my rifle and entered the fray. The spirit to conquer that brute was contagious. When the last few feet of new rope lay in sight, Chester hurriedly tied the last ball of white line to the end. Bob was panting and swearing. "More rope! . . . We'll lick him yet. Somebody get more rope. I'm losin' heah."

"Just tied on the last piece," replied Chester.

Then followed a short intense struggle to stop the fish, before he

[191]

had all the rope. Heisler nearly went overboard hanging on to his, but he lost it. That was the last I saw clearly, for my eyes grew red with the effort I was making. We knew indeed we were whipped, at least all of us knew except Bob. For when I gave the order to take a half hitch with the ropes and let the fish pull free of the irons Bob groaned loudly. Then he panted: "Got to—hand it—to old Rhinoceros."

14

THE DREADNAUGHT POOL

The 1910's and 1920's were active decades for the exchange of angling information among the different nations of Europe and America, particularly between the United States and Great Britain. Zane Grey read the British journals and corresponded with their contributors, comparing notes on tackle and techniques. The British, in turn, read ZG because he described wild places where rivers ran to the sea between fir trees three hundred feet high and where rainbow trout became new fish known as the steelhead.

But the British had a legend-land of their own—where you fished beneath volcanoes in crystal waters so cold that if they ever stopped flowing, they would turn to ice—or so natives said. Here, too, rainbow trout, first introduced from Oregon in 1883, flourished and averaged ten pounds apiece—and they didn't need to run to the sea to reach this size.

Many traveling anglers before ZG had commented on New Zealand's fabulous fishing, and American outdoor magazines were recommending trips there as early as 1900. Zane Grey read accounts of New Zealand anglers catching 200 pounds of trout a day, and he grew restless.

The stirrings he felt were a mingling of curiosity, doubt, and competitiveness. The articles he read only said that the trout had been "caught on fly." But what kind of fly? What pattern? And what about the size and fighting quality of these fish? If New Zealand and American tackle were comparable, then either New Zealand rainbows were deadheads compared to their American cousins or Americans were poorer anglers than their New Zealand colleagues. He just *had* to go see for himself.

An invitation from the government at Wellington was sent to America's foremost author and premier sportsman, and on December 30, 1925, he and Captain Mitchell were aboard the Royal Mail Packet *Makura* steaming through the Golden Gate on the first of many visits to lands far below the equator.

*

New Zealand overwhelmed Zane Grey—both the courtesy of its people and the abundance of its wildlife. First he fished salt water—and forever changed New Zealand angling habits by his success. ZG caught the first broadbill swordfish even taken in New Zealand waters, as well as a record 450-pound striped marlin and a record 111-pound yellowtail. He caught a 784-pound black marlin, his largest billfish to that time, and Captain Mitchell went one better with a black marlin 24 pounds shy of the magic thousand-pound mark, thereby establishing a new world record for all species of fish caught on rod and reel.[1]

---

[1] This record was something of an embarrassment to Mitchell. After all, it's never good politics for a second-in-command to show up the Chief. But this was a minor strain compared to the one which eventually shattered their friendship. By 1931 Mitchell's remittances were no longer coming from England, and ZG had taken him on as an employee, as well as companion, for $450 a month plus expenses. While in Tahiti a dispute arose over something Captain Mitchell was supposed to have said, and the argument ended with ZG's firing Mitchell. Mitchell sued for breach of contract under a French law which gave him, as a former employee, the possibility of attaching all ZG's Tahitian possessions—

[194]

Then came the trip inland to Lake Taupo and the Waihoro and Waihaha rivers. Here at last Zane Grey learned of the techniques that made possible the great catches of trout he'd heard of in the States:

I could not understand how one fisherman could catch a ton of rainbow trout in a month, fishing only the best of the days. After I learned about the heavy tackles and the spinners, and especially the night fishing with flies, I was a great deal better informed.

And relieved—for ZG felt American angling honor was fully vindicated in the lightweight *quality* of his tackle, even though his party would not likely equal the *quantity* of any of the New Zealand trout-catching records.

Here's the story of his favorite New Zealand pool from *Tales of the Angler's Eldorado* composed in Catalina from notes in May, 1926.

GWR

THE DREADNAUGHT POOL

Hoka, our genial Maori guide,[1] whom I had begun to like very well indeed, averred one morning that the trout had begun to run up the river. Both Captain Mitchell and I verified this. But to make these rainbows rise to an ordinary fly was something which would take the patience of a saint, not to mention a good degree of skill. The Captain finally did it, and so did I, but at the expense of infinite labor. We resorted to large Rogue River flies, mostly number four, and then to salmon flies number two, and finally we got to dressing our own flies. This was fun for me. Some of the outlandish lures I dressed up should have scared a rainbow trout out of his wits. Nevertheless they answered the purpose, and one of them, a fly so extraordinary that I could not make another like it,

---

which included the half-million dollar *Fisherman II*. A lengthy legal battle was avoided only after ZG agreed to keep Mitchell on as an employee—but at a reduced salary.

[1] Hoka Down was one of eleven men to whom *Tales of the Angler's Eldorado* was dedicated. ZG describes him as "Maori guide of the Tongariro, whose big heart shone in his ever-ready smile, and who instilled in me the fishing faith of his forefathers."

turned out to be a "killer." The only difficulty about large flies was that they were hard to cast. By diligent practice and strenuous effort, however, I at length achieved considerable distance, making an average of sixty feet, often seventy, and rarely even eighty feet. And when I saw that gaudy fly shoot out to such extreme distance I certainly felt exultant and vain.

We had word of another record catch of eleven fish at the mouth of the Tongariro. This was given us by Mr. Gilles, the nail driver, who stopped at our camp on an errand. He saw the fish and vouched for their weight; a fourteen-pound average, with largest weighing sixteen and one-half pounds. All caught on a fly at night! But no other information had been vouchsafed. I asked Mr. Gilles many questions about this remarkable catch, very few of which could he answer. He was himself a fisherman of long experience, and it was his opinion the trout were caught by the fisherman letting out a large fly or spinner a hundred or two hundred feet from the boat, and then drawing it back by hand until he had a strike. I shared this opinion.

By climbing to the bluff above the river, when the sun was high, we could see the big trout lying deep in the pale-green crystal water; ten-, twelve- and fifteen-pound rainbows, and an occasional brown trout, huge and dark, upward to twenty pounds. This was a terrible, although glad, experience for Captain Mitchell and me. To sight such wonderful fish and not get a rise from them! Alma Baker[2] took it more philosophically, and considered the privilege of seeing them quite enough. Cap and I, however, wanted to feel one of those warriors at the end of a line. In the pool below camp we tried at sunrise, through the day, at sunset and then after dark. Fly-fishing at night was an awful experience for me. I got snarled in the line. I continually hit my rod with my fly, and half the time it spun round the rod, entailing most patient labor. Moreover, I was standing through the chill of night in ice-cold water. Finally I whipped the big hook in the back of my coat. That gave me sufficient excuse to go back to camp. What joy the camp fire! Captain Mitchell returned presently, wet and shivering. He did not complain of the

---

[2] A well-known British angler, who helped make the arrangements for ZG's trip to New Zealand.

cold water, but he lamented a great deal over the loss of his best fly. He had snagged it on a rock and nearly drowned himself trying to rescue it.

*

Next morning while the rest of the party were at breakfast I stole down the bank and made a cast into the swirling waters. I made another, and when I tried to retrieve the line, lo! it was fast to something that moved. I struck, and I hooked a trout. For fear he might rush out into the swift current I held him harder than I would otherwise, and thus tired him out before he could take advantage of me. When I was sure of him, a fine seven-pounder rolling in the clear water, I yelled loudly. The whole breakfast contingent rushed pell-mell to the bank, and to say they were amazed would be putting it mildly.

That was a prelude to a strenuous day for all of us. Baker elected to fish the pools below camp, where he did not have to wade. Hoka took Captain Mitchell and me, accompanied by Morton,[3] up the river.

"Only a little way, about a mile," said Hoka, with the smile that always robbed me of a retort. It was a long, long mile before we even got off the road; and even a short mile in heavy waders, three pairs of woolen socks, and iron-studded clumsy wading boots was always quite sufficient. I can pack a gun and walk light-footed far up and down canyons, but wading paraphernalia burdens me down.

Hoka led us into a fern trail, one of those exasperating trails where the ferns hook your fishing line and leader and will not let go. Then he arrived at a precipitous bluff under which an unseen river roared musically. It was not the Tongariro. The Captain naturally wanted to know how we got down.

"We go right over," replied Hoka, and with that remark he disappeared. We heard crashings in the ferns. Next I went "right over." I held my rods high above my head and trusted my seven-league eight-ton boots to the depths. When at last I arrived at a comparative level, I awaited to see what would happen to my comrades. I knew there would be a fall all right. Soon I heard what might have been a rhinoceros plowing down the ferny cliff; but it

---

[3] A New Zealand photographer.

was only Captain Mitchell who arrived beside me hot, furious, forgetful of all save his precious pipe, which a tenacious fern still clung to. The real fun, however, came with Morton. Our genial cinematographer was burdened with cameras, also a pair of iron-hoofed boots that I had insisted he wear. I have no idea how Morton got down, unless he fell all the way. We heard him talking vociferously to the obstructing ferns. At last he arrived, red of face, and grimly hanging on to his load.

Hoka was waiting for us with his disarming smile.

"You came down easy," he said. "But this panel over the river will be hard."

"Huh! What's a panel?" I asked. "Hoka, I've begun to have suspicions about you."

He soon showed us the panel. It was no less than a rickety pole bridge, swung on wires attached to branches of trees, and spanning a dark rushing little river that must have been beautiful at some other time. Just now it seemed treacherous. How the current swept on, down, rushing, swirling, gurgling under the dark overreaching trees!

Hoka went first. He weighed seventeen stone, which in our language is over two hundred pounds; and I felt that if the panel held him, it would certainly hold me. He crossed safely and quite quickly for so large a man; I went next. Such places rouse a combative spirit in me, and that made the crossing something different. Nevertheless when I was right in the middle, where the thin crooked poles bent under my heavy boots, I gazed down into the murky water with grim assurance of what might happen if the poles broke. I got across, proving how unnecessary the stirring of my imagination often is.

Once safe on the bank I was tempted to yell something facetious to Morton and Mitchell, but I desisted, for this was hardly the place for humor. They reached our side without mishap, and then again we beat into the jungle of ferns and *ti* trees. It was hard going, but soon I heard the mellow roar of the Tongariro, and with that growing louder and louder I found less concern about difficulties. We came at length into an open thicket of *ti* brush, bisected by shallow waterways and dry sandy spaces, through which we emerged to the wide boulder-strewn river bank.

"This pool here is called Dreadnaught," said Hoka, pointing to a huge steep bluff strikingly like the shape of a dismantled man-of-war. It stood up all alone. The surrounding banks were low and green. After one glance, I gave my attention to picking my steps among the boulders, while Hoka kept on talking. "My people once fought battles here. They had a *pa* on top of this bluff. I'll show you graves that are wearing away. The skulls roll down into the river. My people, the Maoris, were great fighters. They stood up face to face, and gave blow for blow, like men."

At last I found a seat on a log, laid aside my rods, camera and coat, and looked about. The Tongariro ran sweeping down in the S shape, between bright soft green banks; a white swift river, with ample green water showing, and rapids enough to thrill one at the idea of shooting them in a Rogue River boat. The end of the last rapids piled against the hull of the Dreadnaught bluff. A little rippling channel ran around to the right, out of sight, but it must soon have stopped, for the high embankment was certainly not an island.

I began to grow more interested. The bluff had a bold bare face, composed of three strata; the lowest a dark lava studded thickly with boulders, the next and middle one a deep band of almost golden sand, and the topmost a gray layer of pumice in the top of which I saw the empty graves of the bygone Maoris.

The current deflected from the base of the bluff, sheered away and swept down through the pool, farther and farther out, until it divided into three currents running into three channels.

The lower and larger end of that pool fascinated me. Under the opposite bank the water looked deep and dark. A few amber-colored rocks showed at the closer edge of the current. It shoaled toward the wide part, with here and there a golden boulder gleaming far under the water. What a wonderful pool! It dawned on me suddenly. The right channel, or one farthest over, ran glidingly under the curving bank, and disappeared. I could not see the level below. Points of rock and bars of boulders jutted out from a luxuriantly foliaged island. The middle channel was a slow wide shallow ripple, running far down. A low bare gravel bar rose to the left, and stretched to where the third channel roared and thundered in a deep curving rapid. Here most of the river rushed on, a deep narrow chute, dropping one foot in every three feet, for over a hundred yards.

I had to walk to the head of the rapid to see where the water ran,

[199]

heaping up waves higher and higher, down the narrow channel that curved away under another high wooded bluff. Most of the water of the pool glided into the channel, growing swift as it entered. Green crystal water! I could see the bottom as plainly as if the depth had been ten inches instead of ten feet. How marvelously clear and beautiful! Round rocks of amber and gold and mossy green lay imbedded closely, like a colorful tiling.

My gaze then wandered back over the head of the pool, where the Captain stood hip deep, casting far across into the current. And it wandered on down to the center, and then to the lower and wide part of the pool. What a magnificent place to fish! I made up swiftly for my laggard appreciation. I could see now how such a pool might reward a skillful far-casting angler, when the rainbows were running. After a long climb up rapids, what a pool to rest in! There might even be a trout resting there then. So I picked up my rod and strode down to the river.

A clean sand bar ran out thirty yards or more, shelving into deep green water. Here a gliding swirling current moved off to the center of the pool, and turned toward the glancing incline at the head of the narrow rapid. The second and heavier current worked farther across. By wading to the limit I imagined I might cast to its edge. I meant to go leisurely and try the closer current first. It was my kind of place. It kept growing upon me. I waded in to my knees, and cast half across this nearer current. My big fly sank and glided on. I followed it with my eye, and then gave it a slight jerky movement. Darker it became, and passed on out of my sight, where the light on the water made it impossible for me to see. I had scarcely forty feet of line out. It straightened below me, and then I whipped it back and cast again, taking a step or two farther on the sand bar.

My line curved and straightened. Mechanically I pulled a yard or so off my reel, then drew perhaps twice as much back, holding it in loops in my left hand. Then I cast again, letting all the loose line go. It swept out, unrolled and alighted straight, with the fly striking gently. Was that not a fine cast? I felt gratified. "Pretty poor, I don't think," I soliloquized, and stole a glance upriver to see if the Captain had observed my beautiful cast. He was so engrossed in his own angling, he did not know I was on the river. Then I looked quickly back at my fly.

[200]

It sank just at the edge of the light place on the water. I lost sight of it, but knew about where it floated. Suddenly right where I was looking on this glancing sunlit pool came a deep angry swirl. Simultaneously with this came a swift powerful pull, which ripped the line out of my left hand, and then jerked my rod down straight.

"Zee-eee!" shrieked my reel.

Then the water burst white, and a huge trout leaped in spasmodic action. He shot up, curved and black, his great jaws wide and sharp. I saw his spread tail quivering. Down he thumped, making splash and spray.

Then I seemed to do many things at once. I drew my rod up, despite the strain upon it; I backed toward the shore; I reeled frantically, for the trout ran upstream; I yelled for Morton and then for Captain Mitchell.

"Doc, he's a wolloper!" yelled the Captain.

"Oh, biggest trout I ever saw!" I returned wildly.

Once out of the water I ran up the beach toward Captain Mitchell, who was wading to meet me. I got even with my fish, and regained all but part of the bag in my line. What a weight! I could scarcely hold the six-ounce rod erect. The tip bent far over, and wagged like a buggy whip.

"Look out when he turns!" called Mitchell.

When the fish struck the swift current, he leaped right before me. I saw him with vivid distinctness—the largest trout that I ever saw on my line—a dark bronze-backed and rose-sided male, infused with the ferocity and strength of self-preservation; black-spotted, big-finned, hook-nosed. I heard the heavy shuffle as he shook himself. Then he tumbled back.

"Now!" yelled Captain Mitchell, right behind me.

I knew. I was ready. The rainbow turned. Off like an arrow!

"Zee! Zee! Zee!" he took a hundred yards of line.

"Oh Morton! Morton! . . . *Camera!*" I shouted hoarsely, with every nerve in my body at supreme strain. What would his next jump be? After that run! I was all aquiver. He was as big as my big black marlin. My tight line swept up to the surface as I have seen it sweep with so many fish. "He's coming out!" I yelled for Morton's benefit.

Then out he came magnificently. Straight up six feet, eight feet and over, a regular salmon leap he made, gleaming beautifully in the sun. What a picture! If only Morton got him with the camera I would not mind losing him, as surely I must lose him. Down he splashed. "Zee!" whizzed my line.

I heard Morton running over the boulders, and turned to see him making toward his camera. He had not been ready. What an incomparable opportunity lost! I always missed the greatest pictures! My impatience and disappointment vented themselves upon poor Morton, who looked as if he felt as badly as I. Then a hard jerk on my rod turned my gaze frantically back to the pool, just in time to see the great rainbow go down from another grand leap. With that he sheered round to the left, into the center of the wide swirl. I strode rapidly down the beach and into the water, winding my reel as fast as possible. How hard to hold that tip up and yet to recover line! My left arm ached, my right hand shook; for that matter, my legs shook also. I was hot and cold by turns. My throat seemed as tight as my line. Dry-mouthed, clogged in my lungs, with breast heaving, I strained every faculty to do what was right. Whoever said a trout could not stir an angler as greatly as a whale?

One sweep he made put my heart in my throat. It was toward the incline into the rapids. If he started down! But he ended with a leap, head upstream, and when he soused back he took another run, closer inshore toward me. Here I had to reel like a human windlass.

He was too fast; he got slack line, and to my dismay and panic he jumped on that slack line. My mind whirled, and the climax of my emotions hung upon that moment. Suddenly, my line jerked tight again. The hook had held. He was fairly close at hand, in good position, head upriver, and tiring. I waded out on the beach; and though he chugged and tugged and bored he never again got the line out over fifty feet. Sooner or later—it seemed both only a few moments and a long while—I worked him in over the sand bar, where in the crystal water I saw every move of his rose-red body. How I reveled in his beauty! Many times he stuck out his open jaws, cruel beaks, and gaped and snapped and gasped.

At length I slid him out upon the sand. I never looked down upon such a magnificent game fish. No artist could have caught with his brush the shining flecked bronze, the deep red flush from jaw to tail, the amber and pearl. He would have to have been content to catch the grand graceful contour of body, and the wolf-jawed head, the lines of fins and tail.

He weighed 11½ pounds. I tied him on a string, as I liked to do with little fish when I was a boy, and watched him recover and swim about in the clear water.

Meanwhile Morton stood there using language because he had failed to photograph those first leaps, and Captain Mitchell went back to his fishing. Presently a shout from him drew our attention. He had broken his rod on the cast.

The Captain waded out and approached us, holding the two pieces for my inspection. The middle ferrule had broken squarely, and the Captain anathematized the rod in several languages.

"But, Cap, you've had it for years. Even the best of rods can't last forever," I protested. "We'll take turn about using mine."

He would not hear of this, so I returned to fishing, with my three companions all on the *qui vive*. I thought to try the same water, and to save that wonderful space out there between the currents for the last.

*

As if by magic of nature the Dreadnaught Pool had been transformed. The something that was evermore about to happen to me in my fishing had happened there. There! The beautiful pool glimmered, shone, ran swiftly on, magnified in my sight. The sun was westering. It had lost its heat and glare. A shadow lay under the bluff. Only at the lower end did the sunlight make a light on the water, and it had changed. No longer hard to look upon!

I waded in up to my knees and began to cast with short line, gradually lengthening it, but now not leisurely, contentedly, dreamingly! My nerves were as keen as the edge of a blade. Alert, quick, restrained, with all latent powers ready for instant demand, I watched my line sweep out and unroll, my leader straighten, and the big dark fly alight. What singularly pleasant sensations attended the whole procedure!

I knew I would raise another rainbow trout. That was the urge, wherefore the pool held more thrill and delight and stir for me. On the fifth cast, when the line in its sweep downstream had reached its limit, I had a strong vibrating strike. Like the first trout, this one hooked himself; and on his run he showed in a fine jump—a fish scarcely half as large as my first one. He ran out of the best fishing

[203]

water, and eventually came over the sand bar, where I soon landed him, a white and rose fish, plump and solid, in the very best condition.

"Fresh-run trout," said Hoka. "They've just come up from the lake."

"By gad! Then the run is on," returned Captain Mitchell with satisfaction.

This second fish weighed 5¾ pounds. He surely had all the strength of an eight-pound steelhead in his compact colorful body. I was beginning to understand what the ice water of the Tongariro meant to the health and spirit of a rainbow.

"Cap, make a few casts with my rod while I rest and hug the fire," I said. "That water has ice beaten a mile."

"Not on your life," replied the Captain warmly. "I've a hunch it's your day. Wade in; every moment now is precious."

So I found myself out again on the sand bar, casting and recasting, gradually wading out until I was over my hips and could go no farther. At that I drew my breath sharply when I looked down. How deceiving that water! Another step would have carried me over my head. If the bottom had not been sandy I would not have dared trust myself there, for the edge of the current just caught me and tried to move me off my balance; but I was not to be caught unawares.

Apparently without effort, I cast my fly exactly where I wanted to. The current hungrily seized it, and as it floated out of sight I gave my rod a gentle motion. Halfway between the cast and where the line would have straightened below me, a rainbow gave a heavy and irresistible lunge. It was a strike that outdid my first. It almost unbalanced me. It dragged hard on the line I clutched in my left hand. I was as quick as the fish and let go just as he hooked himself. Then followed a run the like of which I did not deem possible for any fish short of a salmon or a marlin. He took all my line except a quarter of an inch left on the spool. That brought him to the shallow water way across where the right-hand channel went down. He did not want that. Luckily for me, he turned to the left and rounded the lower edge of the pool. Here I got line back. Next he rushed across toward the head of the rapid. I could do nothing but hold on and pray.

[204]

Twenty yards above the smooth glancing incline he sprang aloft in so prodigious a leap that my usual shout froze in my throat. Like a deer, in long bounds he covered the water. The last rays of the setting sun flashed on this fish, showing it to be heavy and round and deep, of a wonderful pearly white tinted with pink. It had a small head which resembled that of a salmon. I had hooked a big female rainbow, fresh run from Taupo, and if I had not known before that I had a battle on my hands I knew it on sight of the fish.

Fearing the swift water at the head of the rapid, I turned and plunged pell-mell out to the beach and along it, holding my rod up as high as I could. I did not save any line, but I did not lose any, either. I ran clear to the end of the sandy beach where it verged on the boulders. A few paces farther on roared the river.

Then with a throbbing heart and indescribable feelings I faced the pool. There were 125 yards of line out. The trout hung just above the rapid and bored deep, to come up and thump on the surface. Inch by inch I lost line. She had her head upstream, but the current was drawing her toward the incline. I became desperate. Once over that fall she would escape. The old situation presented itself—break the fish off or hold it. Inch by inch she tugged the line off my reel. With all that line off and most of it out of the water in plain sight, tight as a banjo string, I appeared to be at an overwhelming disadvantage. So I grasped the line in my left hand and held it. My six-ounce rod bowed and bent, then straightened and pointed. I felt its quivering vibration and I heard the slight singing of the tight line.

The first few seconds were almost unendurable. They seemed an age. When would line or leader give way or the hook tear out? But nothing broke. I could hold the wonderful trout. Then as the moments passed I lost that tense agony of apprehension. I gained confidence. Unless the fish wheeled to race for the fall I would win. The chances were against such a move. Her head was up current, held by that rigid line. Soon the tremendous strain told. The rainbow came up, swirled and pounded and threshed on the surface. There was a time then when all old fears returned and augmented; but just as I was about to despair, the tension on rod and line relaxed. The trout swirled under and made upstream. This move I signaled with a

[205]

shout, which was certainly echoed by my comrades, all lined up behind me, excited and gay and admonishing.

I walked down the beach, winding my reel fast, yet keeping the line taut. Thus I advanced fully a hundred yards. When I felt the enameled silk come to my fingers, to slip on the reel, I gave another shout. Then again I backed up the beach, pulling the trout, though not too hard. At last she got into the slack shallow water over the wide sand bar.

The fish made short hard runs out into the deeper water, yet each run I stopped eventually. Then they gave place to the thumping on the surface, the swirling breaks, the churning rolls, and the bulldog tug, tug, tug. The fight had long surpassed any I had ever had with a small fish. So strong and unconquerable was this rainbow that I was fully a quarter of an hour working her into the shallower part of the bar. Every time the deep silvery side flashed, I almost had heart failure. This fish would go heavier than the 11½-pound male. I had long felt that in the line, in the rod; and now I saw it. There was a remarkable zest in this part of the contest.

The little rod wore tenaciously on the rainbow, growing stronger, bending less, drawing easier. After what seemed an interminable period there in this foot-deep water, the battle ended abruptly with the bend of the rod drawing the fish head-on to the wet sand.

Certainly I had never seen anything so beautiful in color, so magnificent in contour. It was mother-of-pearl tinged with exquisite pink. The dots were scarcely discernible, and the fullness of swelling graceful curve seemed to outdo nature itself. How the small thoroughbred salmon-like head contrasted with the huge iron-jawed fierce-eyed head of the male I had caught first! It was strange to see the broader tail of the female, the thicker mass of muscled body, the larger fins. Nature had endowed this progenitor of the species, at least for the spawning season, with greater strength, speed, endurance, spirit and life.

"Eleven pounds, three-quarters!" presently sang out the Captain. "Some rainbow, old man. Get in there and grab another."

"Won't you have a try with my rod?" I replied. "I'm darn near froze to death. Besides I want to put this one on the string with the others."

He was obdurate, so I went back into the water; and before I knew what was happening, almost, I had fastened to another trout. It did not have the great dragging weight of the other two, but it gave me a deep boring fight and deceived me utterly as to size. When landed, this, my fourth trout, weighed 6¾, another female, fresh run from the lake, and a fine rainbow in hue.

"Make it five, Doc. This is your day. Anything can happen now. Get out your line," declared Mitchell, glowing of face.

The sun had set as I waded in again. A shimmering ethereal light moved over the pool. The reflection of the huge bluff resembled a battleship more than the bluff itself. Clear and black-purple rose the mountain range, and golden clouds grew more deeply gold. The river roared above and below, deep-toned and full of melody. A cold breeze drifted down from upstream.

I cast over all the water I had previously covered without raising a fish. Farther out and down I saw trout rising, curling dark tails out of the gold gleam on the water. I waded a foot farther than ever and made a cast, another, recovered line, and then spent all the strength I had left in a cast that covered the current leading to the rising trout. I achieved it. The fly disappeared, my line glided on and on, suddenly to stretch like a whipcord and go zipping out of my left hand. Fast and hard! What a wonderful thrill ran up and down my back, all over me!

"Ho! Ho! . . . Boys, I've hung another!" I bawled out. "Say, but he's taking line! . . . Oh, look at him jump! . . . Two! . . . Three . . . Four, by gosh! . . . Oh, Morton, if we only had some sunlight! What a flying leap! . . . *Five!*"

The last jump was splendid, with a high parabolic curve, and a slick cutting back into the water. This rainbow, too, was big, fast, strong and fierce. But the fish did everything that should not have been done and I did everything right. Fisherman's luck! Beached and weighed before my cheering companions; 9½ pounds; another silvery, rosy female rainbow, thick and deep and wide!

Then I forced Captain Mitchell to take my rod, which he would not do until I pleaded I was frozen. But what did I care for cold? I made the day a perfect one by relinquishing my rod when I ached to wade in and try again.

The day, however, had begun badly for Captain Mitchell and so

[207]

it ended. He could not raise a trout. Then we left the rousing fire
and strode off over the boulders into the cool gathering twilight.
Hoka carried two of my trout, Captain two, and Morton one. We
threaded the *ti*-tree thicket and the jungle of ferns, and crossed the
perilous panel in the dark, as if it had been a broad and safe bridge.

My comrades talked volubly on the way back to camp, but I was
silent. I did not feel my heavy wet waders or my leaden boots. The
afterglow of sunset lingered in the west, faint gold and red over the
bold black range. I heard a late bird sing. The roar of the river
floated up at intervals. Tongariro! What a strange beautiful high-
sounding name! It suited the noble river and the mountain from
which it sprang.

15

COLORADO TRAILS

Fortunately for mankind, fraternal rivalry is usually less bloody than Cain and Abel's, though it's at least that old. Despite Zane Grey's affection and almost paternal concern for his younger brother, R. C., ZG relished every opportunity of one-upping "Reddy." From his standpoint, R. C. rather enjoyed this give-and-take and even managed to give as much as take.

This rivalry is one of the themes of "Colorado Trails," first serialized in *Outdoor Life* starting March, 1918, and later made a part of *Tales of Lonely Trails* (1922). But there is another, more important, theme in the following selections: ZG's disenchantment with the killing part of hunting. Most non-hunters will be bewildered by this distinction: Aren't killing and hunting the same?" they may ask. Not necessarily. ZG's passion for the chase, his pleasure in the horses and hounds, and his love of the camp fire at night—all part of hunting—are clearly distinguishable from his dislike for the execution of cornered game.

When Arizona enacted game restrictions for the first time in 1930, the state refused ZG special permission to hunt out of season even though he was Arizona's most famous citizen. ZG felt "grossly insulted." He pointed out that "in twelve years my whole bag of game has been five bears, three bucks and a few turkeys. I have written fifteen novels with Arizona background . . . [and] my many trips all over the state have cost me $100,000. So in every way I have not been an undesirable visitor." While ZG's suggestion that Arizona be willing to trade an out-of-season bearskin for more good publicity seems unsavory, we should consider the possibility that he generated the entire conflict as a means of cutting himself off from his killing past. ZG must have known that Arizona would not embarrass itself with a special license—especially after all the *bad* publicity he'd created on the subject. And so that year, he abandoned his lodge in the Tonto Basin and never hunted again.

This decision would have come as no surprise to anyone remembering a difficult trip west of Denver in 1917 and later converted to "Colorado Trails."

GWR

COLORADO TRAILS

Riding and tramping trails would lose half their charm if the motive were only to hunt and to fish. It seems fair to warn the reader who longs to embark upon a bloody game hunt or a chronicle of fishing records that this is not that kind of story. But it will be one for those who love horses and dogs, the long winding dim trails, the wild flowers and the dark still woods, the fragrance of spruce and the smell of camp fire smoke. And as well for those who love to angle in brown lakes or rushing brooks or chase after the baying hounds or stalk the stag on his lonely heights.

We left Denver on August 22nd over the Moffet road and had a long wonderful ride through the mountains. The Rockies have a sweep, a limitless sweep, majestic and grand. For many miles we crossed no streams, and climbed and wound up barren slopes. Once across the divide, however, we descended into a country of black forests and green valleys. Yampa, a little hamlet with a past prosperity, lay in the wide valley of the Bear River. It was picturesque but idle, and a better name for it would have been Sleepy Hollow. The main and only street was very wide and dusty, bordered by old boardwalks and vacant stores. It seemed a deserted street of a deserted village. Teague, the guide, lived there. He assured me it was not quite as lively a place as in the early days when it was a stage center for an old and rich mining section. We stayed there at the one hotel for a whole day, most of which I spent sitting on the boardwalk. Whenever I chanced to look down the wide street it seemed always the same—deserted. But Yampa had the charm of being old and forgotten, and for that reason I would like to live there a while.

On August 23rd we started in two buckboards for the foothills, some fifteen miles westward, where Teague's men were to meet us with saddle and pack horses. We arrived at the edge of the foothills about noon. It appeared to be the gateway of a valley, with aspen groves and ragged jack-pines on the slopes, and a stream running down. Our driver called it the Stillwater. That struck me as strange, for the stream was in a great hurry. R. C. spied trout in it, and schools of darkish, mullet-like fish which we were informed were grayling. We wished for our tackle then and for time to fish.

Teague's man, a young fellow called Virgil, met us here. He did not resemble the ancient Virgil in the least, but he did look as if he had walked right out of one of my romances of wild riders. So I took a liking to him at once.

But the bunch of horses he had corralled there did not excite any delight in me. Horses, of course, were the most important part of our outfit. And that moment of first seeing the horses that were to

[211]

carry us on such long rides was an anxious and thrilling one. I have felt it many times, and it never grows any weaker from experience. Many a scrubby lot of horses had turned out well upon acquaintance, and some I had found hard to part with at the end of trips. Up to that time, however, I had not seen a bear hunter's horses; and I was much concerned by the fact that these were a sorry looking outfit, dusty, ragged, maneless, cut and bruised and crippled. Still, I reflected, they were bunched up so closely that I could not tell much about them, and I decided to wait for Teague before I chose a horse for anyone.

In an hour Teague trotted up to our resting place. Beside his own mount he had two white saddle horses, and nine pack animals, heavily laden. Teague was a sturdy rugged man with bronzed face and keen gray-blue eyes, very genial and humorous. Straightway I got the impression that he liked work.

"Let's organize," he said, briskly. "Have you picked the horses you're goin' to ride?"

Teague led from the midst of that dusty kicking bunch a rangy powerful horse, with four white feet, a white face and a noble head. He had escaped my eye. I felt that here at least was one horse.

The rest of the horses were permanently crippled or temporarily lame, and I had no choice, except to take the one it would be kindest to ride.

"He ain't much like your Silvermane or Black Star," said Teague, laughing.

"What do you know about them?" I asked, very much pleased.

"Well, I know all about them," he replied. "I'll have you the best horse in this country in a few days. Fact is I've bought him an' he'll come with my cowboy, Vern. . . . Now, we're organized. Let's move."

We rode through a meadow along a spruce slope above which towered the great mountain. It was a zigzag trail, rough, boggy, and steep in places. The Stillwater meandered here, and little breaks on the water gave evidence of feeding trout. We had several miles of meadow, and then sheered off to the left up into the timber. It was a spruce forest, very still and fragrant. We climbed out up on a bench, and across a flat, up another bench, out of the timber into the patches of snow. Here snow could be felt in the air. Water was

[212]

everywhere. I saw a fox, a badger, and another furry creature, too illusive to name. One more climb brought us to the top of the Flattop Pass, about eleven thousand feet. The view in the direction from which we had come was splendid, and led the eye to the distant sweeping ranges, dark and dim along the horizon. The Flat-tops were flat enough, but not very wide at this pass, and we were soon going down again into a green gulf of spruce, with ragged peaks lifting beyond. Here again I got the suggestion of limitless space. It took us an hour to ride down to Little Trappers Lake, a small clear green sheet of water. The larger lake was farther down. It was big, irregular, and bordered by spruce forests, and shadowed by the lofty gray peaks.

The camp was on the far side. The air appeared rather warm, and mosquitoes bothered us. However, they did not stay long. It was after sunset and I was too tired to have many impressions.

Our cook appeared to be a melancholy man. He had a deep quavering voice, a long drooping mustache and sad eyes. He was silent most of the time. The men called him Bill, and yelled when they spoke, for he was somewhat deaf. It did not take me long to discover that he was a good cook.

Our tent was pitched down the slope from the cook tent. We were too tired to sit round a camp fire and talk. The stars were white and splendid, and they hung over the flat ridges like great beacon lights. The lake appeared to be inclosed on three sides by amphitheatric mountains, black with spruce up to the gray walls of rock. The night grew cold and very still. The bells on the horses tinkled distantly. There was a soft murmur of falling water. A lonesome coyote barked, and that thrilled me. Teague's dogs answered this prowler, and some of them had voices to make a hunter thrill. One, the bloodhound Cain, had a roar like a lion's. I had not gotten acquainted with the hounds, and I was thinking about them when I fell asleep.

Next morning I was up at five-thirty. The air was cold and nipping and frost shone on grass and sage. A red glow of sunrise gleamed on the tip of the mountain and slowly grew downward.

The cool handle of an axe felt good. I soon found, however, that I could not wield it long for lack of breath. The elevation was close to ten thousand feet and the air at that height was thin and rare.

[213]

After each series of lusty strokes I had to rest. R. C., who could handle an axe as he used to swing a baseball bat, made fun of my efforts. Whereupon I relinquished the tool to him, and chuckled at his discomfort.

After breakfast R. C. and I got out tackles and rigged up fly rods, and sallied forth to the lake with the same eagerness we had felt when we were boys after chubs and sunfish. The lake glistened green in the sunlight and it lay like a gem at the foot of the magnificent black slopes.

The water was full of little floating particles that Teague called wild rice. I thought the lake had begun to work, like eastern lakes during dog days. It did not look propitious for fishing, but Teague reassured us. The outlet of this lake was the head of White River. We tried the outlet first, but trout were not rising there. Then we began wading and casting along a shallow bar of the lake. Teague had instructed us to cast, then drag the flies slowly across the surface of the water, in imitation of a swimming fly or bug. I tried this, and several times, when the leader was close to me and my rod far back, I had strikes. With my rod in that position I could not hook the trout. Then I cast my own way, letting the flies sink a little. To my surprise and dismay I had only a few strikes and could not hook the fish.

R. C., however, had better luck, and that, too, in wading right over the ground I had covered. To beat me at anything always gave him the most unaccountable pleasure.

"These are educated trout," he said. "It takes a skillful fisherman to make them rise. Now anybody can catch the big game of the sea, which is your forte. But here you are N. G. . . . . Watch me cast!"

I watched him make a most atrocious cast with his double flying. But the water boiled, and he hooked two good-sized trout at once. Quite speechless with envy and admiration I watched him play them and eventually beach them. They were cutthroat trout, silvery-sided and marked with the red slash along their gills that gave them their name. I did not catch any while wading, but from the bank I spied one, and dropping a fly in front of his nose, I got him. R. C. caught four more, all about a pound in weight, and then he had a strike that broke his leader. He did not have another leader, so we walked back to camp.

Wild flowers colored the open slopes leading down out of the

[214]

forest. Goldenrod, golden daisies, and bluebells were plentiful and very pretty. Here I found my first columbine, the beautiful flower that is the emblem of Colorado. In vivid contrast to its blue, Indian paintbrush thinly dotted the slopes and varied in color from red to pink and from white to yellow.

My favorite of all wild flowers—the purple asters—were there too, on tall nodding stems, with pale faces held up to the light. The reflection of mountain and forest in Trappers Lake was clear and beautiful.

In the afternoon R. C. and I went out again to try for trout. I found a place between two willow banks at the lake's outlet where trout were breaking on the surface. It took a long cast for me, but about every tenth attempt I would get a fly over the right place and raise a fish. They were small, but that did not detract from my gratification. The light on the water was just right for me to see the trout rise, and that was a beautiful sight as well as a distinct advantage. I had caught four small fish when a shout from R. C. called me quickly downstream. I found him standing in the middle of a swift chute with his rod bent double and a long line out.

"Got a whale!" he yelled. "See him—down there—in that white water. See him flash red! . . . Go down there and land him for me. Hurry! He's got all the line!"

I ran below to an open place in the willows. Here the stream was shallow and very swift. In the white water I caught a flashing gleam of red. Then I saw the shine of the leader. But I could not reach it without wading in. When I did this the trout lunged out. He looked crimson and silver. I could have put my fist in his mouth.

"Grab the leader! Yank him out!" yelled R. C. in desperation. "There! He's got all the line."

"But it'd be better to wade down," I yelled back.

He shouted that the water was too deep and for me to save his fish. This was an awful predicament for me. I knew the instant I grasped the leader that the big trout would break it or pull free. The same situation, with different kinds of fish, had presented itself many times on my numberless fishing jaunts with R. C. and they all crowded to my mind. Nevertheless I had no choice. Plunging in to my knees I frantically reached for the leader. The red trout made a surge. I missed him. R. C. yelled that something would break. That was no news to me. Another plunge brought me in touch with

[215]

the leader. Then I essayed to lead the huge cutthroat ashore. He was heavy. But he was tired and that provided hope. Near the shore as I was about to lift him, he woke up, swam round me twice, then ran between my legs.

When, a little later, R. C. came panting downstream I was sitting on the bank, all wet, with one knee skinned, and I was holding his broken leader in my hands. Strange to say, he went into a rage! Blamed me for the loss of that big trout! Under such circumstances it was always best to maintain silence and I did so as long as I could. After his paroxysm had spent itself and he had become somewhat near a rational being once more, he asked me:

"Was he big?"

"Oh—a whale of a trout!" I replied.

"Humph! Well, how big?"

Thereupon I enlarged upon the exceeding size and beauty of that trout. I made him out very much bigger than he actually looked to me and I minutely described his beauty and wonderful gaping mouth. R. C. groaned and that was my revenge.

The next day, September 1st, we rode down along the outlet of Big Fish to White River and down that for miles to fish for grayling. The stream was large and swift and cold. It appeared full of ice water and rocks, but no fish. We met fishermen, an automobile, and a camp outfit. That was enough for me. Where an automobile can run, I do not belong. The fishing was poor. But the beautiful open valley, flowered in gold and purple, was recompense for a good deal of bad luck.

A grayling, or what they called a grayling, was not as beautiful a fish as my fancy had pictured. He resembled a sucker or mullet, had a small mouth, dark color, and was rather a sluggish-looking fish.

*

We spent many full days under the shadow of Whitley's Peak. After the middle of September the aspens colored and blazed to the touch of frost, and the mountain slopes were exceedingly beautiful. Against a background of gray sage the gold and red and purple aspen groves showed too much like exquisite paintings to seem real. In the mornings the frost glistened thick and white on the grass; and after the gorgeous sunsets of gold over the violet-hazed ranges the air grew stingingly cold.

[216]

Bear-chasing with a pack of hounds has been severely criticized by many writers and I was among them. I believed it a cowardly business, and that was why, if I chased bears with dogs, I wanted to chase the kind that could not be treed. But like many another I did not know what I was writing about. I did not shoot a bear out of a tree and I would not do so, except in a case of hunger. All the same, leaving the tree out of consideration, bear-chasing with hounds is a tremendously exciting and hazardous game. But my ideas about sport are changing.

The more I hunt the more I become convinced of something wrong about the game. I am a different man when I get a gun in my hands. All is exciting, hot-pressed, red. Hunting is magnificent up to the moment the shot is fired. After that it is another matter. It is useless for sportsmen to tell me that they, in particular, hunt right, conserve the game, do not go beyond the limit, and all that sort of thing. A rifle is made for killing. When a man goes out with one he means to kill. He may keep within the law, but that is not the question. It is a question of spirit, and men who love to hunt are yielding to and always developing the primitive instinct to kill. The meaning of the spirit of life is not clear to them. An argument may be advanced that, according to the laws of self-preservation and the survival of the fittest, if man stops all strife, all fight, then he will retrograde. And this is to say if a man does not go to the wilds now and then, and work hard and live some semblance of the life of his progenitors, he will weaken. It seems that he will, but I am not prepared now to say whether or not that would be well. The Germans believe they are the race fittest to survive over all others—and that has made me a little sick of this Darwin business.

To return, however, to the fact that to ride after hounds on a wild chase is a dangerous and wonderfully exhilarating experience, I will relate a couple of instances, and I will leave it to my readers to judge whether or not it is a cowardly sport.

One afternoon a rancher visited our camp and informed us that he had surprised a big black bear eating the carcass of a dead cow.

"Good! We'll have a bear tomorrow night," declared Teague. "We'll get him even if the trail is a day old. But he'll come back tonight."

Early next morning the young rancher and three other boys rode into camp, saying they would like to go with us to see the fun. We were glad to have them, and we rode off through the frosted sage that crackled like brittle glass under the hoofs of the horses. Our guide led toward a branch of a park, and when we got within perhaps a quarter of a mile, Teague suggested that R. C. and I go ahead on the chance of surprising the bear. But we did not see any bear near the carcass of the cow. Old Jim and Sampson were close behind us, and when Jim came within forty yards of that carcass he put his nose up with a deep and ringing bay, and he shot by us like a streak. He never went near the dead cow! Sampson bayed like thunder and raced after Jim.

"They're off!" I yelled to R. C. "It's a hot scent! Come on!"

We spurred our horses and they broke across the open park to the edge of the woods. Jim and Sampson were running straight with noses high. I heard a string of yelps and bellows from our rear.

"Look back!" shouted R. C.

Teague and the cowboys were unleashing the rest of the pack. It surely was great to see them stretch out, yelping wildly. Like the wind they passed us. Jim and Sampson headed into the woods with deep bays. I was riding Teague's best horse for this sort of work and he understood the game and plainly enjoyed it. R. C.'s horse ran as fast in the woods as he did in the open. This frightened me, and I yelled to R. C. to be careful. I yelled to deaf ears. This is the first great risk—a rider is not going to be careful! We were right on top of Jim and Sampson with the pack clamoring mad music just behind. The forest rang. Both horses hurdled logs, sometimes two at once. My old lion chases with Buffalo Jones had made me skillful in dodging branches and snags, and sliding knees back to avoid knocking them against trees. For a mile the forest was comparatively open, and here we had a grand and ringing run. I received two hard knocks, was unseated once, but held on, and I got a stinging crack in the face from a branch. R. C. added several more black and blue spots to his already spotted anatomy, and he missed, just by an inch, a solid snag that would have broken him in two. The pack stretched out in wild staccato chorus, the little Airedales literally screeching. Jim got out of our sight and then Sampson. Still it was even more thrilling to follow by sound rather than sight. They led up a thick, steep slope. Here we got into trouble in the windfalls of timber and the pack drew away from us, up over the mountain. We were half-way up when we heard them jump the bear. The forest seemed full of strife and bays and yelps. We heard the dogs go down again to our right, and as we turned we saw Teague and the others strung out along the edge of the park. They got far ahead of us. When we reached the bottom of the slope they were out of sight, but we could hear them yell. The hounds were working around on another slope, from which craggy rocks loomed above the timber. R. C.'s horse lunged across the park and appeared to be running off from mine. I was a little to the right, and when my horse got under way, full speed, we had the bad luck to plunge suddenly into soft ground. He went to his knees, and I sailed out of the saddle fully twenty feet, to alight all spread out and to slide like a plow. I did not seem to be hurt. When I got up my horse was coming and he appeared to be patient with me, but he was in a hurry. Before we got across the wet place, R. C. was out of sight. I decided that instead of worrying about him I had better think about myself. Once on hard ground, my horse fairly charged into the woods and we broke brush and branches as if they had been punk. It was again open forest, then a rocky slope, and then a flat ridge with aisles between the trees. Here I heard the melodious notes of Teague's hunting horn, and following that, the full chorus of the hounds. They had treed the bear. Coming into still more open forest, with rocks here and there, I caught sight of R. C. far ahead, and soon I had glimpses of the other horses, and lastly, while riding full tilt, I spied a big, black, glistening bear high up in a pine a hundred yards or more distant.

Slowing down, I rode up to the circle of frenzied dogs and excited men. The boys were all jabbering at once. Teague was beaming. R. C. sat on his horse, and it struck me he looked sorry for the bear.

"Fifteen minutes!" Teague exclaimed with a proud glance at Old Jim standing with forepaws up on the pine.

Indeed it had been a short and ringing chase.

While I fooled around trying to photograph the treed bear, R. C. sat there on his horse, looking upward.

"Well, gentlemen, better kill him," said Teague, cheerfully. "If he gets rested he'll come down."

It was then I suggested to R. C. that he do the shooting.

"Not me!" he exclaimed.

[219]

The bear looked really pretty perched up there. He was as round as a barrel and black as jet and his fur shone in the gleams of sunlight. His tongue hung out, and his plump sides heaved, showing what a quick, hard run he had made before being driven to the tree. What struck me most forcibly about him was the expression in his eyes as he looked down at those devils of hounds. He was scared. He realized his peril. It was utterly impossible for me to see Teague's point of view.

"Go ahead—and plug him," I replied to my brother. "Get it over with."

"You do it," he said.

"No, I won't."

"Why not—I'd like to know?"

"Maybe we won't have so good a chance again—and I want you to get your bear," I replied.

"Why it's like—murder," he protested.

"Oh, not so bad as that," I returned, weakly. "We need the meat. We've not had any game meat, you know, except ducks and grouse."

"You won't do it?" he added, grimly.

"No, I refuse."

Meanwhile the young ranchers gazed at us with wide eyes, and the expression on Teague's honest, ruddy face would have been funny under other circumstances.

"That bear will come down an' mabbe kill one of my dogs," he protested.

"Well, he can come for all I care," I replied, and I turned away.

I heard R. C. curse low under his breath. Then followed the spang of his .35 Remington. I wheeled in time to see the bear straining upward in terrible convulsion, his head pointed high, with blood spurting from his nose. Slowly he swayed and fell with a heavy crash.

*

The next bear chase we had was entirely different medicine.

Off in the basin under the White Slides, back of our camp, the hounds struck a fresh track and in an instant were out of sight. With the cowboy Vern setting the pace, we plunged after them. It was rough country. Bogs, brooks, swales, rocky little parks, stretches of timber full of windfalls, groves of aspens so thick we could

[220]

scarcely squeeze through—all these obstacles soon allowed the
hounds to get far away. We came out into a large park, right under
the mountain slope, and here we sat our horses listening to the
chase. That trail led around the basin and back near to us, up the
thick green slope, where high up near a ledge we heard the pack
jump this bear. It sounded to us as if he had been roused out of a
sleep.

"I'll bet it's one of the big grizzlies we've heard about," said
Teague.

That was something to my taste. I have seen a few grizzlies. Riding to higher ground I kept close watch on the few open patches up
on the slope. The chase led toward us for a while. Suddenly I saw a
big bear with a frosted coat go lumbering across one of these open-
ings.

"Silvertip! Silvertip!" I yelled at the top of my lungs. "I saw
him!"

My call thrilled everybody. Vern spurred his horse and took to
the right. Teague advised that we climb the slope. So we made for
the timber. Once there, we had to get off and climb on foot. It was
steep, rough, very hard work. I had on chaps and spurs. Soon I was
hot, laboring, and my heart began to hurt. We all had to rest. The
baying of the hounds inspired us now and then, but presently we
lost it. Teague said they had gone over the ridge and as soon as we
got up to the top we would hear them again. We struck an elk trail
with fresh elk tracks in it. Teague said they were just ahead of us. I
never climbed so hard and fast in my life. We were all tuckered out
when we reached the top of the ridge. Then to our great disappointment we did not hear the hounds. Mounting we rode along
the crest of this wooded ridge toward the western end, which was
considerably higher. Once on a bare patch of ground we saw where
the grizzly had passed. The big, round tracks, toeing in a little,
made a chill go over me.

We climbed and rode to the high point, and coming out upon
the summit of the mountain we all heard the deep, hoarse baying of
the pack. They were in the canyon down a bare grassy slope and
over a wooded bench at our feet. Teague yelled as he spurred down.
R. C. rode hard in his tracks.

But my horse was new to this bear-chasing. He was mettlesome, and he did not want to do what I wanted. When I jabbed the spurs into his flanks he nearly bucked me off. I was looking for a soft place to light when he quit. Long before I got down that open slope, Teague and R. C. had disappeared. I had to follow their tracks. This I did at a gallop, but now and then lost the tracks, and had to haul in to find them. If I could have heard the hounds from there I would have gone on anyway. But once down in the jack-pines I could hear neither yell nor bay. The pines were small, close together, and tough. I hurt my hands, scratched my face, barked my knees. The horse had a habit of suddenly deciding to go the way he liked instead of the way I guided him, and when he plunged be-tween saplings too close together to permit us both to go through, it was exceedingly hard on me. I was worked into a frenzy. Suppose R. C. should come face to face with that old grizzly and fail to kill him! That was the reason for my desperate hurry. I got a crack on the head that nearly blinded me. My horse grew hot and began to run in every little open space. He could scarcely be held in. And I, with the blood hot in me, too, did not hold him hard enough.

It seemed miles across that wooded bench. But at last I reached another slope. Coming out upon a canyon rim I heard R. C and Teague yelling, and I heard the hounds fighting the grizzly. He was growling and threshing about far below. I had missed the tracks made by Teague and my brother, and it was necessary to find them. That slope looked impassable. I rode back along the rim, then for-ward. Finally I found where the ground was plowed deep and here I headed my horse. He had been used to smooth roads and he could not take these jumps. I went forward on his neck. But I hung on and spurred him hard. The mad spirit of that chase had gotten into him, too. All the time I could hear the fierce baying and yelping of the hounds, and occasionally I heard a savage bawl from the bear. I literally plunged, slid, broke a way down that mountain slope, rid-ing all the time, before I discovered the footprints of Teague and R. C. They had walked, leading their horses. By this time I was so mad I would not get off. I rode all the way down that steep slope of dense saplings, loose rock slides and earth, and jumble of splintered cliff.

Then before I realized it I was at the foot of the slope, in a narrow canyon bed, full of rocks and trees, with the din of roaring

[222]

water in my ears. I could hear nothing else. Tracks everywhere, and when I came to the first open place I was thrilled. The grizzly had plunged off a sandy bar into the water, and there he had fought the hounds. Signs of that battle were easy to read. I saw where his huge tracks, still wet, led up the opposite sandy bank.

Then, downstream, I did my most reckless riding. On level ground the horse was splendid. Once he leaped clear across the brook. Every plunge, every turn I expected to bring me upon my brother and Teague and that fighting pack. More than once I thought I heard the spang of the .35 and this made me urge the roan faster and faster.

The canyon narrowed, the stream bed deepened. I had to slow down to get through the trees and rocks. And suddenly I was overjoyed to ride pell-mell upon R. C. and Teague with half the panting hounds. The canyon had grown too rough for the horses to go farther and it would have been useless for us to try on foot. As I dismounted, so sore and bruised I could hardly stand, old Jim came limping in to fall into the brook where he lapped and lapped thirstily. Teague threw up his hands. Old Jim's return meant an ended chase. The grizzly had eluded the hounds in that jumble of rocks below.

"Say, did you meet the bear?" queried Teague, eyeing me in astonishment and mirth.

Bloody, dirty, ragged, and wringing wet with sweat, I must have been a sight. R. C., however, did not look so very immaculate, and when I saw he also was lame and scratched and black, I felt better!

16

TAHITI WATERS—
THE LATEST ANGLERS' EL DORADO

The first time Zane Grey saw Tahiti, he didn't like it. He had stopped over for a day on his way to New Zealand and reacted like many tourists who only see Papeete's weary waterfront:

> *The beachcomber, always a romantic if pathetic figure, became by actual contact somewhat disconcerting to me, and wholly disgusting. . . . I spent a full day in this world-famous South Sea Island port—it was long enough for me!*

ZG's negative feelings increased—when he found no quantity of wildlife. Therefore, it's a wonder that Zane Grey ever returned to the Society Islands, and even more wonderful that he made Tahiti his headquarters during many visits spanning several years. He even bought eight acres along the south shore of the island, where he built a permanent camp. The reason for all this change of heart, of course, was fishing.

Many odd tales and legends draw men to Tahiti, but none so peculiar as those which inspired Zane Grey. Even while angling New Zealand waters, he heard stories of toothless Tahitian sharks that fasten themselves to their prey and suck off large sections of flesh (stories "verified" by natives who had been thus disfigured); tales of a mysterious Polynesian marlin whose sword is an extension of its underjaw (just the opposite of all other billfish); and rumors of forty-pound bonefish and hundredweight *mahimahi* (dolphin fish) weighed in Papeete's market. However, the most intriguing rumors concerned giant phantom swordfish ranging in lengths of more than twenty feet to one thirty-three foot monster captured and dragged into the shallows of a Marquesas' island and there butchered, before a reliable witness or camera could be found. However, the bill was saved, and it was reputed to be curved and over five feet long. Thus in June of 1928 ZG arrived in Tahiti with his New Zealand boatmen, tons of camp equipment and tackle, and his three-masted schooner, the *Fisherman*, to begin the first of several long stays.

Though *Tales of Tahitian Waters*, in which ZG tells the story of his thousand-pound marlin, was published in 1931, his public did not really appreciate the variety of the trophy game fish to be found in the Society Isles until July, 1932, when *Outdoor Life* published "Tahiti Waters: The Latest Anglers' El Dorado." In this article Zane Grey describes big wahoo, tuna and a 170-pound Pacific sailfish. But ZG also described two other species dear to the hearts of big-game anglers, and here's the story of their capture.

GWR

TAHITI WATERS—
THE LATEST ANGLERS' EL DORADO

I am sure that I owe to Charles Nordhoff[1] the discovery of the great game fishing in Tahitian waters.

When we dropped anchor at Papeete my intention was to fish a little around the island, and then make for the Paumotus and the Marquesas, which groups of islands were my objective. We fished quite a little between Moorea and Tahiti, but as we were unable to catch bait and did not see any fish, I decided that perhaps there was something in what American yachtsmen had claimed about the absence of game fish around Tahiti.

Then I was to learn how Nordhoff, when out with the natives after bonito, had seen many swordfish and sailfish, the size of some of which seemed incredible. I am bound to admit now that Nordhoff was very conservative in his estimates. He strongly advised me to stay and give Tahiti an exhaustive fishing. This I did as related in my book *Tales of Tahitian Waters*.

The spring of 1931 was my fourth season at Tahiti, during which time I had fine sport and caught three very notable fish—a black marlin of 810 pounds, a world-record sailfish 170 pounds, and a mako shark, the only known fish of this species that was ever caught in these waters.

It should be recorded that fishing at Tahiti is the hardest of any that I have tried. And any visiting angler must have his own tackle, and make arrangements in advance for boat and engineer. As the sport there is in its infancy, these are not easy to procure. But it can be done, and the enthusiastic angler with time and money can be assured of an unforgettable experience.

My protégés, the Guilds, who live at Tahiti, started from scratch without any previous experience whatever, and they made a mag-

---

[1] Mr. Nordhoff and James Norman Hall were the co-authors of *Mutiny on the Bounty* published in 1932. They had met as Army pilots in World War I and pledged that if they managed to survive that holocaust, they'd find a place inhabited by more gentle and sensible people than the Europeans and Americans who had produced such blood-letting. Their final choice was Tahiti. Zane Grey's older son, Romer, still has a chart of Tahitian waters once used by his father with several notes in Charles Nordhoff's hand indicating the best fishing spots, species and seasons.

nificent success of it. They began with a little launch they bought from me, and some tackle I gave them, and some few days out with Captain Mitchell and me. The story of their blunders and struggles against tremendous odds is not the least interesting of my *Tales of Tahitian Waters*. I called them Ham-Fish and Carrie-Finn.

It took Carrie-Finn two years to catch her first marlin. She had strikes from many fish, and had a score hooked before she got one.[2] I mention this here, not only because I want to emphasize their remarkable perseverance against obstacles, and their ultimate graduation into great anglers, but also to prove my contention that for anglers who want only a little sport as well as those who aim at the heights, Tahiti has no peer in the Seven Seas.

My first important catch at Tahiti in 1931 was a 150-pound mako shark. This species has been reported from various waters away from New Zealand, its natural habitat, but no verification of the claim has been substantiated to my knowledge.

In March, while trolling for swordfish off Paea I raised a white and blue fish that leaped high out of the water on the strike. It did not resemble a marlin in any particular, yet I took it for one. I hooked the fish and was working hard on him when the hook tore out. My chagrin gave way to amazement when we sighted the fish returning for part of the bait still left on the hook. I had reeled most of the line in. When I saw the fish distinctly I shouted: "It's a mako!" Peter[3] certainly responded to that call. As he was from New Zealand himself, the word *mako* was magic to him.[4] When the darn fool fish took the bait again, right under our noses, we knew it was a mako, entirely aside from classification by sight.

"Whoopee! Mako!" bawled Peter.

I jerked with all my might and believed I had made fast to the shark. Nevertheless he pulled free. Still he had not had enough!

---

[2] In the November, 1932, issue of *Field and Stream*, Carrie-Finn tells her story of "My Tahiti Marlin."

[3] Peter Williams was ZG's salt-water guide during his first visit to New Zealand and thereafter on other South Sea adventures.

[4] The word *mako* is Maori in origin, but, ironically, ichthyologists today insist that the Pacific mako is actually the bonito shark, *Isurus glaucus*. The "true mako," *Isurus oxyrhinchus*, is found only in the Atlantic Ocean.

This is a feature of the mako that is great. You can scarcely hurt, whip, or faze him. He came a third time, looking for more. Peter had swiftly hauled in my line to put on another bait. I let it down. The mako swam around it several times, evidently leery of the strange contrivance. Something to eat with a string and a pull in it! Eventually either his hunger or his pugnaciousness got the better of discretion, for he charged the fresh bait and rushed away. I put on a stiff drag and lunged back with all my strength. This time I knew I had hooked him. But mako or not, he refused to leap, which was disappointing to us. After a brief tussle I bested him and dragged him in to the gaff. The instant that steel touched him—souse—crash! "Same old mako stuff!" I yelled. We landed him, and could see no difference in the slightest way from a New Zealand mako.

I remember another shark I had hooked at Vairao two years before. I had let down a live bait, got a tremendous strike, and hooked something heavy. It ran a little way, then came up—a huge blue and white fish, nearly twenty feet long, that evidently saw the boat, for he darted away with inconceivable rapidity. The line simply melted off the reel. At four hundred yards it snapped. We had always wondered about the fish. Now we identified him—an enormous mako shark.

March 5 was a day of full moon, always a period of uncertainty at Tahiti. It promised to be a hot clear day, with a heavy sea and strong wind. On the way out we met the native who caught flying fish for us. He had a unique method. He put out in his outrigger canoe to leeward of the reef a few hundred yards. His tackle consisted of a dozen or more little floats of light wood, six or eight feet of line to each, mounted with tiny hooks and baited with shrimp. These he scattered around the smooth patch of water and kept his eye upon the floats. When he saw one bob under, reappear and glide away with a ducking motion, then he knew he had a flying fish, so he would paddle over and haul it in. One morning he caught eleven in short order. But that was exceptional. On this particular March morning he had only one. From past experience I knew well that a single bait could get an angler into a heap of trouble. This very thing happened that day.

We ran out several miles off Vairao. The sea was rough and blue,

[229]

with whitecaps showing. While I trolled the one flying fish, the rest of the outfit searched the sea for sign of birds and bonito. In vain!

As it was pretty rough I decided to run in under the lee of the mountains and try to raise a sailfish. My tackle was a hickory rod, six hundred yards of 39-thread line[5] on a nine-inch Coxe reel. My leader was twenty feet long and the hook, a Sobey Pflueger 10. This rig was small enough to be all right for an ordinary sailfish, ideal for a big one, and it would serve pretty well if I had the bad luck to hook a heavy marlin. That is the only way you can fish successfully in these crystal-clear hot waters of the tropics. I had learned to my sorrow that light tackle means only grief. You will hook what you do not expect, and toil in vain.

We were well back in the lee and not a mile from the reef when our first mate, Jimmy, yelled in his deep voice: "Beeg feesh!" I sighted this fish myself just about the same instant. It was a long brown shape on the left side, far back of the teaser, and coming pretty fast. I stood up. The leathery shape resembled a porpoise. But as he shot in toward us I recognized a swordfish shape and pealed out: "There he is!"

He rushed that flying fish, his black fin out of the water, and simply absorbed it in a great swirl. He swept away in plain sight, curved and came back. I knew he had my bait by the way the swivel of the leader cut the surface.

"That bloaker wants some more," yelled Peter.

"Sorry we can't oblige him, Pete, for this is the only bait we have," I replied.

Whereupon I put on the drag, reeled in until the line was tight and struck him hard. He lunged out of sight, leaving a circling swirl of green water where he had been. When I struck again I came up on a tremendous weight, and I knew that whatever the fish was, I had him hooked.

He got going fast and faster, and at the end of perhaps a hundred yards he leaped. We all yelled bloody murder. Peter and I: "Black marlin!" and the natives some name in Tahitian. The second leap was long and low, broadside on, and gave us a chance to estimate his size. He was a dazzling blue-green and silver, a lengthy fish, and

---

[5] Approximately 117-pound test.

very deep in his shoulders. He struck up a huge splash, went under to heave out in so magnificent a leap that I was stunned with the wonder of it. Then he sounded and headed out to sea.

"Up against it, Peter," I said, grimly, as I faced the ridged sea and the hard job. But there was a degree of exultation in it, too—the fight ahead—the obstacles to overcome.

My angling principles do not approve of following a fish, if he can be stopped and fought. But I doubt that I could have stopped this fellow very quickly, even if I had had him on my big tackle. Peter was evasive as to his size and weight. "He's a big fish," was Peter's only comment. To that I replied: "He's long and four feet deep. He'll go a thousand pounds. . . . But it's a thousand to one I'll ever land him in this sea."

"I'll take that bet," averred Peter.

So we followed him while I hauled and pumped and wound steadily. Mile after mile he led us out, until we cleared the extreme east end of Tahiti and went out in the open sea, where the great green combers rolled. I had to admit that the new boat was a comfort to fish out of. I did not mind the sea at all, except that I worried about the finish of the fight, if it ever came to that. I managed to turn the fish, and he led us back a few miles, for which we were extremely grateful.

Three hours—four hours—five hours—how they fly in a battle like this! At the end of five and a half hours I stopped the black marlin. He began to act queerly, to fool around, to change his tactics. But he was still mighty powerful and not yet exhausted. Then to my regret he began what I had feared—to sound. I had to let him go.

When he got down a thousand feet I knew the pressure of water would kill him. "He's cooked," said Peter. It was my idea that I was the same. Down twelve-, thirteen-, fourteen-hundred-odd feet. Then he stopped. Probably at that moment he gave up the ghost.

"Well boys, he's whipped. Now let's take stock of the job, and see what can be done," I said.

The rod was bent in a curve and rested on the gunwale. It had the solidity of a rock. I could not raise it off the gunwale, or move it in the slightest. The line stretched like wet gut and sang like a telephone wire in the cold wind. We drifted and we talked. Peter put down fifteen hundred feet of line, with a heavy lead and grap-

[231]

pling hook, but could not tell whether he reached the fish or not. The sea was not so heavy as it had been, still it made my chance appear hopeless. The fact that the wonderful Swastika line[6] held was the only thing to keep me calculating. By holding the bell of the reel with both gloved hands I was able to keep the line from slipping off when a huge swell lifted up.

Perhaps we had drifted for a quarter of an hour before I noted that the angle of my line had changed. First it had been straight down and now it took an angle of 45 degrees. That gave me an idea.

"Throw the clutch in and turn her hard toward my line. I'll see if I can get some back," I said hopefully.

The engine roared, the wheel whirled, the boat turned to short ahead. The tension on the rod eased. I hauled and wound in a frenzy, and I recovered about ten yards of line before we had to stop.

"It worked," I shouted. "Throw her out. We'll drift and try that again."

In ten minutes the angle of my line slanted off to windward. We tried that plan again. It worked still better. I got in more line. I had to work strenuously, but felt that the short time justified any exertion. I could rest up each time. This method we kept up three long hours. It took skill, judgment, and endurance. We got back fully nine hundred feet when Peter conceived a brilliant idea.

"Let's cut that line and thread it on your big rod."

I wondered why I had not thought of that before. They wound the line off my Hardy reel. Then Peter reached down to grasp the line which held my fish and very carefully pulled until he had slack. "Pull some off. Then cut—and tie a running bowline knot."

It was accomplished in a few seconds, and there I had the great fish on my big outfit, with only five hundred feet of line to recover. The danger, of course, was that with the more powerful rod and reel, and the same line, already stretched and strained to hazard, I might break the fish off. Moreover we could not get so much of an angle

---

[6] A superior category of line manufactured by Ashaway Line & Twine Company, Ashaway, Rhode Island. For obvious reasons, this trade name was abandoned later in the decade.

by drifting. But I made headway, and though almost beaten, felt that I could last.

Sharks came around the boat—ugly, yellow, uncanny devils. The boys got out the lance and threw it whenever the sharks came close. That is a new sport we have developed, and to anyone who hates sharks it is surely thrilling. The lance is a heavy blade eighteen inches long, and screwed into a long pole with a line at the end to recover it. You aim and throw as you would a baseball. The thing goes like a shot and when that blade connected with a shark it was just too bad for him.

At the end of nine and a half hours I dragged the black marlin to the surface. He was huge, almost deformed, black as a black opal, with a short rather light spear. The sharks had mutilated him considerably, but we believed we could patch him up well enough to photograph.

The sun had set, the sea was still rough, and we were ten miles off land. We had to tow the fish in. Darkness came on, the moon rose, the clouds over the black mountain were grand in the extreme. I sat out on top, in a heavy coat, and rested while I watched. I was pretty severely used up and sagged more as time passed.

At eight o'clock we got inside the point into calmer water. I flashed my searchlight which was answered from camp. That was a help and comfort. We got in at nine-thirty, to meet all my party and half of Vairao at the dock.

The black marlin weighed 810 pounds as he was. That was a disappointment to me. But despite his length of twelve feet and more and his great depth he was thin. If he had been thick and fat he would have weighed over a thousand. Nevertheless he surely was a superb specimen of that species and lent an added stimulus and thrill to the beginning of our cruise.

[233]

17

THE FIRST THOUSAND-POUNDER

This is the story of the big one—the fish that Zane Grey spent a king's ransom pursuing across two oceans for more than two decades. But the triumph of this tale of perseverance is leavened with postmortem disappointment.

In 1939, the year Zane Grey died, Michael Lerner of the United States and Clive Firth of Australia founded an international association establishing guidelines for keeping records of salt-water game fish. Among the many restrictions insuring fair play are two that disqualified ZG's biggest catch: no one but the angler can touch any part of the tackle during the fight; and if a fish is shot, harpooned, or mutilated in any way, it is not eligible for a world record.

But the disappointment for Zane Grey fans runs deeper than the sacrifice of this first thousand-pounder. In recent years, the International Game Fish Association has created restrictions that eliminate nearly all the early records. Among other refinements, the organization insists on testing a sample of the line used to catch the submitted fish. The work of the pioneers is being jettisoned. The last of ZG's records, his 111-pound New Zealand yellowtail, has been replaced by another New Zealand fish of identical size caught in 1961. There's generally no memory of pre-1939 catches. While it's right and natural that larger fish be caught and honored, it's sad that the achievements of the great pioneers are in no way commemorated. There is no recollection of Zane Grey's 582-pound broadbill swordfish, his 63-pound dolphin, his 758-pound bluefin tuna, or his 1,036-pound tiger shark. Only ichthyologists remember Zane Grey—and then rather modestly—for science has honored him by naming one of his favorite game fish, the Pacific sailfish, *Istiophorus greyi*.

*

There are other ironies associated with Zane Grey's success in Tahiti. Not long after publishing his discovery of giant marlin off Papeete, new and more convenient marlin grounds were discovered off the west coast of South America and the Kona coast of Hawaii. A fabulous fishing region was found in the vicinity of a little-known cape in Peru—Cabo Blanco. Several thousand-pounders were taken, and on August 4, 1953, Alfred C. Glassell, Jr., landed a 1,560-pound black marlin—still the heaviest billfish ever to be taken on rod and reel. More recently thousand-pound marlin have been caught off Cairns, Australia, while Zane Grey's achievements in Tahiti fade into the haze of big-game angling's past.

But ZG predicted that Tahiti would one day top the list of ocean angling hotspots, and in 1966 a huge marlin caught on a commercial handline by two local fishermen was brought into Papeete that vindicated his faith and staggered the angling world's imagination. When the fish was cut into sections and weighed for authentication, the pieces totaled *2,400 pounds!*

And even if the International Game Fish Association never recognized Zane Grey's catch as the forerunner to that ton-and-a-quarter marlin, ZG's story of its capture provides its own immortality.

GWR

THE FIRST THOUSAND-POUNDER

Time is probably more generous to an angler than to any other individual. The wind, the sun, the open air, the colors and smells, the loneliness of the sea or the solitude of the stream, work some kind of magic.

Morning disclosed dark, massed, broken clouds, red-edged and purple-centered, with curtains of rain falling over the mountains.

I took down a couple of new feather jigs—silver-headed with blue eyes—just for good luck. They worked. We caught five fine bonito in the lagoon, right off the point where my cottage stands. Jimmy[1] held up five fingers: "Five bonito. Good!" he declared, which voiced all our sentiments.

Cappy[2] had gone up the lagoon toward the second pass, and we tried to catch him, to give him a fresh bait. As usual, however, Cappy's natives were running the wheels off his launch, and we could not catch him. The second pass looked sort of white and rough to me. Cappy went out, however, through a smooth channel. Presently we saw a swell gather and rise to close the channel and mount to a great, curling white-crested wave which broke all the way across. Charley,[3] who had the wheel, grinned at me: "No good!" We turned inshore and made for the third pass, some miles on, and got through that wide one without risk. Afterward Cappy told me Areireia[4] knew exactly when to run through the second pass.

We headed out. A few black noddies skimmed the dark sea, and a few scattered bonito broke the surface. As usual—when we had them —we put out a big bonito on my big tackle and an ordinary one on the other. As my medium tackle holds one thousand yards of 39-thread line[5] it will seem interesting to anglers to speak of it as medium. The big outfit held fifteen hundred yards of line—one

---

[1] A six-foot, four-inch Tahitian who, according to Romer, was the most expert of any of ZG's crew at handling the heavy cane poles used in bonito fishing.

[2] Captain Laurie Mitchell.

[3] Another Tahitian crewman.

[4] Mitchell's guide.

[5] 117-pound test.

thousand of 39-thread and five hundred yards of 42[6] for backing; and this story will prove I needed it.

Off the east end there was a brightness of white and blue where the clouds broke, and in the west there were trade-wind clouds of gold and pearl, but for the most part a gray canopy overspread mountain and sea. All along the saw-toothed front of this range inshore the peaks were obscured and the canyons filled with down-dropping veils of rain.

What a relief from late days of sun and wind and wave! This was the kind of sea I loved to fish. The boat ran easily over a dark, low, lumpy swell. The air was cool, and as I did not have on any shirt, the fine mist felt pleasant to my skin. John[7] was at the wheel. Bob[8] sat up on top with Jimmy and Charley, learning to talk Tahitian. The teasers and heavy baits made a splashing, swishy sound that could be heard above the boil and gurgle of water from the propellers. We followed some low-skimming boobies for a while, and then headed for Captain M.'s boat, several miles farther out. A rain squall was obscuring the white tumbling reef and slowly moving toward us. Peter sat at my right, holding the line which had the larger bonito. He had both feet up on the gunwale. I noticed that the line on this reel was white and dry. I sat in the left chair, precisely as Peter, except that I had on two pairs of gloves with thumb-stalls in them. I have cut, burned, and skinned my hands too often on a hard strike to go without gloves. They are a nuisance to wear all day, when the rest of you, almost, is getting pleasantly caressed by sun and wind, but they are absolutely necessary to an angler who knows what he is doing.

Peter and I were discussing plans for our New Zealand trip next winter—boats, camp equipment, and what not. And although our gaze seldom strayed from the baits, the idea of raising a fish was the farthest from our minds.

Suddenly I heard a sounding, vicious thump of water. Peter's feet went up in the air.

---

[6] 126-pound test.

[7] John Loef was a California auto mechanic who asked Zane Grey what it was like to go fishing. One day ZG took him along and eventually trained him into one of his best boatmen.

[8] Bob Carney, a photographer and ZG's son-in-law.

[238]

"*Ge-zus!*" he bawled.

His reel screeched. Quick as thought I leaned over to press my gloved hand on the whizzing spool of line. Just in time to save the reel from overrunning!

Out where Peter's bait had been showed a whirling, closing hole in the boiling white-green water. I saw a wide purple mass shooting away so close under the surface as to make the water look shallow. Peter fell out of the chair at the same instant I leaped up to straddle his rod. I had the situation in hand. My mind worked swiftly. It was an incredible wonderful strike. The other boys piled back to the cockpit to help Peter get my other bait and the teasers in.

Before this was even started, the fish ran out two hundred yards of line, then turning to the right he tore off another hundred. All in a very few seconds! Then a white splash, high as a tree, shot up, out of which leaped the most magnificent of all the leaping fish I had ever seen.

"GIANT MARLIN!" screamed Peter. What had happened to me I did not know, but I was cold, keen, hard, tingling, motivated to think and do the right thing. This glorious fish made a leap of thirty feet at least, low and swift, which gave me time to gauge his enormous size and his species. Here at last on the end of my line was the great Tahitian swordfish! He looked monstrous. He was pale, shiny gray in color, with broad stripes of purple. When he hit the water he sent up a splash like the flying surf on the reef.

By the time he was down I had the drag on and was winding the reel. Out he blazed again, faster, higher, longer, whirling the bonito around his head.

"Hook didn't catch!" yelled Peter, wildly. "It's on this side. He'll throw it."

"No, Peter! He's fast," I replied. Still I kept working like a windmill in a cyclone to get up the slack. The monster had circled in these two leaps. Again he burst out, a plunging leap which took him under a wall of rippling white spray. Next instant such a terrific jerk as I had never sustained nearly unseated me. He was away on his run.

"Take the wheel, Peter," I ordered, and released the drag. "Water! Somebody pour water on this reel! ... *Quick!*"

The white line melted, smoked, burned off the reel. I smelled the scorching. It burned through my gloves. John was swift to plunge a bucket overboard and douse reel, rod, and me with water. That, too, saved us.

"After him, Pete!" I called, piercingly. The engines roared and the launch danced around to leap in the direction of the tight line.

"Full speed!" I added.

Then we had our race. It was thrilling in the extreme, and though brief it was far too long for me. Five hundred yards from us—over a third of a mile—he came up to pound and beat the water into a maelstrom.

"Slow up!" I sang out. We were bagging the line. Then I turned on the wheel-drag and began to pump and reel as never before in all my life. How precious that big spool—that big reel handle! They fairly ate up the line. We got back two hundred yards of the five hundred out before he was off again. This time, quick as I was, it took all my strength to release the drag, for when a weight is pulling hard it releases with extreme difficulty. No more risk like that!

He beat us in another race, shorter, at the end of which, when he showed like a plunging elephant, he had out four hundred and fifty yards of line.

"Too much—Peter!" I panted. "We must—get him closer—go to it!"

So we ran down upon him. I worked as before, desperately, holding on my nerve, and when I got three hundred yards back again on the reel, I was completely winded, and the hot sweat poured off my naked arms and breast.

"He's sounding . . . Get my shirt . . . Harness!"

Warily I let go with one hand and then with the other, as John and Jimmy helped me on with my shirt and then with the leather harness. With that hooked on to my reel and the great strain transferred to my shoulders, I felt that I might not be torn asunder.

"All set. Let's go," I said, grimly. But he had gone down, which gave me a chance to get back my breath. Not long, however, did he remain down. I felt and saw the line rising.

"Keep him on the starboard quarter, Peter. Run up on him now . . . Bob, your chance for pictures!"

I was quick to grasp that the swordfish kept coming to our left, and repeatedly on that run I had Peter swerve in the same direction, in order to keep the line out on the quarter. Once we were almost in danger. But I saw it. I got back all but one hundred yards of line. Close enough! He kept edging in ahead of us, and once we had to turn halfway to keep the stern toward him. But he quickly shot ahead again. He was fast, angry, heavy. How his tail pounded the leader! The short powerful strokes vibrated all over me.

"Port—port, Peter!" I yelled, and even then, so quick was the swordfish, I missed seeing two leaps directly in front of the boat as he curved ahead of us. But the uproar from Bob and the others was enough for me. As the launch sheered around, however, I saw the third of that series of leaps—and if anything could have loosed my chained emotion of the instant, that unbelievably swift and savage plunge would have done so. But no more dreaming! I was there to think and act.

By the same tactics the swordfish sped off a hundred yards of line and by the same we recovered them and drew close to see him leap again, only two hundred feet off our starboard, a little ahead, and of all the magnificent fish I have ever seen, he excelled. His power to leap was beyond credence. Captain M.'s big fish, that broke off two years before, did not move like this one. True, he was larger. Nevertheless, this swordfish was so huge that when he came out in dazzling swift flight, my crew went simply mad. This was the first time my natives had been flabbergasted. They were as excited, as carried away, as Bob and John. Peter, however, stuck at the wheel as if he were after a wounded whale which might any instant turn upon him. I did not need to warn Peter not to let that fish hit us. If he had he would have made splinters out of our launch. Many an anxious glance did I cast toward Cappy's boat, two or three miles distant. Why did he not come? The peril was too great for us to be alone at the mercy of that beautiful brute if he charged us either by accident or by design. But Captain could not locate us, owing to the misty atmosphere, and missed seeing this grand fish in action.

How sensitive I was to the strain on the line! A slight slackening directed all my facilities to ascertain the cause. The light on the moment was bad, and I had to peer closely to see the line. He had not slowed up, but he was curving back and to the left again.

"*Port, Peter*—PORT!" I commanded.

[241]

We sheered, but not enough. With the wheel hard over, one engine full speed ahead, the other in reverse, we wheeled like a top. But not swift enough for that Tahitian swordfish.

The line went under the bow.

"Reverse!" I called, sharply.

We pounded on the waves, slowly caught hold, slowed, started back. Then I ordered the clutches thrown out. It was a terrible moment and took all my will not to yield to blank panic.

When my line ceased to pay out I felt that it had been caught on the keel. I surrendered for an instant to agony. But no! That line was new, strong. The swordfish was slowing. I could yet avert catastrophe.

"Quick, Pete! Feels as if the line is caught," I cried, unhooking my harness from the reel.

Peter complied with my order. "Yes, by cripes! It's caught. Overboard, Jimmy! Jump in! Loose the line!"

The big Tahitian in a flash was out of his shirt and bending to dive.

"No!—Hold on, Jimmy!" I yelled. Only a moment before I had seen sharks milling about. "Grab him, John!"

They held Jimmy back, and in a second I plunged my rod over the side into the water, so suddenly that the weight of it and reel nearly carried me overboard.

"Hold me—or it's all—day!" I panted, and I thought that if my swordfish had fouled on keel or propellers I did not care if I did fall in.

"Let go my line, Peter," I said, making ready to extend the rod to the limit of my arms.

"I can feel him moving, sir," shouted Peter, excitedly. "By jingo! He's coming! . . . It's free! It wasn't caught!"

I felt such intense relief I could not recover my balance. They had to haul me back into the boat. I shook all over as one with the palsy, so violently that Peter had to help me get the rod in the rod-socket of the chair. An instant later came the strong electrifying pull on the line, the scream of the reel. Never such sweet music! He was away from the boat—on a tight line!

"Close shave, sir," said Peter, cheerily. "It was like when a whale turns. . . . We're all clear, and after him again."

[242]

The gray pall of rain bore down on us. I was hot and wet with sweat, and asked for a raincoat to keep me from being chilled. Enveloped in this, I went on with my absorbing toil. Blisters began to smart on my hands, especially one on the inside of the third finger of my right hand, certainly a queer place to raise one. But it bothered me, hampered me. Bob put on his rubber coat and, protecting his camera more than himself, sat out on the bow, waiting.

My swordfish, with short, swift runs took us five miles farther out, and then welcome to see, brought us back, all this while without leaping, though he broke water on the surface a number of times. He never sounded after that first dive. The bane of an angler is a sounding fish, and here in Tahitian waters, where there is no bottom, it spells catastrophe. The marlin slowed up and took to milling, a sure sign of a rattled fish. Then he rose again, and it happened to be when the rain had ceased. He made one high, frantic jump about two hundred yards ahead of us, and then threshed on the surface, sending the bloody spray high. All on board were quick to see that sign of weakening, of tragedy—blood.

Peter turned to say, coolly, "He's our meat, sir."

I did not allow any such idea to catch my consciousness. Peter's words, like those of Bob and John, and the happy jargon of the Tahitians, had no effect upon me whatever.

It rained half an hour longer, during which we repeated several phases of the fight, except slower on the part of the marlin. In all he leaped fifteen times clear of the water. I did not attempt to keep track of his threshings.

After the rain passed, I had them remove the rubber coat, which hampered me, and settled to a slower fight. About this time the natives again sighted sharks coming around the boat. I did not like this. Uncanny devils! They were the worst of these marvelous fishing waters. But Peter said: "They don't know what it's all about. They'll go away."

They did go away long enough to relieve me of dread, then they trooped back; lean, yellow-backed, white-finned wolves.

"We ought to have a rifle," I said. "Sharks won't stay to be shot at, whether hit or not."

It developed that my swordfish had leaped too often and run too swiftly to make an extremely long fight. I had expected a perceptible weakening and recognized it. So did Peter, who smiled gladly. Then I taxed myself to the utmost and spared nothing. In another hour, which seemed only a few minutes, I had him whipped and coming. I could lead him. The slow strokes of his tail took no more line. Then he quit wagging.

"Clear for action, Pete. Give John the wheel. . . . I see the end of the double line. . . . There!"

I heaved and wound. With the end of the double line over my reel I screwed the drag up tight. The finish was in sight. Suddenly I felt tugs and jerks at my fish.

"*Sharks!*" I yelled, hauling away for dear life.

Everybody leaned over the gunwale. I saw a wide shining mass, greenish silver, crossed by purple bars. It moved. It weaved. But I could drag it easily.

"*Mauu! Mauu!*" shrilled the natives.

"Heave!" shouted Peter, as he peered down.

In a few more hauls I brought the swivel of the leader out of the water.

"By God! They're on him!" roared Peter, hauling on the leader. "Get the lance, boat hook, gaffs—anything. Fight them off!"

Suddenly Peter let go the leader and jerking the big gaff from Jimmy, he lunged out. There was a single enormous roar of water and a sheeted splash. I saw a blue tail so wide I thought I was crazy. It threw a six-foot yellow shark into the air!

"Rope him, Charley," yelled Peter. "Rest of you fight the tigers off."

I unhooked the harness and stood up to lean over the gunwale. The swordfish rolled on the surface, extending from forward of the cockpit to two yards or more beyond the end. His barred body was as large as that of an ox. And to it sharks were clinging, tearing the tail. Charley looped the great tail and that was a signal for the men to get into action.

One big shark had a hold just below the anal fin. How cruel, brutish, ferocious! Peter made a powerful stab at him. The big lance-head went clear through his neck. He gulped and sank. Peter stabbed another underneath, and still another. Jimmy was tearing at sharks with the long-handled gaff, and when he hooked one he was nearly hauled overboard. Charley threshed with his rope; John did valiant work with the boat hook, and Bob frightened me by his daring fury as he leaned far over to hack with a cleaver. Bob is lean and long and powerful. Also he was angry. Whack! He slashed a shark that let go and appeared to skip up into the air.

"On the nose, Bob. Split his nose! That's the weak spot on a shark," yelled Peter.

Next shot Bob cut deep into the round stub nose of this big black shark—the only one of that color I saw—and it had the effect of dynamite. More sharks appeared under Bob, and I was scared stiff.

"Take that! . . . And that!" sang out Bob, in a kind of fierce ecstasy. "You will try to eat our swordfish!—Dirty, stinking pups! . . . Aha! On your beak, huh! . . . Wow, Pete, that sure is the place!"

"Look out, Bob! For God's sake—look out!" I begged, frantically, after I saw a shark almost reach Bob's arm.

Peter swore at him. But there was no keeping Bob off those cannibals. Blood and water flew all over us. The smell of sharks in any case was not pleasant, and with them spouting blood, and my giant swordfish rolling in blood, the stench that arose was sickening. They appeared to come from all directions, especially from under the boat. Finally I had to get into the thick of it, and at that armed only with a gaff handle minus the gaff. I did hit one a stunning welt over the nose, making him let go. If we had all had lances like the one Peter was using so effectively we would have made short work of them. One jab from Peter either killed or disabled a shark. The crippled ones swam about belly up or lopsided, and stuck up their heads as if to get air. Of all the bloody messes I ever saw this was the worst.

"Makes me remember—the war!" panted Peter, grimly.

And it was Peter who whipped the flock of ravenous sharks off. *Chuck!* went the heavy lance, and that was the end of another. My heart apparently had ceased to function. To capture that glorious fish only to see it devoured before my eyes!

"Run ahead, Johnny, out of this bloody slaughter-hole, so we can see," called Peter.

John ran forward a few rods into clear water. A few sharks followed, one of them to his death. The others grew wary, and swam around and around.

[245]

"We got 'em licked!" said Peter. "Whoever saw the like of that? The bloody devils!"

Bob took the lance from Peter, and stuck the most venturesome of the remaining sharks. It appeared then that we had the situation in hand again. My swordfish was there still, his beautiful body bitten here and there, his tail almost severed, but not irreparably lacerated. All around the boat wounded sharks were lolling with fins out, sticking ugly heads up, to gulp and dive.

There came a letdown then and we exchanged the natural elation we felt. The next thing was to see what was to be done with the monster, now that we had him. I vowed we could do nothing but tow him to camp. But Peter made the attempt to lift him on the boat. All six of us, hauling on the ropes, could not get his back half out of the water. So we tied him fast and started campward.

Halfway in we spotted Cappy's boat. He headed for us, no doubt attracted by all the flags the boys had strung up. There was one, a red and blue flag that I had never flown. Jimmy tied this on his bamboo pole and tied that high on the mast. Cappy bore quickly down on us and ran alongside, he and all of his crew vastly excited.

"What is it? Lamming big broadbill?" he yelled.

My fish did resemble a broadbill in his long black beak, his wide-spread flukes, his purple color, shading so dark now that the broad bars showed indistinctly. Besides, he lay belly up.

"No, Cappy. He's a giant Tahitian striped marlin, one of the kind we've tried so hard to catch," I replied, happily.

"By gad! What a monster! . . . I'm glad, old man. My word, I'm glad! I didn't tell you, but I was discouraged. Now we're sitting on top of the world again."

"We've got him, Captain," said Peter, "and he's some fish. But the damn sharks nearly beat us."

"So I see. They are bad. I saw a number. . . . Have you got any fresh bonito?"

We threw our bait into his boat and headed for camp again. Cappy waved, a fine happy smile on his tanned face, and called: "He's a walloper. I'm sure glad."

We ran for the nearest pass, necessarily fairly slow, with all that weight on our stern. The boat listed half a foot and tried to run in a circle. It was about one o'clock and the sky began to clear. Bob raved about what pictures he would take.

[246]

We were all wringing wet, and some of us as bloody as wet. I removed my soaked clothes and gave myself a brisk rub. I could not stand erect, and my hands hurt—pangs I endured gratefully.

We arrived at the dock about three o'clock, to find all our camp folk and a hundred natives assembled to greet us. Up and down had sped the news of the flags waving.

I went ashore and waited impatiently to see the marlin hauled out on the sand. It took a dozen men, all wading, to drag him in. And when they at last got him under the tripod, I approached, knowing I was to have a shock and prepared for it.

But at that he surprised me in several ways. His color had grown darker and the bars showed only palely. Still they were there and helped to identify him as one of the striped species.[9] He was bigger than I had ever hoped for. And his body was long and round. This roundness appeared to be an extraordinary feature for a marlin spearfish. His bill was three feet long, not slender and rapier-like, as in the ordinary marlin, or short and bludgeon-like, as in the black marlin. It was about the same size all the way from tip to where it swelled into his snout, and slightly flattened on top—a superb and remarkable weapon. Singularly, he had a small head, only a foot or more from where his beak broadened to his eye, which, however, was as large as that of a broadbill swordfish. He had a straight under maxillary. The pectoral fins were large, wide, like wings, and dark in color. The fin-like appendages under and back of his lower jaw were only about six inches long and quite slender. In other spearfish these are long, and in sailfish sometimes exceed two feet and more. His body, for eight feet, was as symmetrical and round as that of a good big stallion. He carried this roundness back to his anal fin, and there further accuracy was impossible because the sharks had eaten most of the flesh from these fins to his tail. On one side, too, they had torn out enough meat to fill a bushel basket. His tail was the most splendid of all the fish tails I have ever observed. It was a perfect bent bow, slender, curved, dark purple in color, finely ribbed, and expressive of the tremendous speed and strength the fish had exhibited.

This tail had a spread of five feet, two inches. His length was

---

[9] Zane Grey called his catch the giant Tahitian striped marlin; marine scientists have more recently identified the fish as a huge Pacific blue marlin.

fourteen feet, two inches. His girth was six feet, nine inches. And his weight, as he was, 1,040 pounds.

Every drop of blood had been drained from his body, and this with at least 200 pounds of flesh the sharks took would have fetched his true and natural weight to 1,250 pounds. But I thought it best to have the record stand at the actual weight, without allowance for what he had lost. Nevertheless, despite my satisfaction and elation, as I looked up at his appalling shape, I could not help but remember the giant marlin Captain had lost in 1928, which we estimated at twenty-two or twenty-three feet, or the twenty-foot one I had raised at Tautira, or the twenty-eight foot one the natives had seen repeatedly alongside their canoes. And I thought of the prodigious leaps and astounding fleetness of this one I had caught. "My heaven!" I breathed. "What would a bigger one do?"

18

THE WHALE KILLERS OF TWO FOLD BAY

Zane Grey was such a prolific writer and so far ahead of schedule when he died on October 23, 1939, that his publisher didn't get out his last book, *Boulder Dam*, until 1963. Still other material was found after ZG's death, including our next selection, which was first published in the Hearst Sunday Supplement, *American Weekly*, on June 26, 1955.

"The Whale Killers of Two Fold Bay," or as the *American Weekly* editors renamed it, "Strange Partners of Two Fold Bay," resulted from ZG's first visit to Australia in 1936. While there, he got thousands of film feet of shark and marlin fishing at Bermagui, Narooma, Eden, and other fishy locations, and managed to capture an 840-pound "white death" shark and a 1,036-pound world record tiger shark taken within sight of Sydney Harbor.

"The Whale Killers," however, has little to do with ZG's angling triumphs. Zane Grey may have heard this tale from Dr. David Stead of the Sydney Museum; or perhaps Peter Williams, ZG's boatman for more than ten years and himself a former whaler, picked up the story on the docks in Eden. Whatever the source, Zane Grey accepted as fact the widely believed killer whale story of Two Fold Bay, and he quickly gathered the details and converted them to his own use.

One interesting aspect of this story's 1955 publication is that many of its readers then were unwilling to accept the intelligence and organizational ability ZG ascribes to killer whales. Now, less than two decades later, with several captive killers to study and a Disney film on the subject, the charge of anthropomorphism won't be as prevalent. But canismorphism—giving whales the qualities of dogs—could be a fair criticism, for "The Whale Killers" is nothing more or less than the excitement of an Arizona bear hunt transferred to Australian waters. And while a purist may be put off by possible errors, like the alleged roaring of a wounded whale (a California whaler once told me: "It's a pitiful thing that such a mighty mountain of a fish dies squeaking like a mouse"), the rest of us will sit back and let the familiar personalities of R. C. and Romer, Don and Moze, and ZG himself—all thinly disguised—sweep us along on new adventure.

GWR

THE WHALE KILLERS OF TWO FOLD BAY

Look," cried whaler Davidson, "there he breaches again!" The three other men in the tiny whaleboat scanned the water in the direction of their leader's outstretched arm.

Almost as Davidson spoke the huge humpback whale appeared on the calm surface of Two Fold Bay, some six hundred yards distant, engaged in a furious battle with a school of deadly orca, known more commonly as killer whales. At this juncture, the first of the accompanying boats from the little Australian fishing village of Eden came within hailing distance of their leader. "Hey, Dad," yelled one of the younger men in the first boat to Davidson, "what happened? Did he break off?"

"No, son," replied the elder, "the whale was attacked by a school of orca and we had to cut the line."

"Aw!" groaned the young man. "Why didn't you hang on a little longer?"

Young Davidson's boat came up and passed his father's and went on; all eyes were intent on the fury ahead. The elder Davidson had to call twice to make them stop. The other boats came along then and the rowers rested on their oars.

Suddenly young Davidson shouted: "They're bearing down on us!"

"So they are," responded Barkley excitedly. "If that whale or those orca should happen to come up under us, it would be all over!"

"Back away, men," ordered Davidson.

Meanwhile, the orca and the whale had sounded again and there was only an oily slick on the water where they had gone down. Then the sea opened suddenly again directly in front of the boat. The great blunt nose of the whale emerged beyond a white ripple, and there was a loud puff of expelled breath and then a whistling intake. Not an orca was in sight. Young Davidson suddenly straightened and raised the great harpoon high over his head. In magnificent action, he cast the iron. It sped true to the mark and sank half its length in the shiny hump. The young men in the boat with Davidson screamed their elation. The whale lunged and, crashing the water, disappeared. In another instant the boat stood almost on end, its stern sunk deeply and the bow rising to an angle of 45 degrees. Young Davidson clung to the thwarts while his comrades hung onto the seats to keep from being spilled out. The whale line stretched out stiff and straight, and in that precarious position the boat sped over the surface leaving two enormous white furrows behind.

"By God," cried Barkley, one of Davidson's companions, "that boy has fastened onto the whale again. What an arm! He's a born harpooner."

"He's a born fool!" rasped out the father, and standing up he cupped his hands to his mouth and thundered: *"Cut that line!"*

But young Davidson gave no heed, even if he did hear, which was improbable. The boat raced on and increased its speed. The leader ordered the other boats to row hard in pursuit. It was evident that Davidson, the father, was deeply concerned over the fate of his son and the others, in view of the tales related by whalers of orca capsizing small boats and attacking men in the water. While his companions worked furiously at the oars, he scanned the bay ahead. They rowed a mile or more before he spoke. Finally he said to the others, with great relief: "Thank God, they're still afloat! There! The whale is on the surface again and the orca are tearing into him. John's boat is up with them. The bloody fools are still fast to the whale!" In the succeeding moments while the three boats were gaining, the whale was driven down seven times but he was prevented from making any long runs. At last the leader's boat came within hailing distance.

"Cut that line, I tell you!" roared the father in stentorian tones.

This time young Davidson turned and waved his hand. "Looks good, Dad," he shouted. "These orca are doing us a good turn!"

"You young fool," bellowed Davidson, "they'll turn your boat over in a second!"

"Dad, we were scared stiff. Two of the orca came up to us and one went right under the boat, the other bit at the line, but he only pulled. Seems to me that if these orca were going to harm us they would have done it."

"That beats me," said Barkley, laying hold of Davidson's arm. "He may be talking sense. Don't make him cut the line."

It was evident that young John could not be forced from his object. The whale and his enemies sank once more and the skiff began to sail over the water again.

In several moments the whale rose again to try for a short blow before he was attacked and literally smothered by the pack of killers. There were at least a dozen of them. A big white spotted orca leaped high out of the water and landed squarely upon the whale's nose in what appeared to be a most singular and incredible

[252]

action. Boats and quarry were soon in the lee of the headland on the south shore and well in the smooth waters in the bay. The whale showed five times at shortening intervals. Then, some miles up the bay, he began to swim in circles. The attack of the orca had frustrated his escape and exhausted him. The orca continued to harry the whale whenever he rose, and the huge black and white fellows doggedly kept leaping upon his nose. These beasts must have weighed five or six tons, and, every time, they managed to submerge the nose of the whale before it could draw a good full breath.

The fray worked into shoal water, increasing the furious activity of the orca. The whale now floundered in three fathoms not far from the shore where friends and families of the whalers had come down to see the battle. From whaler Davidson's boat there rang a sharp command: "Pull close, John. Spear him the next time he comes up." The boatmen pulled the slack line in and laid it in the bow while young Davidson stood with his ten-foot lance waiting for the critical moment. The whale heaved up again, slowly rolling and gasping, this time the orca paying little attention to the boat in their furious attack. However, as the rowers pulled their boat closer to the whale, the orca left off their attack, but could be seen cruising around in front. As the first skiff came right upon the rolling quarry, young Davidson elevated the huge spear and plunged the ten feet of steel, with all his strength, deep into the vitals of the great beast. A geyser of blood shot high into the air. The whale let out a gasping, gurgling roar and began to beat the water with his tail in great white splashes. Quickly the boatmen backed water to a safe distance. All eyes were turned upon the death throes of the great humpback. He slapped the water with thunderous crashes. He rolled in a sea of blood. His great head came out, jaws gaping, with the huge juicy tongue hanging out. Immediately the orca were upon him, tearing the tongue out of his mouth, and then as the whale slowly sank, they could be seen biting out great mouthfuls of blubber. The whale sank slowly to the bottom in less than three fathoms of water. Presently the orca disappeared and the great humpback lay dying in convulsions in a great cloud of murky water. As soon as the blood had drifted away on the current, the second boat put down a huge hook and anchored it in the whale. Then all

boats rowed ashore where the whalers climbed out to the wild acclaim of their friends and families. As far as the whale was concerned, it would be necessary to wait a day or so until internal gases
built up to bring the beast to the surface. Then he could be towed
ashore and cut up.

Excitement ran high in Eden that night. The capture of the
whale presaged the beginning of an industry after a discouraging time
of many years during which great numbers of huge tiger sharks had
continually torn up the fishermen's nets, destroying the normal fishing industry along this part of the Australian coast.

Orca, the giant ancient enemy of whales, had been known along
the coast of New South Wales and Two Fold Bay for over seventy
years. That is about as long as the memory of the oldest inhabitant.
Of course, killer whales must have ranged up and down this coast
for thousands of years, as long indeed as whales have inhabited these
waters.

However, there had to be a whale industry before any notice was
taken of the orca and their predatory habit of chasing whales. A
peculiar kind of whaling had been developed by Davidson and his
men at Two Fold Bay, probably as primitive as was ever devised by
man. The whalers used what were little more than large rowboats,
harpoons with long ropes, and long-poled lances with which to put
the finishing stroke to the whales. Their method had been largely
unsuccessful in that they had been afraid to go out into the open sea
after their quarry. They patrolled the mouth of the bay until a
whale came in. Then they would attack it and take a chance on
being able to hold the whale within the confines of the bay. However, most of the whales they sighted had been too wary, and the
few monsters they actually harpooned soon departed with most of
their inadequate gear. However, because of the persistence of some
of the younger men under Barkley, who had been a whaler in New
Zealand, and the fact that the normal fishing industry of Eden was
dying, the whalers had kept up their dogged efforts.

The capture of the first whale depended a great deal upon the
formation of Two Fold Bay. It is a body of water difficult to describe. The mouth of the bay is comparatively narrow and the inlet
soon runs shallow towards the upper end, folding back upon itself,
to account for its picturesque name. The background is about the

[254]

same as everywhere along the New South Wales coast, very rugged
and wild with white sandy beaches, green benches, and forests of
eucalyptus running up to the mountain ranges which grow purple
in the distance. The little town of Eden is not only picturesquely
situated, but felicitously named.

This particular morning the whalers had been unusually lucky
and had sighted whales only a couple of miles out and well within
the calm water area of the bay. The elder Davidson's boat was first
to come within throwing distance of one of the giant humpbacks.
Barkley, heaving the heavy iron harpoon, had made fast to a whale
and the fight was on, to the grim concern of the older men and the
yelling chorus of the younger. The whale made off with three or
four hundred yards of rope and then slowed down. The three other
boats followed, rowing as swiftly as they could, but losing ground.
But, as usually happened, Davidson's craft was towed to the mouth
of the bay. Presently the whale came to the surface and began to
thrash around in a commotion of white water. Barkley, standing in
the bow holding to the rope, suddenly let out a yell: "*Orca*, by
Lord!" and pointed ahead. "Look, look! See those big black fins
standing up? They belong to bull orca whale killers. Bad luck! It's
as much as our lives are worth to go near that bunch!"

Davidson and the other two men in the boat saw the big black
fins swirling and splashing around the whale, forcing him down,
and Davidson cried: "Bad luck, indeed! We'll have to cut him
loose," and he made a move with a naked blade.

Barkley motioned him to stop. "Let's wait and see. There's five
hundred yards of good rope out there and we can't afford to lose it."
The whale sounded and the orca disappeared. The strain on the
whaling line slackened. Presently, as the men waited in tense excitement, the big humpback came to the surface surrounded by the
thumping, splashing school of orca. The boat was close enough for
the fishermen to hear the bellowing roar of the whale and the vicious splashing of the killer whales.

Barkley had heard a whale roar before in its terror, but the other
men had not. It was a strange, strangling sound. Then one of the
orca leaped into the air, a huge black glistening body with white
spots, and landed squarely on top of the whale. Sounding with a
tremendous splash of his tail, the big humpback went out of sight as

[255]

did his tormentors. Again the whale line went whistling off the bow. As the boat gathered momentum and rose on its stern, fairly flying through the water, Davidson leaped forward and cut the line. The boat settled down, slid ahead a few yards and finally came to a stop. The whalers, gray faced and sweating, eyed each other in silence. Finally Barkley, wiping his face, spoke: "I guess there wasn't anything else to do, but it's hard to swallow the loss of all that fine rope and the whale, too."

"We're lucky to get rid of him," spoke up one of the other men.

This would have been the end of it had not the younger men rashly made fast to the whale again and, with what seemed the almost incredible aid of the orca, succeeded in capturing him.

That night the men of Eden speculated excitedly on their good luck.

"Men," said Barkley, "I've got to believe my own eyes! These orca are as keen and bold as any hounds that ever chased a stag. Nearly every whale killed in deep water sinks to the bottom. The orca know this. If they kill a whale in the open sea, it will sink before they can satisfy their hunger. This bay is a trap, which accounts for the orca often hanging out here and patrolling the mouth until a school of whales comes along. Then they deliberately separate one from the others and drive him inshore. That accounts for the skeletons of whales we occasionally find here in shallow water. But, of course, every battle with a whale doesn't end successfully for the orca. They're intelligent enough to see that we're a help. They intercepted this whale and sent him back."

Young John answered, "As the chase kept on, they showed less fear of us."

"Well," spoke up John's father, "I wonder—it remains to be seen whether they'll do it again."

On the second day, about noon, while the whalers were at work cutting up their humpback, a scout came running down to the wharf to shout the exciting news that there was white water in the offing. Whaler Davidson took his glass and went to an elevated place to take a look. A school of whales was passing the mouth of the bay and one of them had already been cut adrift from his fellows and was being hemmed in and driven into the bay by the whale killers.

Davidson went back to his men with the exciting information, and two boats made ready to go out.

When they were about a mile off, it was evident that there was a big school of orca and that they were proceeding with remarkable energy to prevent the whale from getting back down the bay. According to Davidson, who had the glass: "There's a small bunch right at him and a larger number back a ways in a half circle and then a line of others stretched across the bay where the water is deep."

The whale, finding himself in shoaling water, made determined and persistent efforts to break the line of his tormentors, but whenever he charged back, a half dozen bulldogs of the sea charged him and tore at his head, compelling him to sound and turn. From the shore watchers could see the long green shadow moving up the bay and also the flashing black and white orca at his head. The pursuit in a straight line soon ended, and a ring of orca encircled the whale. He was a big humpback whale much larger than the first one, and he still had tremendous power. However, he was unable to prevent the orca from driving him up the bay to shallow water. They were on top of him every moment, and as his efforts to rise to breathe were frustrated, he grew bewildered, frantic, and nearly helpless, although the pursuing orca still kept a safe distance from his tremendous tail. There came a time when the humpback slid up on his side with a crooked-fin orca the whalers had dubbed Humpy, hanging on to his lip like a bulldog. What a strange blubbering roar the whale made! It was a loud noise and could be heard far beyond the village. Presently the whale shook free of Humpy and went plunging again, round and round. He was so big and powerful that the orca could not stop him, and Old Tom, as the whalers had named the orca with the white spots, could not wholly shut up the whistling blowhole. It was the opinion of some of the whalers that this humpback might have escaped his relentless enemies if he had had deep water. But between him and the dark blue water of the bay were stretched two lines of menacing orca that charged him in a body when he headed towards the opening.

It became apparent before long that the orca would require the help of the whalers to finish the humpback. Davidson sent out his son and a crew of four, also a second boat with four more men. The

[257]

men were still afraid of the orca, but there did not seem to be any reason for this. The orca, with the exception of Old Tom and Humpy, kept away from the boats. And it was astonishing and incredible to see their renewed ferocity when the whalers came upon the scene. Young Davidson soon harpooned the whale, which lunged out and then tried to burrow in the mud at the bottom in its mad endeavor to sound. But the whale was prevented from going any distance in a straight line. He was driven around to where a harpooner in the second boat soon made fast to him. They had him from two sides now. When the second harpoon went home, it struck a vital place, for it energized the whale to a tremendous rolling and heaving and a mighty buffeting of the water with his great tail. Out the long black head came again with the white smoke from the blowhole accompanied by a strangling whistle. Three of the orca were now hanging onto his lips, wiggling their shiny bodies with fierce and tenacious energy. Old Tom cut the water in a grand leap to alight fairly on the side of the whale's head and slip off, raising a great splash. That appeared to be a signal for the remaining orca to charge in close. In a maelstrom of white and bloody water, the whale and his attackers fought a few moments in a most ferocious manner. At the end of this attack, the whale heaved up with his great jaws spread and as he sank back, the orca in a solid mass tore at the enormous tongue.

Not long after the carnage had settled, several huge triangular-shaped fins were seen headed out to sea. So far as the orca were concerned, the engagement was ended. They swam away leaving the whalers with a seventy-foot humpback, and establishing the fact for all who had seen the incident that they had leagued themselves with the whalers.

Thus began a strenuous season for the whalers and all who were concerned in the disposition of the great carcasses. The inhabitants of Eden labored early and late. Seldom did they have a whale cut up and his carcass towed away to the other side of the bay when the orca would drive in another victim.

All through June the partnership between the whalers and the orca grew more successful. The news had long since traveled all over Australia, and many visitors made the long journey to the little hamlet to verify the strange and romantic tale. During July the whalers processed seven whales, which was about all they could handle with their limited equipment. Then toward the close of that month, the whales passed by in fewer numbers until only a stray was seen here and there. When at last they were gone, the orca were seen no more. The whalers speculated upon what had become of them and concluded that they had followed the whales. They were all sorry to see the orca go, hardly hoping that they would ever turn up again. But on the first of June the next year, on the very first day the whalers went out, they were amazed and delighted to see the orca patrolling the mouth of the bay. Old Barkley expressed the opinion that he thought they were as glad to see the whalers as the whalers were to see the orca! He proved his point when Old Tom, Old Humpy, and another orca they had dubbed Hooker, deliberately swam close to the boat to look them over—as if to identify them!

The orca were back, and it was a certainty that the well-known leaders of the pack, and others that had been named the summer before, had returned to Two Fold Bay. Barkley identified Big Ben and Typee, while the elder Davidson recognized Big Jack and Little Jack and an enormous lean orca without any white marks they called Blacky. In less than two hours from the time the orca showed themselves to the whalers, they had a humpback headed into the bay. In due course they drove it into shallow water where the combined energies of whalers and orca soon added another humpback to their list.

There were more whales that summer and more orca to help in the pursuit of them. When that season ended, it was an established fact that a crew of whalers had enlisted a school of whale killers to help them in their work.

Even more remarkable, on at least two occasions, the orca had driven in a whale and helped to kill it, but made absolutely no attempt to tear at the tongue, the juicy morsel that attracted them so powerfully. After the kill had been executed and the whale had sunk to the bottom, the orca had left without further molestation.

Davidson had done a good deal of thinking about this and had talked to his comrade Barkley about it. They decided that if the whale killers did not tear out the tongue of a crippled whale and otherwise chew him up, it meant that they were not hungry. The

[259]

deduction to be made, then, was that this intelligent school of orca, or at least the leaders, Old Tom, Humpy, Hooker, and one or two others, cut a whale adrift from its herd, chased him inland, and deliberately helped kill him for no other reason than to maintain their partnership with the whalers.

One night Davidson saw his conclusion borne out in a startling manner. Shortly after he had gone to bed, he was awakened by a succession of loud rapid reports almost like pistol shots. He listened, wonderingly. His house was some distance from the bay, but he had often heard the splashing of great sharks or the blowing of porpoises and other marine sounds that went on in the dead of night. When it occured again, somewhat more clearly, he decided it was a fish of some kind.

Davidson called to his son, who slept in the next room: "John, slip on some clothes and grab a lantern and go down to the wharf and see what's making that noise."

"What noise?" asked John, sleepily.

"Don't you hear it? Listen."

Again the sound rang out—short, sharp, powerful smacks on the water. John let out a whoop and his bare feet thudded on the floor. "Sure, I hear that!" he shouted. "Something's up for sure." He dresed, lighted a lantern, and rushed out.

He was gone so long that the elder Davidson nearly fell asleep waiting for him. But at last a light gleamed through the murky darkness, accompanied by the rapid tread of bare feet. John entered, letting the cool misty air in with him.

"Dad, what do you think?" he burst out. "Our band of orca have brought in a big whale and some of them are lobtailing while the others are fighting the whale. Struck me funny. What would they be doing that for?"

"No reason in the world, son, except to wake us up and tell us to come down and do our part! Go wake up the men and hurry down to the wharf," he ordered, as he got out of bed. Davidson dressed hurriedly, putting on his great raincoat; and lighting the lantern, he sallied forth into the black night. Several times before he reached the wharf, he heard loud buffetings on the water. As he drew closer, he also caught the sharp splashes and quick blows that he recognized were made by orca. Then he heard the strangled obstructed puff of a whale trying to breathe. A second later came the unmistakable and fearsome sound of the whale roaring like a wounded bull.

"By Halifax!" Davidson uttered. "I thought I had seen and heard everything before, but this beats me all hollow." He halted on the wharf and cast the beam of his lantern out upon the dark waters. He could see fifty feet or more from where he stood and as he watched, there came a surge of the water, a short deep whistle and intake of air, and a huge orca, blacker than the night, with his white spots showing like phosphorescence, plunged in the track of the lantern to show the gleaming eye and the tremendous seven-foot fin of Old Tom. Davidson yelled with all his might. It was as if he was halloing to the orca. The orca made a plunging souse and vanished. Then out of the darkness came rapid cracking slaps of the giant tail on the water, loud and sharp as the shots from a rapid-fire gun.

Davidson stood there marveling. The lobtailing ceased. Out there in the bay, a hundred or two hundred yards, resounded the rush and slap and roar of battle between a cornered whale and his enemies. Then lights appeared from all directions and soon Davidson was joined by a dozen men. They were excited, eager, and curious to know what it was all about.

"Our pet hounds have chased in a whale and they're fighting him out there," replied the chief.

"What can we do?" asked Barkley. "It's dangerous enough in the daytime, let alone at night."

"There's no danger for us if we keep out of the way of the whale."

"But we ought to wait until more light," objected Hazelton.

"It's a long while till dawn. Our orca have brought in a whale, and they have signaled us to come and help. We couldn't let them down now. We'll take four boats. I'll call for volunteers."

Twelve of the score or more men signified their willingness to take the risk. This was enough to man the boats. When all was in readiness, leader Davidson shouted for them to follow him and headed out over the black waters of the bay. While two of the crew rowed the lead boat, another held the lantern high and Davidson stood in the bow of his boat with his harpoon in readiness. "Back water," he called, presently. "Steady. Rest your oars! Now everybody listen. We got to tell by the sound." From the thrashing and swishing of the water, it appeared that the whale and his attackers were approaching the boats. After an interval of quiet when undoubtedly the whale and the orca were underwater, there came a break just ahead and as the long black snout of the whale appeared, it emitted a resounding blast as loud as a steam whistle. Davidson poised the harpoon aloft. He was a big man and he easily held the heavy iron. As the whale came sliding by, he cast the harpoon with unerring and tremendous force. In the light of the lantern, it appeared to sink half its length in the side of the whale.

"*Get away! Get away!*" boomed Davidson as he sank to his knees with the line in his hands.

With a thunderous surge the whale answered the inthrust of the steel. He leaped half out of the water. As he came down, big waves rocked the boat, nearly capsizing it. Then the whole pack of orca were upon their victim. The sounds of watery combat and the frenzied plunging of the whale united in a deafening din. Orca and whale passed out of the lantern's illumination. Davidson yelled at the top of his lungs, but his words were indistinct. The lights of the other boats came close. The whale sounded with his demons hanging on to him, and in the sudden quiet, yells became distinguishable.

"I'm fast, men, good and hard," called the leader. "The line is going out. He's circling. Better hang close to me so that when he comes round you can get another iron in him. . . . Mike, lend a hand here. They're blocking him—turning him. We can risk a tow *. . . Hey, you all back there, hang close to us, it's getting hot!*"

Davidson's boat was now being hauled through the water at a considerable rate. The line showed the whale to be circling, but the lantern, which had been set down, cast very little light ahead. However, the lanterns of the crew behind Davidson helped. Suddenly the line slacked, the boat slowed down, the turmoil of orca and whale ceased again. "He's sounded," yelled Davidson. "Now look out!" His warning cry was echoed by the men in the nearest boat. They had seen a gleam in the water ahead in time for them to row aside, just missing the blunt nose of the whale as it heaved out. Again that whistling strangled intake of breath, a hollow rumbling roar, then the surge of a tremendous body in friction against the water, and after that the swift cutting splashes of the orca and the dull thuds of their contact with the whale. Nevertheless, the second boat did not escape an upset. It capsized and all the men were thrown into the water. The third boat sped to the rescue, and just as quickly, young Davidson, in the bow of the fourth boat, with a magnificent throw, made fast to the sliding black flanks of the whale. The two boats towed by the whale passed the others and sped into the night. Soon the orca stopped the crippled whale and killed it. When gray dawn broke soon after, the orca had left the scene of carnage and the whale had sunk.

*

The successful summer passed and another followed. The fame of the whale killers continued to spread abroad, bringing many people to the bay, and the little hamlet of Eden grew apace. The whaling business flourished, and there was some talk of installing more modern methods of hunting the leviathans. But nothing ever came of it. The whalers preferred their own method and the help that was given them by the orca. So the years passed bringing few changes. The older whalers passed on or moved away or gave up their work to sit in the sun and tell tales about their great experiences with the orca. Davidson's son, John, became the leader of the whalers, and other younger men took the place of the old. For thirty years there was little alteration in the number and actions of the orca. Led by Old Tom and Humpy and Hooker, this pack of sea wolves patrolled the mouth of Two Fold Bay and grew well nigh perfect in their system of driving whales into the quiet waters within reach of the harpoons. And as they grew more proficient in their attacks, they also grew friendly with their human allies.

It was related of Old Tom that he grew mischievous and liked to play pranks, some of which gave the whalers a great deal of concern. Several times he made off with the anchor of a small boat, dragging the boat behind him. This was play, and after a while the whalers seemed to enjoy the experience as much as the orca. But the first time that Old Tom took the line fastened to a harpooned whale and ran off with it, the whalers were frightened and concerned, and had a difficult time recovering it. There didn't seem to be any reason for this behavior except playfulness on the part of the big fellow. The remarkable thing was that this trick of Old Tom's never lost them a whale.

He and old Humpy often swam alongside the small boats with

[263]

every appearance of friendly interest. The whalers never entirely gave up their fear of falling overboard when orca were around. A heritage of confidence had come down to them from the older whalers, but it applied only to Old Tom and Humpy and Hooker and possibly one or two others. The young whalers were still afraid of the less tame and friendly orca.

Most notable of all stories told by the old whalers, and handed down to their sons, was the time the orca, either by mistake or design, drove a sperm whale into the bay. Sperm and blue whales were rare along the coast, and the whaling men had given the sperms a wide berth. Owing to the superior bulk and speed of this species, and the fact that they have great teeth in the lower jaw, and habitually charge boats when attacked, sperm whales are considered most formidable and dangerous foes. That day, two boats went out ahead, the crews composed of younger men. Then two other boats, with some experienced whalers among the crews, followed the first two and found them fast to a whale they didn't know was a sperm. The older men, reluctant to show a shy spirit by cutting this whale loose, came to the assistance of the bold young whalers. They fought the big beast all the way up the bay to the shoal water. Here again the whalers were treated to an exhibition of the amazing intelligence of the orca. When the sperm headed toward one of the skiffs, Old Tom and his partners would lay hold of the side of the whale, carefully avoiding the great jaw, and fight him and nag him until he changed his course. This was one whale Old Tom did not try to stop breathing, for a major reason: the blowhole of the sperm was clear out at the end of his nose and much nearer the formidable jaws and huge teeth than in other species of whale. As a consequence, this fight was a longer one, fiercer and harder than any the whalers had ever seen. It was owing, of course, to the superior strength and stamina of the sperm, and the impossibility of the orca's interfering with his breathing. But when the whale reached the shallow water, the whole pack attacked him and they made up in ruthless fury what they had lost in the way of technique. The men now pressed in and tried to get another harpoon in the sperm.

The whalers had noticed a number of huge tiger sharks following in the wake of the bloody mess and this fact did not lend any pleasure to the thought of a capsized boat. John Davidson's skiff

[264]

finally drew in close to the sperm and John, by a very long throw, got his harpoon into the side of the whale—but it did not hold. Suddenly the sperm turned as on a pivot. The slap of his great tail staggered the boat and threw John into the water. Cries of alarm rose from the other whalers. The boat from which John had fallen passed him with its momentum, and before the crew could back water, two of the great orca deliberately swam up to Davidson. The sperm whale was still close, rolling and thrashing around, and everywhere were other orca and a number of the big gray tiger sharks. One of the men standing in the bow of the skiff with a rope yelled at the top of his lungs: "It's Old Tom and Humpy! They're not going to hurt John!"

And marvelous to relate, that is the way it was. Old Tom and Humpy, who had been friends with the whalers for fifty years, swam one on each side of Davidson and guarded him for the distance of some yards until his own swimming and a rope tossed from the first boat made his rescue possible. The orca actually followed until John was safe in the boat.

The fight with the sperm was then renewed; and in time, when the whale's weakening enabled the whalers to get in two more harpoons, the fight eventually ended with victory for the men from Eden. Orca and sharks chewed up the whale pretty badly, but they could not injure the great head which formed at least a third of this species' body and which contained the valuable sperm oil. However, several of the orca seemed to have been injured in this fray. One was seen to swim away after the others as if he were crippled.

No yarn handed down from the old whalers to the young compared to this one. And the young whalers made the most of it! From that day, Old Tom and Humpy became heroes. But when Old Tom's body washed ashore in Two Fold Bay shortly afterward, the villagers were stunned. Some were in favor of sending the skin to Sydney to be mounted, but the whalers would have none of this. They built a memorial for Old Tom right there in Eden.

Humpy and the other orca well-known to the whalers were often seen in the ensuing years. But whales finally became so scarce that the whalers did not go out, and the orca took to other hunting grounds. Finally the whaling business waned and died, but never the romance and wonderful doings of the orca whale killers. It was said by many that the friendly orca had all died, but others thought they'd roamed on to better hunting waters.

There are men now living in Eden who will take pleasure in verifying the story I have here told. Some will tell it conservatively; others will embellish it with the most remarkable fishing yarns that were ever invented. And they say an occasional fight between orca and whales can be seen to this day off the mouth of Two Fold Bay.

19

THE NORTH UMPQUA, OREGON

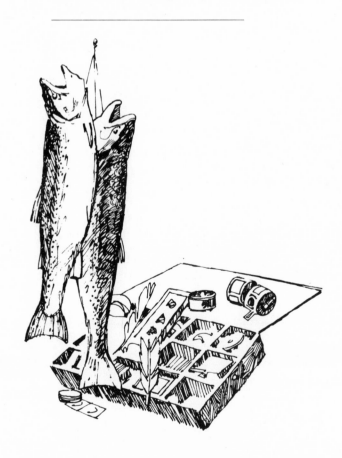

In some respects, Oregon's Umpqua River has changed little since ZG fished its North Fork. In fact, many of the names given to choice pools by the Grey family during their regular visits in the 1930's have stuck, so that today's residents are familiar with Ledges, Divide Pool, Split Rock Hole, and Takahashi Pool. The last-mentioned, by the way, honors Zane Grey's cook, George Takahashi, who accompanied ZG for twenty years on various hunting and fishing adventures and was the first man to clear all the brush from alongside this particular pool so that backcasts wouldn't hang up. It was a day-long effort, but George caught the first steelhead out of this pool and today it's still one of the best on the North Umpqua.

But some unpleasant features of the river described by ZG in 1934 also have little changed. Occasional fishing with "Dupont sinkers" (alias, dynamite caps) still goes on, and in 1970 several hundred Chinook salmon were destroyed in one pool alone—approximately 20 percent of the entire spawning run that year.

In addition, ZG's fears that the automobile might invade the region became a reality nearly twenty years after his death with the completion of a road through some of his favorite haunts. And dams at the upper end of the North Fork have put a limit on the number of tributary creeks available for spawning salmon and steelhead.

However, the years have created some good. Gill-netting is no longer permitted at the mouth of any Oregon river (the Columbia excepted), and in 1968 the state legislature declared the steelhead a game fish. Now the only legal commercial fishery for steelhead is conducted by the Columbia River gill-netters, who are allowed to market the sea-run rainbows that are too large to pass through their 7¼-inch mesh. (They call these fish "incidental catch.")

Finally, the hatcheries that ZG railed against should instead be commended for their work. In all likelihood without them, timbering, pollution, and development would have caused the virtual disappearance of the Pacific Northwest anadromous fishes. Yet we can understand the sentiments of an aging angler, who had taken native gamesters from many of the finest waters in North America, protesting against the mechanics of put-and-take fishing. Very simply, ZG suspected hatchery fish lacked the "wild spirit" of true game fish.

All but the introduction to "The North Umpqua, Oregon" was published as "North Umpqua Steelhead" in the September, 1935, issue of *Sports Afield*. ZG's introduction was eliminated because the magazine's editors felt it was too "cranky" and might offend some readers. By contemporary standards of environmental concern, Zane Grey's words are not cranky enough.

GWR

THE NORTH UMPQUA, OREGON

It ought to be a guarantee that I am honest and sincere about this noble river, practically unknown to the world, when I confess that I have given up the Rogue, and the fishing lodges I own at Winkle Bar, on the most beautiful and isolated stretch, to camp and fish and dream and rest beside the green-rushing, singing Umpqua.

Before I go on to tell of the Umpqua, to show how its fishing is superior to any river in the United States, and comparable only to the great rivers of Newfoundland or the far-famed Tongariro of New Zealand, I want to get a few things off my chest.

This summer was my third on the Umpqua, and about completed my study of conditions and possibilities.

The people of Oregon, and more especially, those who live on or near the Umpqua, are as a whole deaf and dumb and blind to the marvelous good of this river, and if they do not wake up, its virtue and beauty and health will be lost to them.

It is difficult to talk to people who are not particularly interested in the value of a river. Nevertheless rivers are as important as land, and infinitely more capable of interesting travelers, tourists, anglers.

As a contrast to the personnel in some Forest Reserves I find the supervisors, rangers and game wardens of the Umpqua keenly aware of the value of the river, and of its possibilities. But they have so little power, except over the timber of the forest. The water of the noble Umpqua fell into the hands of private promotors, who are simply waiting to exploit it. When they build the dams and cut the timber, with all the attendant ballyhoo about good to the people, that will be the end of the Umpqua. It will merely be history repeating itself. I never knew any company, in any one of the many National Forests, to do anything but harm. And in many preserves I could point out where forest fires and devastation have tremendously increased. The automobile is the worst foe of forests and rivers.

Outside of Canada there is no stream in the United States that can hold a candle to the Umpqua for wet or dry fly-fishing. This year there was an unprecedented run of steelhead. It was all the more astonishing in view of the net fishing at the mouth and the salmon racks up the river. The commercial interests have been strong enough politically to get steelhead trout regulated under the name "salmon." They are not salmon. But it is perfectly obvious why this characterization has been imposed upon the people. The law says it is illegal to net trout.

It is also perfectly obvious that the Fish and Game Commission, so far as the Umpqua is concerned, have no interest in the future. What interests them is where the money comes from *now*. And that comes from the nets at the mouth of the river.

Any scientific angler, any good naturalist, let alone an ichthyologist, could expose the blunders made in the so-called conservation of fish. For example, U. S. fish hatcheries are mostly rackets. In very few cases do they increase the number of fish, despite the millions of eggs hatched and the millions of young fry released in the river. But that sounds swell in the newspapers, in the fisheries reports. It's a lot of baloney. It's just another example of Vanishing America.

In the cold tributaries of the Umpqua millions of young fry freeze to death. Those that survive get eaten up pronto. If the hatcheries were of any value at all they would take the *summer* steelhead for their eggs. But they merely stop these steelhead from getting up to their spawning grounds.

So far as we can ascertain, Canton Creek and Steamboat Creek are the natural spawning streams for steelhead. The Chinooks, what few get over the racks in high water, go on up the Umpqua. Both Canton and Steamboat creeks should be closed. We found evidences of huge numbers of steelhead being dynamited by pot-hunters from over the divide. The rangers and wardens do their best, but they cannot be everywhere at once, and the freedom of the creeks to so-called fishermen makes it easy for the murdering of vast numbers of steelhead full of eggs.

Unless strong measures are adopted by the people of Oregon, this grand river will go the way of the Rogue. And it will be a pity because the value of the Umpqua, with its wonderful steelhead, is inestimable.

I may be an outsider, but I love the Umpqua, and I know what it needs to be saved for Oregonians first and outsiders afterwards. But I had better, in this article, confine myself to the fish and fishing.

*

Fifty miles or so above its junction with Steamboat Creek the Umpqua has its source in the high ranges and probably receives most of its ice-cold water from an underground outlet in Diamond Lake. For many miles down, this rushing river seldom feels the sun. Great fir trees and canyon walls shade it. Numerous small brooks and creeks augment its flow. There are two big waterfalls and innumerable rapids. Ten miles above Steamboat, cutthroat and rainbow trout up to five pounds are abundant. We know that steelhead run up at least that far. There is a good trail up the river, and two homesteaders. Not until you reach Steamboat on the way down does the Umpqua know anything about fishermen, or automobiles. It is virgin. It has unsurpassed beauty. Deer and bear and cougar, wolves and coyotes are abundant.

From Steamboat an auto road makes the Umpqua accessible to anglers. That is to say it is easy to see the river from the road. But there are only a few places where you can get down to the river without great exertion and a risking of your neck, and a very decided chance of your being hit by a rattler. There is a succession of long channels, cut in solid granite, and white rapids. We call many of the former, pools.

The Umpqua is the most dangerous river to wade, and therefore to fish, that I know this side of Canada. In June it is high, swift, heavy and cold. It would be bad for any fisherman to slip in. And the rocks are more slippery than slippery elm! July it begins to drop, half an inch a day, and by August you can reach most of the water. This summer, which was hot and dry, making the Umpqua lower than ever known before, it was possible for some young and vigorous fishermen, like my boys, to wade it without waders. At that I have seen them come back to camp blue in the face, shivering as with the ague, and yelping for the fire. I would not advise wading the Umpqua very much without waders.

It is not a good river for spoon and bait fishermen. I watched upwards of several dozen hardware fishermen this summer, and very few of them caught steelhead. Some of them get good bags of small trout. I am not one of the many who advocate closing the Umpqua to spoon fishermen. That is arbitrary, and would be inclined to affront many Oregonians who live near the river. My idea has been to educate spoon fishermen, and I have succeeded with several.

There are two reasons why this should be easy: first, a spoon fisher-man by a few casts in any stretch of water spoils the fishing in that particular place for fly fishermen all the rest of that day. A good angler with the fly, especially the dry fly, can spend all day in a hundred-yard stretch of water. It is obvious that only a fish hog, or an unthinking fisherman, will go down the river, spoiling all the water for others who start in behind him. The second reason has no ethical or sporting side. It is merely that even a novice can, as soon as he learns a little about casting, get more rises, hook more steel-head, and have infinitely more sport than the spooner. Only the expert spoon fisherman can contend with an expert fly fisherman, and even the very best ones would get nowhere in a contest with Burnham[1] or Romer. The question of tackle is negligible. You can buy useable fly tackle almost as cheap as spoon tackle.

I have had many requests by letter to tell what kind of tackle we use and how we fish. Romer, like Burnham, is partial to light tackle. This summer, as usual, he started with five-and-a-half-ounce Leonards and Grangers, Halford lines, and .357 Hardy leaders. These English leaders are tapered, nine feet in length, and they cost plenty. In spite of his skill, and delicate handling of big fish, and his wonderful daring in wading and, in a pinch, swimming the Umpqua, Romer began right at the outset to lose many steelhead. He broke two tips, and many leaders. He graduated to six-ounce rods and .345 leaders. And when he quit on September 21st, his last fish, an 11¾-pound steelhead, about which I will tell later—he was using my favorite leader, .341.

Romer fishes fine and far away. He is a disciple of Burnham. He can cast a hundred feet with ease. But he begins on a pool by keeping out of sight and fishing close. He is like an Indian in his wary approach. He never scares any trout. He preferred always, until this summer, small flies, numbers six and eight, and he used a good many English flies.

As is well-known, the Parmachene Belle and Hair Coachman are the best flies on the Umpqua during June and July. But toward the middle of the latter month the fish stopped rising to these patterns.

---

[1] Fred Burnham, an angling friend from California who first put Zane Grey on to the Umpqua.

[272]

The old Turkey-and-Red failed to raise them, and the Turkey-and-Gold that Joe Wharton[2] made for me soon lost its effectiveness. I had Wharton make a pattern after the New Zealand Gold Demon, adding hair and jungle cock. It was good for a while. Then that too slowed up, and we were hard put to find flies that would raise fish.

I had always been partial to larger flies, number four and number three. And I had Loren and Joe Debernardi[3] get busy with the fly-tying kits. It was my idea, but Loren hit upon a fly that beat any I ever used, and it was quite different in pattern and color from all the others. With that fly, and others similar, we had the most magnificent sport that I ever heard of on a steelhead river. We really made Umpqua steelhead fishing no less than salmon fishing. And I mean Atlantic salmon fishing.

My bag of steelhead was impressive. Sixty-four in all, including three over eleven pounds, five of nine, a dozen around eight, and so on down to five pounds. Of course, I let a good many fish go. We never kept any we could not use, except a big one that we wanted to photograph. And these we smoked. Steelhead properly smoked and salted are most delectable.

But that number sixty-four does not say anything. It was the steelhead I raised and could not hook, and those that I hooked and could not land which counted. My favorite rod was a Hardy, seven ounces, with an extension butt I used after I hooked a fish. It was a wonderful rod. I do not see how it stood all the fights I had. Some of the steelhead I caught took over an hour to subdue. One that I did not catch, and never even saw, battled for two and a half hours and took me half a mile down the river where I would certainly have drowned but for Joe.

Curious to relate, this fish and the two largest I got fast to were all hooked in the same place—a pool we called Island Pool. It was a channel in a bend with rocky islands here and there. The water was swift. Below was a rapid, then a long succession of small islands, and

---

[2] A former Rogue River guide and owner of a distinctive tackle shop in Grant's Pass. At one time there were only two stores in the United States that sold Halford lines: Abercrombie & Fitch in New York City and Joe Wharton's in Grant's Pass, Oregon. He later became the town's mayor.

[3] Another Oregon guide.

[273]

then a series of white rapids. The one I caught out of this hole weighed 11¼. I was one hour and five minutes on this bird. At that I never got him fairly, for he ran down the river so fast I could not follow. He took a hundred and sixty yards of the hundred and ninety-two yards I had on my reel—this was the Crandall[4] new camouflage salmon line, with one hundred fifty yards of the strongest and finest silk backing—the most wonderful line I have ever used.

Joe ran down river and, wading out to the islets below, he succeeded in catching hold of my line. He held the steelhead for a while in the swift current, then carefully handlined him up river, until the fish took a notion to run again. This happened three times, and the last time he got the steelhead close up to him, or even with him, then he had to let go.

"Big pink buck!" yelled Joe. "He's tired. Put the wood to him!"

I was over a hundred yards above Joe. How I ever pumped that steelhead up to me, inch by inch, I cannot tell. But eventually I did, and led him ashore and beached him on a flat rock. Then breathless and wet and exhausted by excitement and exertion, I sat down to gaze spellbound at this magnificent steelhead. He was over thirty inches long, deep and thick, with a tail spread of eight inches, and a blending of silver and rose exquisitely beautiful.

The second whale I hooked in that hole, I did not see rise. I felt a heavy drag and thought my fly had caught. It had, as a galvanizing vibrant pull proved. I saw a long white fish wiggle and jerk in the shadow of the green water. Then he came upstream slowly. He swam all the way up the Island Pool to where it was shallow. And there in scarcely three feet of water he fooled around in plain sight. Joe nearly fell off the rocks in his frenzy to get that fish. I nearly collapsed. For we could see him, and he was forty inches long, ten deep, a pink fresh-run steelhead that must have been lifted over the salmon racks by the netters at the hatchery. Sometimes they dip out a few steelhead and release them up river. Gus, my driver,[5] saw them lift out six, all over twenty pounds, and one they said would go

---

[4] Ever since 1832, the Crandall family of Rhode Island has owned and operated the Ashaway Line & Twine Company which provided ZG with all his fresh and salt-water lines.

[5] Gus Bagnard, a schoolmate and fishing companion of Loren's from Altadena.

twenty-eight. No other way could those giant steelhead get above the racks. Well, this one was so big that I could not do anything but keep the rod up and let him bend it. To make a long and agonizing story short, this monster swam there in plain sight for over a half hour until the hook pulled out. I have lost 1,000-pound swordfish with less misery! Joe swore he would get drunk.

The third huge steelhead I hooked there must have been even larger. We never saw him once. The first one, I forgot to tell, had leaped prodigiously and often. This third one made my reel shriek and smoke as no Newfoundland salmon had done. He ran a hundred yards, then stopped in the current. We ran, fell, waded, climbed, all but swam. At times Joe had to hold me up. I got half or more of the line back, then the son-of-a-gun ran again. This happened five times during that half mile. At last down at the head of a fall above what we call the Divide Pool he hung for half an hour more, then took his hardest run. I was glad he got off, but Joe was sick. I shall never forget what thrills and pangs that steelhead packed into the two-and-a-half-hour battle.

Loren established a remarkable and enviable record of one hundred steelhead for the three months of our stay. A third of these, at least all of the small ones, he carefully unhooked and let go.

During July I used to sit in camp with my glass and watch him fish the ZG Pool. Out of this water he caught forty-three steelhead, and here he learned the fine points of the game. He developed. His luck was nil at first. For weeks it was all he could do to raise a fish a day. But he stuck, and that's the answer. After that he would get up at daylight and try to beat everybody to the Ranger Station Pool at Steamboat. Half the time he beat the fishermen who were camped right on the bank. And did he snake steelhead out of that strange and wonderful hold! Twenty-seven he caught there, and lost twice that many. But when the fish start down, it's time to weep.

Loren's best work came in August in the pools down the river. He would leave early in the afternoon and come back at dark—wet, tired, but with shining eyes. And once only do I recall that he came back without fish. That single exception he had a story that even I dare not tell. Allowing for the exaggeration and inaccuracy of a youngster, it was still a most remarkable fish yarn. Some days he would climb down the almost unscalable mountain, kick rattlers off the rocks, raise from ten to twenty steelhead, hook some, fight them, and catch one or two, or more. Three times he got the limit.

One night—the night—he came back with Gus packing a huge red steelhead that weighed in camp, hours after it had dried out, a little over twelve pounds.

"Here he is, fellows," he flashed with vibrant voice. "Look him over. Thirty-two and one-half inches! Look at that spread of tail. . . . Look at me! Soakin' wet. An' look at this skinned place on my shin! An' look at Gus!—He swam out above that bad rapid—you know, the hole, my hole, where I have hooked an' lost so many—Gus swam out to save the line. I thought he would go over the falls. But he didn't. And this darn fish then swam upstream again. He did that a dozen times. Jump? Oh, it was terrible. Right in our faces! He splashed water right on me. He shook himself—tussled, like a dog. All silver an' red—jaws like a wolf! . . . Oh, boy, I'm tellin' you, it was great!"

I did not need to be told that. It was. And not all the greatness was in the sport, the luck, the fish itself. It is the spirit that counts. The boy or man who can be true to an ideal, stick to a hard task, carry on in the face of failure, exhaustion, seeming hopelessness—he is the one who earns the great reward.

As for Romer, dynamic drama always attended his fishing activities. He could not keep out of trouble with fish. One day he spent the whole long day trying to raise a big steelhead that lay dark against a green rock in the ZG Pool. This fish was so big he could be seen from automobiles on the road, high above the river. Romer must have tried a hundred flies over that fish. He must have rested him almost as many times. He did not come in for supper. We yelled and waved. No use! Finally I sent Joe out to drag him in. But Joe forgot that—forgot all in the passion to raise this steelhead.

I sat in my camp chair with my glass trained on Romer. And I was watching when he at last persuaded or drove this steelhead to rise. I saw the great boil on the water, then the angry upcurl of white water. Romer's piercing yell of triumph and Joe's hoarse yell of exultation came to our ears above the roar of the falls.

I yelled like a maniac, and then all of us lined up on the cliff to watch in intense excitement. That steelhead ran up the river. The channel was tortuous and impossible to wade in a straight line. But

[276]

Romer and Joe followed as best they could. Once a great splash far upstream warned me that this steelhead was going places. He did not show again. He ploughed through two rapids before he broke off. Romer stood as one dazed, looking up the river. Then he turned and waded back toward camp.

We were all sympathy. Romer was pale and grim. His big dark eyes burned. "Eighteen pounds!" he said. "I raised him at noon on a New Zealand fly. And tonight he took a Turkey-and-Gold—after all that time. I think he got sore, like a salmon does when you cast a lot over him."

Another evening I was just getting back to camp when I heard yelling. I ran. When I got out where I could see, the crowd was lined up on the cliff, greatly excited. They yelled and pointed. Then I saw Romer pile into the deep swift channel above the big falls. Long ago I ceased to be scared when he pulled some stunt like this. He is a champion swimmer. He waded out on the other side, his bent rod held high. He could not stop the fish. It went over the falls. Romer plunged in to swim back to the point he had started from. And then straight down the middle of this wide reach in the Umpqua he ran with great strides. We knew, of course, he had hooked another of the bad fighters. There was a ledge of rock extending across the river, with the heavy fall at the far side, and a lesser one on our side. Romer piled right off this ledge to swim the few yards to the head of an island. There he ran again, winding his reel like a madman. Evidently the demon of a fish kept on. At the foot of this island Romer waded a bad rapid that he had never attempted before. He reached another island where we thought he would be marooned. We hurried along the cliff, kept even with him, and climbed down to the bank, yelling encouragement. There was a white millrace between Romer and the shore on our side. He leaped in with bent rod and swam. We saw the rod wag with his powerful strokes. He came out safely, crossed the shallow rocky place, ran to the gravel bar below, and at length clear round the bend he stopped that fish in a deep eddy.

And there, for twenty minutes more, by my watch, Romer pumped and worked on that steelhead before he could lift him. We were all dumbfounded to see the fish which had put up that fight. It was one of the smallest size. In fact it weighed four and a half

[277]

pounds. But what a rare, colorful, quivering, magnificently built steelhead!

"What do you—know about that!" Romer exclaimed, when he could talk. "Froze stiff—for this little fish!"

I happened to be with Romer when he got fast to a big steelhead that, like this little one, was almost unbeatable.

It happened at the Takahashi Pool near sunset on our last day of fishing. We had been far down the river. No luck! I had not even had a rise. Romer whipped the lower reaches in Takahashi while I watched. The sun set. The river sped by, shimmering in amber-green light. The mountain slope was bathed in gold. Insects had begun to chirp. The air had grown cold.

At last Romer climbed a high rock at the head of this Takahashi Pool and cast from there. This is at the foot of a heavy rapid. The waves were white-crested and big, the current fast. Few trout fishermen would ever try such a place. But we raised steelhead out of such water. When our fly dances over these waves, steelhead will rise straight from the bottom in a rush, and come clear out. Sometimes they miss the fly; seldom do they hook themselves; but when they are going fast—what a wonderful experience!

I was watching the fly when a vicious splash flew up and Romer's yell pealed out. I ran to a more advantageous point. This steelhead ran upstream against that current so that the line seethed cuttingly, audible to the ears. Romer stood high with a long line out. He reeled fast, but there was no need, for the bag in the line was as tight as a wire. I ran on up beside him, and got there in time to see this steelhead leap fully six feet out of that white water. He looked enormous and he caught all the gold of the setting sun.

Turning, he made down river with extraordinary speed. I could not keep pace with Romer. At the foot of that long stretch there is a ledge where all hooked steelhead foul the line. This one did. We had a moment of despair. Then the reel sang again. The line was round the ledge but not fouled. Romer got out on the platform of poles Joe had built there for the purpose of releasing our lines when caught. Romer worked there carefully to get free. He reached out so far with his rod that I feared he would fall in. With sunset the canyon had begun to fill with shadow and soon the line was hard to see. But we could hear the reel clear enough. Jerk by jerk it warned us that the line was nearing the spool. Presently it ceased.

[278]

"There!—All—out," cried Romer, tragically.

"What? Not all your line!"

"Yes. What'll I do now?"

The old poignant query in moments of baffled effort!

"My heavens. All that hundred and ninety yards!" Then I remembered the long forked pole Joe and I had used before we built the platform. Finding that, I waded as far as I dared and reached out. The pole was heavy. When I got it extended, it sank of its own weight. Another desperate try while Romer called huskily: "Hurry, Dad!"

I released the line. It sang like a telephone wire. Romer plunged off the platform and made the water fly. I followed. We came out upon the flat ledge round the corner to a long deep stretch of river. Here had always been the ideal place to have it out with a big steelhead. Dusk had mantled the gap between the wooden slopes.

"He's stopped. But I can't get—any line," panted Romer.

"You've got to. It's now or never. What kind of leader and hook have you on?"

"That short salmon leader you gave me—and big hook. I put them on—to try in that rough water."

"Lucky break! Lam it into him before he takes a notion to run again."

"Hook'll tear out. . . . Oh, he's heavy."

"No, it won't. Not this time. Put the wood on him, Romer."

The moment was one of severe strain for more than the tackle and steelhead. But nothing broke. Romer got him headed upstream. Little by little he recovered line. What an endless task it seemed! I believed he was half an hour on that fish before he got to the enameled end. Forty-two yards from the steelhead! I begged Romer not to be afraid to pull him. In a long fight, the hook wears out of a fish's jaw.

The moon came up over the mountain—a full moon, bright as silver, and it made a vast difference. We could see. But another quarter of an hour passed before we saw the first white flash of the big trout. He was far from whipped, at least as badly whipped as Romer wanted.

We were standing in a foot of water with the fish close, weaving and turning right in front of us. Every time he moved his tail he took line.

[279]

"Don't let him have an inch! Hold him!" I remonstrated. "Romer, that steelhead is as tired as he will ever get."

"Oh—Lord!" was all my son replied.

Moments dragged by. And we saw the steelhead on each turn. In that black water, when he flashed in the moonlight, he looked monstrous. Everything was magnified. I never saw such delicate handling of a big fish. Afterward I acknowledged Romer's incredible patience and judgment. But I could not have done it. And I began to sag under the strain. Fifty-five minutes on that ledge! I had not noted the precise hour when the fish was hooked, but it was at sunset. Finally, I could not endure any longer.

"My God—son! Pull him in."

"Not ready—yet," panted Romer, hoarsely.

"Romer, you *know* some of these steelhead *never* get tired."

"All right, Dad. I'll horse him," replied Romer, and tightened up a little. "Never—did this—before. . . . God help you—if I lose him!"

Romer worked the steelhead up on the ledge and approached the shore. I could see the fish, and I would have yelled to Romer if I had not been panic-stricken. Why is it a big fish always has this effect upon a fisherman?

I kept wading in behind the steelhead, determined to fall on him if he got his head turned out again.

Presently he lodged on a shallow place to turn on his side. Gaping with wide jaws, his broad side shining like silver, he galvanized me to action. With a plunge I scooped him out on the bank, where he flopped once, then lay still, a grand specimen if I ever saw one.

"How—much?" whispered Romer, relaxing limp as a rag.

"Fourteen—thirteen pounds!" I pealed out. "Oh, what a fish! Am I glad you got him!"

"Whew!—Is he that big? . . . Gosh, what'll Loren say?"

"It'll be tough on the kid. He's so proud of his record. That twelve-pounder! But Loren can take it."

"Dad, don't weigh this one. We'll say 11¾!"[6]

---

[6] See Appendix A for a different ending to this story.

[280]

20

A TROUT FISHERMAN'S INFERNO

After he was relieved from command in the Far East, General Douglas MacArthur concluded his farewell address to Congress with the refrain from an ancient Army song: "Old soldiers never die; they just fade away." The saying became so popular that inevitably it was parodied, and since then amusing variations on all categories of humanity, from golfers to mothers-in-law, have been heard. The one for anglers goes: "Old fishermen never die; they just smell that way!"

While Zane Grey would doubtless have enjoyed this quip about his favorite sport, he had his own thoughts about an angler's death and after-life. Writing for *Field and Stream* in April, 1910, he describes a Dantesque Hell inhabited by familiar shades. His two brothers, Cedar and Reddy, are there, along with good friends Alvah James and Will Dilg. Other famous fishermen undergoing various kinds of eternal punishment are Charles Frederick Holder, founder of the Catalina Tuna Club, and Robert Davis, avid bass angler, editor of *Munsey's Magazine*, and the man who helped Zane Grey establish the world's first "Porpoise Club" on September 21, 1912, when the two men pitched in to land a harpooned porpoise on rod and reel off Seabright, New Jersey. Judged by contemporary standards of empathy for these sea mammals, this deed alone would have been sufficient to land both anglers in Hell! Yet when the rest of us get there, we can only appeal to our finny magistrates to let us share Zane Grey's special punishment.

GWR

A TROUT FISHERMAN'S INFERNO

Almost endless seemed the last few days before April first, that spring day long looked for by the trout fisherman. But it dawned finally, clear and cold, with a steely gray sky and white frost on the trees; and I was on my way to Beaver Brook.

A buoyant eagerness and expectation lent to my swift steps something of the nameless charm of remembered lonely rambles along many streams of the past. It was half pleasurable, half painful. I climbed the shaggy hills to face the pale sunrise, and then tramped into the woods. There was still a hint of reluctant winter in the wind; little patches of snow lay in the hollows; little lines of ice fringed the edges of the many springs. The trees were all bare, except for small red buds showing on the maples. The dark green of

[282]

hemlock and rhododendron gleamed against the somber gray of the forest.

As I trudged along, careful not to tread on the crimson-spotted newts crawling in the trail, I caught a faint dreamy hum. I stopped and turned my ear to the cool morning breeze. Then I strode on over the frosty leaves, only to stop again. . . . Hark! the deep far-away boom of the rushing brook! It had been a long time since I had heard it; the rainy autumn, the cold dark winter were as if they had never been. The solitude of the woods, the roar of the rapids, roused the strange haunting sense of rest, of solitude, of indefinable aloofness from the tumult of the world. There was the wild quickening leap of the blood, the inexplicable selfish gratification of possession. The dark forest with its dank odor of decayed leaves, of wet earth, of rotting stumps was mine, all mine, as were the rush and roar of rapids, the boom of the deep falls, the hollow laugh of the low ones.

Down the ravine I threaded a way under the shadowy hemlocks, through the tangled thickets of rhododendron, to the brook. It was bank-full of wine-brown water. For me in that moment every swift-curling channel, every bubbling eddy behind a stone, every dark pool under overhanging matted roots, harbored a great, lurking, wolf-headed trout. While baiting my hook with a common earth-worm my fingers trembled, and I laughed to note it. Hands that had withstood the wonderful leap of the tarpon, the tremendous strike of the tuna, the fierce onslaught of the swordfish, failed me here and trembled like a girl's. Well, what of it? I thought. Battles with great game fish were proud memorable achievements of a sportsman's life, but not to be named in the same breath with the pursuit of the bronze-backed bass in swift clear water, of the blue-backed trout in foamy rapids. I do not know why, but it is so. Perhaps the little fish are associated with my boyhood days. What then can take their place? Perhaps the wind in the pines, the sound of the stream, liberate thought and feeling not felicitous in the hard fight with a finny giant of the sea.

I began to fish downstream, my mind in harmony with the racing current. Beaver Brook was a rushing, brawling brown brook, full of bronze boulders and lined by mossy roots, and obstructed by bulging benches, and broken by rapids and barred by windfalls. The water was icy cold and too deep for wading. The banks were steep and thick with rhododendron. My tingling anticipation wore itself out in long climbing and futile fishing. Then the judgment of a trout fisherman reasserted itself. The stream was too high, the water too cold, the trout would not rise. Thereafter my pleasure was in leisurely wending my way down the brook, fishing because hope never dies, noting the many changes in the stream bed, the new cuts, the old pools filled, recognizing old friends in certain falls and great mossy stones and leaning trees. How sweet and melancholy was this meeting with well-remembered places! In a long millrace channel I had once hooked and lost a big trout; here in an eddying foam-flecked hole under a bank I had caught a two-pounder; there from a slippery incline of rock I had fallen in. A gray lichen-covered cliff was reminiscent of many June days and violets and mountain laurel. Memorable these nooks were and sad because of the sudden shock to the mind. They were as well-known almost as my favorite daily walk, my room, my desk, yet they had been forgotten. And now, after nearly twelve months, they burst familiarly upon my vision, keen reminders of the brevity of a year, of the little span of time called human life.

Midday found me seeking a sunny seat where I could rest and eat my lunch. I did not realize how tired I was till I got anchored in a cosy niche of rock. It was very pleasant there and I idly watched my floating line while I ate. Afterwards I lingered, and closing my eyes, leaned back against the stone. The sun beat down warm upon me; the wind seemed to cease its moaning; the roar of the rapids grew into a faint hum; I was drifting, drowsily drifting—

Suddenly I got a vigorous electric strike, and, bounding up, saw the heavy swirl of a powerful fish. I hooked him. He split the center of the brook, lashing the bank with waves, and plunged over a fall, making the reel scream. What a trout! I danced from stone to stone, skimmed the glancing brook, airily leaped from bank to bank, ever watching the great dark blue body, the sweeping tail, the broad wake of the fish far ahead. It seemed that the brook widened, the current flew faster, the falls boomed louder, and the cliff and forest lifted themselves shutting out the light. But these things were no hindrance to me. No width or depth, no slippery stone or slanting log had terrors for me. It was as if I had wings. Fear beset me at times that I might not fly fast enough downstream to ease the strain on the line. It stretched wet and thin, a mere horsehair, but it did not break. Then it was only a cobweb line; still it held the great trout that was growing larger all the time.

I seemed to speed by other fishermen. They beheld me with upraised hands and open mouths, but I heard no cry, and they faded into the gray. Heavy thunder ahead bespoke of a mighty waterfall. The brook constricted in a dark cleft, overhung by bulging cliff and fringe of forest. The light of the sun went out. I balanced myself on a log and tried to hold my fish. The reel burned in my hand; the line paid out to the end; the violence of the jerk pulled me from my last perch. There was no help for it. I must follow him, and I lightly skimmed the current. From the cleft led a glancing incline smooth as glass, and far down it my giant trout shot with the water wreathed in white about him. I had an idea that it would be pleasant to tarry under the green dripping walls of the gorge, but if I did not stay with my fish I could not get back; so I sped downward. The water went so much faster than I that I concluded I would do well to ride, so resting lightly on the foam, I made better headway. Soon I found I could not lift my feet nor release my rod. Faintness and dimness of sight seized upon me. Miles I rode the crest of the current, out at last into a wide marginless pool. Here my monster trout whirled about and lunged for me. All my inner being froze with horror. I saw his long silver-barred jaws, his huge intent eyes, watching, watching in savage mockery. Then he rose for me, a magnificent leap, half out of the water, and seized me with a savage shake of his jaws.

Swift hot agony, one quivering struggle, despairing cry—and I knew I was dead. Black cold night enfolded my spirit. I felt the sharp teeth in my breast, but the pain was gone. Down, down, down! The water rushed upward as my captor plunged into the depths. Then the sound of water ceased. All about us was overpowering silence. We floated downward like falling feathers through space. The thick cold water changed to moist thin air of murky blackness. Faint murmurs began to drift upward. Down, unceasingly down! Was there never an end to this falling? Where was he taking me? I must now have been far beneath the world. Long low wails crept piercingly into my ears. I was descending to the abode of pain

[285]

and woe. The dark cloud walls about me lightened and my feet suddenly touched the sand.

I saw that I stood in a great dim amphitheatre veiled in golden shadows and vapors. The dome was as black as night; the sides were obscured in distance. Subdued voices and whispers and low cries rose about me, and shapeless forms moved to and fro. I was led along the sand for many leagues to the banks of an opaque river where there was great confusion.

"Where am I?" I asked.

"This is the Fisherman's Inferno," replied my captor.

"What are you going to do with me?"

"I don't know. I'm leading you to the judges. We must consult your record."

Then I could see quite plainly, though my sight seemed obscured by a haze. The place was immense, and fearful, yet it was beautiful. Everywhere were scurrying, noiseless brooks and huge mossy stones and giant hemlocks, all dim under the strange veil. Trout were swimming about, walking the sands, sitting on the rocks, and engaged in tasks.

"You must wait your turn," said my captor. "There's a long line. One of the seasons opened today. This is the Seventh Circle. You must have friends, acquaintances here. Look about, perhaps you can see people you'll be glad to meet in hell."

"Is this the lowest circle?" I queried, not that I was not interested, but just because he wished me to have company.

"Oh, no! There's one lower—the Fishhog Circle. I hope you won't be booked for that. This is bad enough."

All the time my eyesight appeared to improve, though I could not rid myself of the filmy blur. Suddenly I espied a handsome man balancing himself upon a slippery rock and leaping to another. He wore white duck trousers and waved a long rod. Though he did not seem very familiar, the peculiar sweep of his rod as he waved it about reminded me of some fisherman I had seen.

"Who's that?" I asked.

"Why that's your brother Cedar!" exclaimed my captor. "Didn't you know he was here?"

"No," I replied. "What's his punishment?"

"He has been condemned to wear white duck and balance himself on those rocks, as you see him—forever."

[286]

"Forever?"

"Forever."

I tried very hard to feel sorry. But somehow I could not. Anguish I had suffered on many a stream returned to me with that remarkable sweep of rod and pose of body; and I had a sense of the inevitable working out of justice, of the fitting nature of some fates.

"Your other brother is here, too," went on my informant.

"Not Reddy?" I implored.

"You have only the two," he replied, reprovingly.

"True. I suppose if I had more they would be here. It ran in the family."

My guide led me along a dim bronze stream to a shadowy bank. There was Reddy, surely, and if my heart had not been dead it would have bled. He was being skittered along by the water. Several colossal trout were standing on the bank holding a stout rod with a stout line and a stout hook. The hook was stuck in a part of Reddy. These lusty trout skittered him back and forth, and suddenly with united effort, tugged mightily on the rod to fling Reddy far back upon the bank. This was repeated before I could turn sadly away. The expression of my brother's face tortured my soul. I remembered his one failing as a fisherman. He did love to strike hard. I had seen him fall off a log or out of a boat because of the violence of his jerk. I recalled a picture of him leaning forward, extending his rod, watching the line run out, as he whispered gleefully: "Say, watch me sock the hook into this one!"

"Your old friend James is here, just round this bend," said my captor.

"Not Alvah James? Why, he hated fish!" I said incredulously. "Many's the time I took him fishing only to have him run back to the girls."

"Yes, he hated fish. Look!"

I saw Alvah in the grasp of several powerful trout. These were leading him to and fro before a bronze cage in which were a bevy of cooing arch-eyed, sweet-lipped mermaids like the sirens of the sea. They were singing and calling to him; he was wrestling with his guards. Then they led him away, and as he passed me the impotent distress of his face was so affecting that I could not speak to him and tell him how glad I was to see him.

I passed close by two more old friends in the toils. Kellogg, who

[287]

had been a demon on minnow-catching for bait, was bound to a stake in the water, and millions of shiners and chubs were nibbling at him, and running into his eyes and mouth to come out his ears. Then there was Bray, a famous and fiendish frog-caster. I asked my guide why this friend should be here in a trout fishermen's hell, when surely he had never caught a trout on a frog.

"No, but he tried, for eleven years. When we got him, we gave him sentence in sympathy for bass and frogs, and there you see him."

Ten Herculean green-backed frogs took turns at casting my unfortunate friend out into the opaque bronze gloom. I could not see where he lit, but I heard the far-off splash, and the rush of water and gurgling cries as they reeled him in.

"Do you want to see Dilg?" inquired my guard.

I hesitated, for I had thought of Dilg. He had been one of the best fishermen I had ever known, the most indomitable, the most enthusiastic. If he was there really getting his desserts I did not want to see him, for it would be a tragedy; yet I could not resist the curiosity and temptation.

I was led under a shady bronze canopy of trees out into the open, where a golden pool shone through the streaky mists. I heard the creak of oars and the splashes of rising fish. Then I saw Dilg rowing hard in a boat. His back was bent, his hair dishevelled, his face sweaty. The muscles of his swollen arms rippled as he plied his weary strokes. A fisherman dandy sat in the stern trolling, and hauling in the fish. A multitudinous school of many-colored, gamy-eyed, strong-finned fish followed his hook, mad to be caught.

"That's awful!" I cried. "All those wonderful fish, yet he can't take up a rod! Say, guide, is his sentence for long?"

"For eternity."

"Poor Dilg!" Recollecting the achievements of this indefatigable angler, I tried to analyze the agony it must have cost him to lose this opportunity, and I shook my head, and turned sorrowing away. What a mastermind had divined the one greatest punishment for him! No Eighth Circle could hold a greater!

My guide held me tightly with his fin, and leading me through crowds of noisy arguing trout, passed by a long tangled mass of heads, gills, fins, silversides, gold-red spots and wide tails. A veritable melee it was and sent up a deafening uproar.

[288]

"Tournament casting," explained he. "Here we take the ex-pounders of this art and practice casting them at targets. There are only two prizes—one for the trout who breaks the most bones of his bait, and the other for the trout who can keep his bait alive longest. No distance casting."

"Then—you do kill some of the poor fishermen—the second time?" I faltered.

"Undoubtedly. It depends, of course, upon the nature of their crime. The tournament casters ought to be killed three times, but we have a rather mild judge and he lets them off easy."

"What—what do you do with them—afterwards?"

"Oh, stuff them and hang them up in our dens. I have a great collection. But you must come to the judge's den. He has the finest mounted collection of any trout in the world: Mark Anthony, Izaak Walton, Grover Cleveland—all the old fellows. But then, of course, our judge has been at it some years, political pull and all that, so we really can't compete with him."

"Thank you, I'd rather not see any—stuffed ones," I replied, weakly. I began to be conscious of the numbness of my legs. In fact, my guide was literally carrying me around. I began to have a dis-trust of his kindness. Then—"Great Heavens! What's that?" I cried.

A tall silversided trout was stalking back and forth along a beach, his head erect, gills agape; and out of his wide pearly-toothed jaws protruded a man's feet encased in rubber wading boots.

"Who's he?" I repeated, recovering somewhat from amazement.

"That'll be Holder, I believe. Looks like his feet. But I'm not sure." My guide hailed the strapping big trout. "Hey, Finspeck, is it your turn to swallow Holder? No? What? Old Dorsal got him now? Well, who's this? Van—Van Dyke. Oh! yes." Turning cheerfully to me, my Virgil of this Purgatory continued: "No, it's not Fred, after all: it's Doc Van Dyke."

Then hearing shuffling sounds and low moans, I whirled to see a striking figure. It resembled a man, but I could not be sure. What an extraordinary thing! It crawled upon all fours and seemed to glitter with shiny scales. The moans, however, were human, and I recognized here another fisherman expiating the crimes of his earthly existence. When he got close I started back first in surprise, then bewilderment, then with something akin to joy. This man was covered with the terrible, barbed, many-hooked, floating baits. They were stuck all over him; only his face, hands and feet were visible. I counted 1,966 before I was satisfied. These, however, were not one-tenth the number he wore.

"Who's that?" I demanded.

"Why, don't you know? Bob Davis, to be sure, and he's got it good!"

"But he's a bass fisherman," I remonstrated.

"Assuredly he is, but in casting one day for a lily pad two hundred yards from the boat, he overcast and hooked Silverjaw, one of our Old Guard trout that happened to swim down into the lake. Why, there have been bass from all over the world come to take a look at this fisherman and stick another wooden bait in him. He's really the greatest drawing card we have."

"But he's in the most awful pain!" I felt cold shudders run over my spirit.

"Pain? Oh! no, you're mistaken," my captor answered, with mingled scorn and mockery. "He's a cold-blooded animal. He has no nerves. The incoming currents to his brain carry no sense of pain from the periphery. The cellular construction of his mesoblast admits no heat, consequently there can be no sensation of pain."

The singular justification presented by this fisherman's case confronted me suddenly with the possibilities of my own. What, then, was in store for me? Manifestly I would soon learn, for my captor hurried me out of the throngs of bustling trout and writhing fishermen, through labyrinthine lanes of bronze, out into the open misty space of sand where a circle of great solemn-eyed trout waited.

"Have you looked up his record?" inquired my captor.

"Yes, it's bad," replied an old gray trout, slapping a huge book with his fin. In abject fright I recognized this trout. He had several long straggling whiskers and each one was an old leader of mine. Evidently the hooks were still fast in his gullet. He looked sour-complexioned, and as if his character had been set during a painful experience.

"Read out the record," ordered the judge. When I saw his beaked nose and hooked jaw I nearly sank into the sand, for I remembered him also. Many a line had he snapped for me. Once I had him in my landing net only to slip on the stones and lose him. My eyes protruded from their sockets as I gazed round the circle. I knew the jury also. There I stood, facing in captor, judge and jury, old trout that I had wronged. What mercy could I expect? I tried not to hear the reading of the record, but my guard held down my hands.

"Dyed in the wool fisherman!—enemy of all the finny people from sunfish to whales—cunning, deceitful bait fisherman—expert with the invisible leaders and the lively minnows—absolutely fatal to inexperienced fish—a menace and a dread to even the old keen-eyed, sharp-scented trout—that terrible scourge of the streams, a manipulator of angleworms, a dirty, wading, implacable fisherman who catches fish."

"Ho, then for the Eighth Circle?"

"No. His record shows one redeeming feature. Never did he catch as many trout as he could. Therefore his punishment must be meted out here."

The wise old trout bent their gray heads close together round the learned judge, and they nodded and held council.

I awaited my fate in a feverish fear that was more dreadful than any I had ever felt in my life upon earth. My future looked desperate, indeed.

"Fisherman," began the gray old judge, with his head cocked wisely to one side, and a gleam of revenge in his dark eye, "it has been your wont to haunt the trout streams. You have claimed to be hunting the spirit of content by the side of the murmuring water. You write that you love the mossy stones, the gnarled old roots, the dripping ferns and violets; and you wade serenely downstream, building your philosophy of life—while you yank murderous hooks into the throats of hungry trout. I shall give you the severest sentence I can under the law of this court."

He paused to lend dignity and weight to his final stroke.

"*You are sentenced to spend eternity here reading your own stories!*"

I fell blindly on my knees.

"Mercy! Mercy! judge. I never deserved that! Mercy!"

"Immutable decree of the Trout Fisherman's Inferno! Lead him away!"

The sonorous command rang in my ears like a bell of doom. My guard dragged me away over the sand; the bronze shafts of light darkened; the murmuring of voices died away, and—

Then I awoke.

"So I took my rod and pail and the two
little bass, and brushed the meadow daisies,
and threaded the familiar green-lined towpath
toward home."

Zane Grey hooked to a bass in the Delaware River during one of his pre-fame excursions to his home in Lackawaxen.

Weekending away from the city had as many delays in 1900 as today—but at least there were no crowds. ZG with his rods and bag waiting for the train at Lackawaxen.

*Zane Grey with a trophy Delaware bass; brother
R.C. with his own trophy: ZG's sweatshirt from
the University of Pennsylvania baseball team.*

(Right) *Mountain lion in dead juniper on the rim of the Grand Canyon. ". . . I was level with the lion, too close for comfort, but in excellent position for taking pictures."* (Below) *Buffalo Jones and Jim Emett packing captured cougar into a saddlebag. "The lioness being considerably longer and larger, was with difficulty gotten into the other pannier, and her head and paws hung out."*

Buffalo Jones and lions in camp.

Old Sultan's mounted skin on the barn at Lackawaxen. Lewis Allsworth Grey (Zane Grey's oldest brother).

Zane Grey and his Mexican guide, Attalano, encamped on the Panuco River (circa 1905). ZG's note on back: "A hut of palm leaves where we spent a night." Note pig, dog, and chicken. ("Byme-By-Tarpon")

On subsequent trips to Mexico and the Florida Keys, Zane Grey made up for the loss of his first tarpon described in "Byme-By-Tarpon" with fish like this near-seven-foot monster.

*Always proud of his small-boat handling, ZG
was more than usually proud on this occasion
with his bride in the bow. He had met her on a
canoeing trip near his Lackawaxen home.*

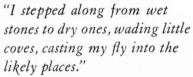

"I stepped along from wet stones to dry ones, wading little coves, casting my fly into the likely places."

On a return to his Lackawaxen home, Zane Grey stands on a hilltop overlooking the confluence of the Delaware (right) and Lackawaxen rivers. His home and outbuildings are seen on the corner of the two rivers where he had some of his best bass and shad fishing.

Over the Glass Mountains on the way to Nonnezoshe.

John Wetherill, first white man to see "Rainbow Bridge," and Zane Grey.

Zane Grey at Nonnezoshe.

Zane Grey with "Lone Angler" Wilborn (Dr. J.A.) at Catalina Island. "Lone Angler" and Zane Grey went to the University of Pennsylvania together.

Fishing aboard the Gladiator *off Catalina.*

The Gladiator, 52-foot, round-bottom cruiser, was ZG's Catalina broadbill swordfishing boat for over ten years. ZG caught 24 broadbill from her, including his 582 pound world record; R.C. caught 18, including the 588 pound broadbill that beat his brother's record. Note the "ZG" flag flying from the masthead. This personal pennant was flown from the masthead of all ZG's boats.

This is the 11½-hour Xiphias Gladius that got away.

On his way between the
mainland and Catalina Islan
ZG gets in a little more wor
on one of his Westerns.

Leaping striped marlin.

ZG's hilltop house overlooking Catalina Harbor
and the Tuna Club (center foreground).

Zane Grey with the 316 pound Catalina striped marlin, his biggest striped marlin catch off that island. This picture hung in ZG's bedroom in Lackawaxen.

(Above) *The vistas—the sheer cliffs and valleys—these are the qualities Zane Grey loved in hunting.* (Left) *ZG and Don, leader of the pack, before a hunt in fresh-fallen snow.*

Zane Grey shooting ahead of lion. "I knelt and leveled my rifle. The lioness showed red against the gray . . . a fine target!"

Mountain lion treed by dogs.

Ready to jump.

(Above) *ZG and brother R.C., after a day's fishing during one of his first visits to Long Key, Florida. One barracuda and three amberjack. Note the cat claw hung from ZG's watch fob. This photograph was made from an old glass plate found in the attic of ZG's Lackawaxen home. ZG tripped the shutter mechanism and ran back to join his brother in the picture.* (Left) *ZG with his 10 pound-2 ounce bonefish that held the Long Key record and whose capture is described in "The Bonefish Brigade."*

The Bonefish Brigade with the fish that nearly toppled ZG's record at Long Key, Florida, 1922. Frank Stick is the young fellow in the middle being threatened with a coconut.

Zane Grey was our first outdoor writer to praise the fighting spirit of the permit which he called "a rare game fish of the coral shoals" in an article published in 1925.

(Right) *Zane Grey with wild turkeys—Tonto Basin.*
(Below) *ZG (in plaid pattern coat) standing with Romer, his Arizona camp crew, and part of the dog pack.*

In Turkey Canyon, Tonto Basin, 1918. Left to right, Ed Haught, Romer Zane Grey, Sievert Nielsen, Lee Doyle.

Romer's first mount and gun— Tonto Basin, 1918.

(Above) *Romer Grey with a pair of turkeys shot by his uncle R.C. and his dad.*
(Right) *ZG scrubbing up in camp after an early-morning outing for deer and turkey.*

ZG was a pioneer in Nova Scotian waters. Here he is on August 22, 1924—ten years before other Americans began to come north for the great tuna fishing found in Nova Scotia—with the then world record of 758 pounds (bluefin tuna).

(Above) *The Nova Scotian
schooner,* Marshal Foch, *built
in 1919 and bought in 1924
by ZG for $17,000. Note the
"ZG" pennant at the masthead.*
(Right) *Leaping blackfish,
first cousin of the orca—1925
cruise of* Fisherman I.
("Fishing Virgin Waters")

(Left) *Zane Grey with tackle on* Fisherman I, *on cruise to Galápagos in 1924. ("Fishing Virgin Waters,"* Tales of Fishing Virgin Seas.*) (Below) A competent photographer in his own right, ZG always managed to have at least one other professional on board during voyages to distant islands. Thus Zane Grey was able to get remarkable shots like this one of a leaping bonito shark.*

PHOTO BY AL TETZLAFF

"The green-purple sea was alive with fish, and the air with birds . . . swift frigate birds . . . more adept at snatching our baits than the yellowtail . . . and other fish. . . ."

Dreadnaught Pool, Tongariro River, New Zealand.

Zane Grey with 11¾ pound rainbow trout caught in the Dreadnaught Pool. Left to right, Capt. Laurie D. Mitchell, Zane Grey, Hoka Down, *Maori guide.*

Zane Grey fishing in Dread-aught Pool.

On their second trip to New Zealand, Zane Grey and his friend Laurie Mitchell competed in a beard-growing contest. It was diplomatically decided to be a draw.

(Above) *Romer Grey and Laurie Mitchell with a day's catch of rainbow trout from the Tongariro River, New Zealand (1927). (Left) ZG listening for the baying of the hounds on a trail near his Arizona base camp.*

Ben Haught, one of Zane Grey's bear-hunting companions ("Colorado Trails").

Zane Grey camp, Tahiti.

Zane Grey spearing first fish after native fish drive on Tahoa Island.

The Fisherman II *was a grander yacht but a poorer vessel than its predecessor. It was uncomfortable in anything but calm waters and exorbitantly expensive to operate; in Tahiti ZG finally abandoned his plans to sail around the world in her.*

Zane Grey camp, Flower Point, Tahiti.

*Zane Grey fishing for nato (a type of perch
known as Tahitian trout) in a stream in Tautira
District, Tahiti.*

New Zealand guides, Peter Williams and
Francis Arlidge, with Zane Grey's sailfish catch
off Bora-Bora, 1929.

(Left) *Tahiti—Zane Grey with bonito bait for giant Tahitian marlin (some bait!)*. (Below) *Zane Grey aboard* Frangipani, *trolling off Tahiti. Hand-held outrigger used long before its official "invention" by Florida guide Tommy Gifford, later in the 30's.* ("The First Thousand Pounder")

Zane Grey hooked on marlin off Tahiti.
("The First Thousand Pounder")

(Left) *Zane Grey with the first 1,000 pound-plus game fish taken on rod and reel. Disqualified by contemporary standards due to the mutilation of the tail by sharks, this was still a notable catch by 1930 standards. Zane Grey named the fish the "giant Tahitian striped marlin" (1,040 pounds even with approximately 200 pounds chewed off the tail), but marine scientists today know this was a huge Pacific blue marlin.* (Below) *Zane Grey fishing fleet, Bay of Islands, New Zealand.* Left to right, *the* Alma G *(ZG's boat), Captain Mitchell's* Sky Blue, *the* Zane Grey *used by R.C. Grey and later by Romer Z. Grey, and the* Red *(camera boat).*

Seining for bait, New Zealand. Zane Grey in foreground, back toward camera. ZG felt fresh bait was a must for trophy marlin.

Pair of orca off Bay of Islands, New Zealand. Note the six-foot spike dorsal fin on the male. Zane Grey was always intrigued by killer whales, a fascination that later led to the story of Two Fold Bay.

First broadbill swordfish to be caught in New Zealand waters (400 pounds). Red Mercury Island, 1926.

(Above) *Zane Grey hooked to 704 pound black marlin, New Zealand, 1926* (Right) *Every evening ZG would have to see to the winding of his linen lines on special dryers to prevent mildew and rot. In the mornings, the lengthy procedure had to be reversed before ZG went out fishing.*

ZG took this closeup of one of his favorite game fish—the Pacific mako, or bonito shark.

Even before his trip West to lasso mountain lions in the Grand Canyon, Zane Grey was a cat fancier. He was especially fond of their lazy grace, which he termed "restful." There was always a cat in his study in Altadena, and at one time he kept nineteen Persian cats in his Lackawaxen home. This shot was taken in front of his tent on Red Mercury Island, New Zealand.

Zane Grey with three Oregon steelhead, North Umpqua River, Oregon, August 1935. He wrote on the back of this shot: "Something to gloat about!"

*Loren Grey continued to fish the Umpqua in
the years following his father's death. Here
he hefts a 10½ pound steelhead taken on a fly.*

APPENDIX A

Loren's version of this last day is a little different. In a story written about the same time his father wrote "The North Umpqua, Oregon," Loren describes his encounter with Romer after he caught the big steelhead this way:

> *Departure day approached with the finality of doom. We all hated to leave, but my sorrow was assuaged by the memories of my battle at Bogus Creek. Only one more evening and my season's record was safe. That afternoon Romer started down the river early, a grim, businesslike look on his face.*
>
> *"Well, good luck, Rome," I ventured a little timidly as he went by my tent.*
>
> *"Umph," was all I could elicit from him.*
>
> *I caught a little one—about three pounds—that evening, but my heart was not in my work. I missed two strikes clean, one from a 10-pounder. I was worried. Somehow Romer had appeared too businesslike.*
>
> *I came home late and sidled rather furtively into the cookshack, my heart in my mouth.*
>
> *"Romer in yet?" I said casually.*
>
> *No one had seen him. I waited. The slow dusk crept over the hills and sank through the river canyon. The low musical roar of the river swelled up into my ears. For a time I forgot everything but that deep comforting song that I was not to know for another year. Eight o'clock came, then nine. Still no Romer . . .*
>
> *Of a sudden, he seemed to burst into the cook-shack, as if from nowhere. He was empty-handed. Slowly, deliberately he set his rod against the wall and unstrapped his knapsack. The silence was deafening. My spirits rose.*
>
> *"Well—what happened?" someone asked.*
>
> *"Oh, really nothing of importance," said Romer noncommittally. He pulled up the flap of his knapsack, and for the first time I noticed that it bulged mysteriously. Then I stared, and goggled. The long shiny thing uncoiled from the knapsack like a snake, until I could have sworn for the moment it was six feet long.*
>
> *"Nothing—nothing but this. . . ." He held up the magnificent, slim shape carelessly. "In the Takahashi Pool. Two hours."*
>
> *"How—much—did he weigh?" I said faintly.*

[341]

"I'm not going to weigh him," said Romer. "I'm going to let you keep your record."

I stared at him. "But—how—how come?" I sputtered.

"Oh, no reason—except it will always be much more interesting for you to be in doubt whether I beat you or not. I'm going to have him mounted, so you can look at him and wonder. . . ."

"Well, if that doesn't beat anything I ever heard," said ZG. "But anyway, you earned him, son. It was a great job."

To this day I don't know whether he shaded me or not . . . it looked to be a toss-up either way. I have a strong suspicion that Romer doesn't know either. . . . The fish hangs on the wall in Romer's office, big and shiny, a vivid reminder of the Umpqua and of friendly rivalry, which is really what makes fishing a paramount sport among men.

APPENDIX B

Principal Outdoor Books and Films

The books listed below were originally published by Harper & Brothers (except *Tales of Lonely Trails*, first published in London by Hodder and Stoughton.) Most are composed of articles and stories that first appeared in various periodicals. Many of these titles were reprinted more than once, and Grosset and Dunlap editions, using Harper's original plates on less expensive paper, are rather common.

1919   *Tales of Fishes*
1922   *Tales of Lonely Trails*
1924   *Tales of Southern Rivers*
1925   *Tales of Fishing Virgin Seas*
1926   *Tales of an Angler's Eldorado New Zealand*
1927   *Tales of Swordfish and Tuna*
1928   *Tales of Fresh Water Fishing*
1928   *Don, The Story of a Dog*
1931   *Zane Grey's Book of Camps and Trails*
1931   *Tales of Tahitian Waters*
1937   *An American Angler in Australia*
1952   *Zane Grey's Adventures in Fishing*

The films listed below were made in the 1920s and 30s and all feature Zane Grey himself. The first two are feature length; the second two, short subjects.

South Sea Adventures
White Death
Fisherman's Pluck
Fighting Mako

[343]

APPENDIX C

Principal Outdoor Stories and Articles
Published in Periodicals

Tracking down Zane Grey's periodical contributions is a task calculated to rattle even the most patient scholar. Some of Zane Grey's stories were reprinted in different magazines under different titles, and ZG himself sometimes sold or gave the same story to more than one publication. Mrs. Zane Grey tried to maintain a list of all of her husband's publications, but he would often submit a story or grant reprint rights without notifying her. A complete list of his outdoor publications would no doubt be considerably longer, but it may be years before all the missing pieces are found and put together. However, the initial work carried out by William J. Clark, G. M. Farley, and Norris F. Schneider has been tremendously helpful.

Whenever an article, either in whole or part, appeared later in book form, I have indicated its title in the right hand column. Starred stories are those which appear in this anthology.

Year	Article Title	Magazine	Book
1902	A Day on the Delaware	Recreation (May)	Tales of Fresh Water Fishing
1903	Camping Out	Field and Stream (Feb)	
1906	James' Waterloo	Field and Stream (Sept)	
1907	Leaping Tarpon	Shield's Magazine (June)	
1907	Three Strikes and Out	Field and Stream (July)	
1907	Byme-by-Tarpon*	Field and Stream (Dec)	Tales of Fishes
1908	Cruising in Mexican Waters	Field and Stream (Jan)	
1908	Lassoing Lions in the Siwash	Everybody's (June)	
1908	Tige's Lion	Field and Stream (June)	
1909	Roping Lions in the Grand Canyon*	Field and Stream (serial beginning in Jan)	Tales of Lonely Trails
1909	The Lord of Lackawaxen Creek*	Outing (May)	Tales of Fresh Water Fishing

Year	Article Title	Magazine	Book
1909	In Defense of Live Bait	*Field and Stream* (June)	
1909	Rabihorcados and the Boobies	*Everybody's* (Sept)	*Tales of Fishes*
1909	Nassau, Cuba and Mexico	N.Y. & Cuba Mail SS Co. (Oct)	
1910	Lightning	*Outing* (March)	
1910	A Trout Fisherman's Inferno*	*Field and Stream* (April)	
1910	Accidents in Camp	*Field and Stream* (June)	
1911	Down an Unknown Jungle River	*Field and Stream* (serial beginning in March)	*Tales of Southern Rivers*
1911	On the Trail of the Jaguar	*Harper's Weekly* (May 6)	*Tales of Southern Rivers*
1911	Water Tigers of the Gulf Stream	*Field and Stream* (Dec)	
1912	Fighting Qualities of Black Bass*	*Field and Stream* (May)	*Tales of Fresh Water Fishing*
1912	Barracuda of Long Key	*Field and Stream* (July)	
1912	Tiger	*Munsey's* (Sept)	
1913	Amberjack of Sombrero Reef	*Field and Stream* (Feb)	
1913	Following the Elusive Tuna	*Field and Stream* (Sept)	
1915	Nonnezoshe*	*Recreation* (Feb)	*Tales of Lonely Trails*
1915	A New Wonder, Nonnezoshe	*World Magazine* (Feb 14)	
1915	Swordfish, the Royal Purple Game	*Recreation* (Dec)	*Tales of Fishes*
1916	Some Rare Fish of the Sea	*Recreation* (Oct)	*Tales of Fishes*
1916	Sailfish	*Recreation* (Dec)	*Tales of Fishes*
1917	Two Fights With Swordfish	*Recreation* (Oct)	*Tales of Fishes*
1918	Catalina Tuna	*Field and Stream* (March)	
1918	Colorado Trails*	*Outdoor Life* (Mar-June)	*Tales of Lonely Trails*
1918	Gladiator of the Sea	*Field and Stream* (April)	*Tales of Fishes*
1918	Gulf Stream Fishing	*Field and Stream* (July)	*Tales of Fishes*
1919	Light Tackle	*Field and Stream* (Jan)	

Year	Article Title	Magazine	Book
1919	Swordfish of the Sea	*Field and Stream* (March)	*Tales of Fishes*
1919	Big Tuna	*Field and Stream* (May)	*Tales of Fishes*
1920	Death Valley	*Harper's* (April 22)	*Tales of Lonely Trails*
1920	Sport of Kings	*California* (L. A. Examiner, April)	
1920	Fishing for Swordfish and Tuna	*Country Gentleman* (May 1)	
1920	Crater Lake Trout	*Country Gentleman* (May 15)	*Tales of Fresh Water Fishing*
1920	Trolling for Trout in Pelican Bay	*Country Gentleman* (June 26)	*Tales of Fresh Water Fishing*
1920	Record Fight With a Swordfish*	*Country Life* (August)	*Tales of Swordfish and Tuna*
1920	Arizona Bear	*Country Gentleman* (Serial beginning Nov.)	
1921	Zane Grey's Deep Sea Angling	*Sportologue* (May)	
1922	Sea Angling	*Izaak Walton Monthly* (Serial beginning August)	
1922	Bonefishing	*Country Gentleman* (Nov)	
1922	The Bonefish Brigade*	*Izaak Walton Monthly* (Dec)	
1923	Blackfish and Swordfish Stories	*Forestry Magazine*	
1923	Tyee Salmon	*Izaak Walton Monthly* (Feb)	*Tales of Fresh Water Fishing*
1923	Steelhead	*Country Gentleman* (Feb 3)	*Tales of Fresh Water Fishing*
1923	Bear Trails	*Country Gentleman* (Mar 3-17)	
1923	The Gladiator of the Sea	*Outdoor America* (March/April)	*Tales of Fishes*
1923	The Whale Killers	*Country Gentleman* (Aug 11)	
1923	Roping Lions in the Grand Canyon*	*Boy's Life* (Nov)	*Tales of Lonely Trails*

Year	Article Title	Magazine	Book
1923	Fishing the Rogue	*Country Gentleman* (Nov 17)	*Tales of Fresh Water Fishing*
1924	Down Into the Desert	*Ladies' Home Journal* (Jan)	
1924	Heavy Tackle for Heavy Fish	*Catalina Islander* (Jan)	*Tales of Swordfish and Tuna*
1924	At the Mouth of the Klamath	*Outdoor America* (Jan)	*Tales of Fresh Water Fishing*
1924	Trails Over the Glass Mountains	*Outdoor America* (Jan)	
1924	Three Broadbill Swordfish	*Outdoor America* (Feb)	
1924	Heavy Tackle for Heavy Fish	*Outdoor America* (Feb)	*Tales of Swordfish and Tuna*
1924	*Xiphias Gladius*	*Country Gentleman* (Feb 9)	*Tales of Swordfish and Tuna*
1924	Trees	*Outdoor America* (March)	
1924	One of the Wonders of the Deep	*Outdoor America* (March)	
1924	Tonto Bear	*Country Gentleman* (Mar 1)	
1924	Help Us Save Vanishing America	*Success* (April)	
1924	Birds of the Sea	*Outdoor America* (June)	
1924	The Fisherman	*Outdoor America* (Serial beginning July)	
1924	Surprise Valley	*Outdoor America* (Aug-Sept)	
1924	Gulf Stream Luck	*Country Gentleman* (Oct 4)	*Tales of Southern Rivers*
1924	Everglades Tarpon	*Country Gentleman* (Oct 11)	*Tales of Southern Rivers*
1924	Fighting Fish	*Country Gentleman* (Oct 18)	
1924	Big Ones We Caught—And Lost	*Country Gentleman* (Oct 25)	
1924	The Wolf Tracker	*Ladies' Home Journal* (Nov)	
1924	A Warning to California	*Outdoor America* (Nov)	
1924	What the Desert Means to Me	*American* (Nov)	

[347]

Year	Article Title	Magazine	Book
1924	End of a Perfect Fishing Day	*Country Gentleman* (Nov 1)	
1925	Permit—A Rare Game Fish of the Coral Shoals	*Outdoor America* (Mar)	
1925	My Bear Cubs	*Cosmopolitan* (May)	
1925	Fishing Virgin Seas	*Catalina Islander* (May)	*Tales of Fishing Virgin Seas*
1925	Zane Grey Goes Fishing in Faraway Seas	*Catalina Islander* (July)	*Tales of Fishing Virgin Seas*
1925	Fishing Virgin Seas	*The Field* (British) July 16	*Tales of Fishing Virgin Seas*
1925	Fishing Virgin Seas	*Pacific Sportsman* (Aug)	*Tales of Fishing Virgin Seas*
1925	Fishing Virgin Seas	*Outdoor America* (Aug)	*Tales of Fishing Virgin Seas*
1925	Don*	*Harper's* (August)	*Don, The Story of a Lion Dog*
1925	Adventures in the Pacific	*Country Gentleman* (Oct)	*Tales of Fishing Virgin Seas*
1925	The Shark of Galapagos	*Country Gentleman* (Nov)	*Tales of Fishing Virgin Seas*
1925	Rooster Fish and Leaping Whales	*Country Gentleman* (Dec)	*Tales of Fishing Virgin Seas*
1926	Thrill of Striking Fish	*Country Gentleman* (Jan)	
1926	Southern California, Out of Doors	Los Angeles *Times* (Jan 1)	
1926	Rocky Riffle on the Rogue	*Field and Stream* (Feb-Aug)	*Tales of Fresh Water Fishing*
1926	Log of the *Gladiator*	*Sunset* (Mar 15)	
1926	My Adventures as a Fisherman	*American* (April)	
1926	Shooting the Rogue	*Country Gentleman* (April-May)	*Tales of Fresh Water Fishing*
1926	Will H. Dilg	*Field and Stream* (June)	
1926	The Man Who Influenced Me Most [Jim Emett]	*American* (Aug)	
1926	Sport in New Zealand Waters	*Field and Stream* (Sept)	
1927	My Son's First Bear	*Country Gentleman* (Feb)	

[348]

APPENDIX C

Year	Article Title	Magazine	Book
1927	The Vanishing American	*Will H. Dilg League Monthly* (July)	
1928	Big Game Fishing in New Zealand	*Scientific American* (Aug)	
1930	Landing the World's Record Tuna	*World* (Jan 26)	*Tales of Swordfish and Tuna*
1930	Big Game Fishing	*Outdoor Life* (April)	
1930	Fishing	*American Legion* (May)	
1930	Giant of the South Seas	*Outdoor Life* (Nov)	
1931	Tales of the South Seas	*Physical Culture* (Serial beginning Feb.)	*Tales of Tahitian Waters*
1931	Modern Sea Angling	*Outdoor Life* (Feb)	
1934	Big Game Fishing in Southern Seas	*Motor Boating* (Jan)	
1934	In Quest of Record Fish	*Motor Boating* (Feb)	
1934	Tahiti, Queen of the Pacific	*Motor Boating* (Mar)	
1934	Big Tuna	*Motor Boating* (April)	
1935	Yes! Lever Action Rifles	*Sports Afield* (May)	
1935	North Umpqua Steelhead*	*Sports Afield* (Sept)	
1936	The Mako Shark	*Field and Stream* (April)	
1936	Fly Fishing	*Horrocks–Ibbetson Co.* (Dec 28)	
1937	World Record Tiger Shark	*Field and Stream* (Feb)	*An American Angler in Australia*
1937	Grey Nurse Sharks	*Field and Stream* (April)	*An American Angler in Australia*
1937	Australian Angling	*Field and Stream* (June)	*An American Angler in Australia*
1937	Marlin and Man Eaters	*Field and Stream* (Aug)	*An American Angler in Australia*
1939	They Came Tough in Tahiti	*Southern Sportsman* (Nov)	
1945	The Biggest Game-fish Ever Landed*	*Esquire* (Sept)	*Tales of Tahitian Waters*
1955	Strange Partners of Two Fold Bay*	*American Weekly* (June 26)